IOWA
TRAVEL

MW01045059

A GUIDE THAT GUID

WHY VISIT IOWA AND NEBRASKA?   I
The Lay of the Land 2 • Flora and Fauna 2 • History 3 • Cultures 5 •
The Arts 5 • Cuisine 6 • Outdoor Activities 7

PLANNING YOUR TRIP   8
When to Go 8 • How Much Will It Cost? 10 • Orientation and
Transportation 10 • Recommended Reading 11

❶ OMAHA AND COUNCIL BLUFFS   14
    ✪ Scenic Route: Loess Hills Scenic Byway   30

❷ LINCOLN AND SOUTHEAST NEBRASKA   32

❸ NEBRASKA'S I-80 TRIANGLE   46

❹ PRAIRIE LAKES COUNTRY   56

❺ OGALLALA AND NORTH PLATTE   64

❻ THE NEBRASKA PANHANDLE   73
    ✪ Scenic Route: Highway 20   84

❼ VALENTINE AND THE SANDHILLS   85

❽ NORTHEAST NEBRASKA   95

❾ SIOUX CITY   104

❿ OKOBOJI, IOWA'S GREAT LAKES   111

⓫ MASON CITY AND CLEAR LAKE   119

⓬ CEDAR FALLS AND WATERLOO   128
    ✪ Scenic Route: Great River Road   140

⓭ DUBUQUE   142

⓮ THE QUAD CITIES   156

⓯ BURLINGTON   166

⓰ IOWA CITY AND CEDAR RAPIDS   175

⓱ MADISON COUNTY   188

⓲ DES MOINES   198

APPENDIX   213
Planning Map 214 • Mileage Chart 216 • Special Interest Tours 217 •
Calendar of Events 223 • Resources 228

INDEX   229

MAP INDEX   232

IOWA NEBRASKA
TRAVEL ✦ SMART®

Kyle Munson

John Muir Publications
A Division of Avalon Travel Publishing

Acknowledgments
To my wife, Ann, for her love and support during the research and writing of this book. Travel writers don't always make fun travel companions. And special thanks to the DeGroff family for their warm Sandhills hospitality.

John Muir Publications
A Division of Avalon Travel Publishing
5855 Beaudry Street
Emeryville, CA 94608

Printed in the United States of America.
First edition. First printing March 2000.

ISSN 1525-3651
ISBN 1-56261-492-4

Editors: Bonnie Norris, Marybeth Griffin Macy, Elizabeth Wolf
Graphics Editor: Ann Silvia
Production: Scott Fowler
Design: Marie J. T. Vigil
Cover Design: Janine Lehmann
Typesetter: Melissa Tandysh
Map Style Development: American Custom Maps—Jemez Springs, NM
Map Illustration: Julie Felton, Kathy Sparkes
Printer: Publishers Press
Front Cover: small—© John Elk III (Snake Alley, Burlington, IA)
            large—© Andre Jenny/Unicorn Stock Photos (Scotts Bluff National Monument, NE)
Back Cover: © Andre Jenny/International Stock (Hogback Covered Bridge, Madison County, Winterset, IA)

Distributed to the book trade by
Publishers Group West
Berkeley, California

IOWA/NEBRASKA TRAVEL·SMART: A GUIDE THAT GUIDES

Most guidebooks are primarily directories, providing information but very little help in making choices—you have to guess how to make the most of your time and money. *Iowa/Nebraska Travel•Smart* is different: By highlighting the very best of the region and offering various planning features, it acts like a personal tour guide rather than a directory.

TAKE THE STRESS OUT OF TRAVEL

Sometimes traveling causes more stress than it relieves. Sorting through information, figuring out the best routes, determining what to see and where to eat and stay, scheduling each day—all of this can make a vacation feel daunting rather than fun. Relax. We've done a lot of the legwork for you. This book will help you plan a trip that suits *you*—whatever your time frame, budget, and interests.

SEE THE BEST OF IOWA AND NEBRASKA

Author Kyle Munson has lived in Iowa for almost 28 years, the last six in Des Moines. He was born in northeast Iowa and raised in southwest Iowa, near the Council Bluffs–Omaha area. He has hand-picked every listing in this book, and he gives you an insider's perspective on what makes each one worthwhile. So while you will find many of the big tourist attractions listed here, you'll also find lots of smaller, lesser-known treasures, such as the Antiquarium, a used bookstore and art gallery in Omaha, and "Carhenge," a full-scale replica of Stonehenge made from wrecked autos, near Alliance, Nebraska. Each sight is described so you'll know what's most—and sometimes least—interesting about it.

In selecting the restaurants and accommodations for this book, the author sought out unusual spots with local flavor. While in some areas of the region chains are unavoidable, wherever possible the author directs you to one-of-a-kind places. We also know that you want a range of options. One day you may crave a gourmet poultry dish at Bistro 43 in Des Moines, while the next day you would be just as happy (as would your wallet) with a ballpark hot dog at Sec Taylor Stadium in Des Moines, home of the Iowa Cubs baseball team. Most of the restaurants and accommodations listed here are moderately priced, but the author also includes budget and splurge options, depending on the destination.

CREATE THE TRIP YOU WANT

We all have different travel styles. Some people like spontaneous weekend jaunts, while others plan longer, more leisurely trips. You may want to cover as much ground as possible, no matter how much time you have. Or maybe you prefer to focus your trip on one part of the state or on some special interest, such as history, nature, or art. We've taken these differences into account.

Though the individual chapters stand on their own, they are organized in a geographically logical sequence, so that you could conceivably fly into Omaha's Eppley Airfield, drive chapter by chapter to each destination in the book, and end up close to where you started. Of course, you don't have to follow that sequence, but it's there if you want a complete picture of the region.

Each destination chapter offers ways of prioritizing when time is limited: In the Perfect Day section, the author suggests what to do if you have only one day to spend in the area. Also, every Sightseeing Highlight is rated, from one to four stars: ★★★★—or "must see"—sights first, followed by ★★★ sights, then ★★ sights, and finally ★ or "see if you have time" sights. At the end of each sight listing is a time recommendation in parentheses. User-friendly maps help you locate the sights, restaurants, and lodging of your choice.

And if you're in it for the ride, so to speak, you'll want to check out the Scenic Routes described at the end of several chapters. They take you through some of the most scenic parts of region.

In addition to these special features, the appendix has other useful travel tools:

- The Planning Map and Mileage Chart help you determine your own route and calculate travel time.
- The Special Interest Tours show you how to design your trip around any of five favorite interests.
- The Calendar of Events provides an at-a-glance view of when and where major events occur throughout the state.
- The Resource Guide tells you where to go for more information about national and state parks, individual cities and counties, local bed-and-breakfasts, and more.

HAPPY TRAVELS

With this book in hand, you have many reliable recommendations and travel tools at your fingertips. Use it to make the most of your trip. And have a great time!

WHY VISIT IOWA AND NEBRASKA?

If cornfields and the occasional movie—say, the one about baseball and the one about covered bridges—dominate your mental image of Iowa, and Omaha and Lincoln are the only places in Nebraska you've ever heard about, get ready for your perceptions to be shattered when you visit.

Rural charm and down-home friendliness do characterize Iowa and Nebraska, but that's not all that these states smack in the middle of the country have to offer. The dour husband and wife of Grant Wood's famous *American Gothic* portrait have given way to a modern heartland where urban culture exists alongside agriculture. If you pass by peaceful Iowa farmsteads as you tour the Bridges of Madison County, or pull off the road to watch a locomotive glide through the wide open landscape of Nebraska's Sandhills, you'll be enjoying a Midwestern moment—just as you will if you pause to study the Egyptian artifacts on display at Omaha's Joslyn Art Museum or dine at a fine Thai restaurant in Des Moines.

To be sure, reminders of the region's rich heritage abound in the states' sightseeing attractions. "There was nothing but land: not a country at all, but the material out of which countries are made," Nebraska author Willa Cather wrote of her native state. This quotation is printed among the exhibits of Grand Island's Stuhr Museum, just one of the places where the past illuminates the present.

From Lewis and Clark, who passed through in 1804, to the thousands that followed the Oregon Trail westward, the flat plains were a wide open

1

page on which travelers began to write their new history. You still get a sense of that openness and optimism from the landscape and the people, whether you're standing at the top of Scotts Bluff National Monument or taking in a scenic view from Iowa's Loess Hills.

"I think one of the greatest losses we suffer is forgetting what it's like to see the world with new eyes," says Iowa artist Brian Andreas, a Decorah resident who exhibits his work in his hometown's Vesterheim Museum. "Everything around us is an event if we stop to see it that way." Andreas isn't alone in the feeling. Iowa and Nebraska's inhabitants still see the world with new eyes. Pioneer spirit is still evident not only in the region's landscape and history, but also in the faces of those who will be the caretakers of Iowa and Nebraska in the twenty-first century.

THE LAY OF THE LAND

From the air, most of Iowa and Nebraska appears to be a patchwork quilt, a flat expanse of cultivated fields and vast plains on which animal herds roam. On the ground, you can drive along I-80 from the Nebraska Panhandle to the Mississippi River and not noticeably change elevation. These two Great Plains states have no terrain that could remotely be described as mountainous, just wide, rolling prairies as beautiful in their own spare way as tall peaks. Pause to look around and you'll agree. A field of tall, waving grasses glowing in the foreground of a summer sunset dazzles the eye.

North-central and southeast Iowa are predominantly flat, but hilly terrain in the northeastern part of the state affords some beautiful vistas, especially along the Mississippi River. To a lesser extent, southwest Iowa is also hilly country. And the Loess Hills, perhaps Iowa's most unusual landscape feature, run parallel to the Missouri River along the state's western border; drive along I-29 and you'll capture great glimpses of them.

Nebraska's Sandhills are a unique land feature, even from a global perspective. The foothills of South Dakota's Black Hills are in the northwestern part of the state. Nebraska even boasts waterfalls—like the 75-foot falls that dumps into the Niobrara River in Smith Falls State Park. Parts of southwest Nebraska resemble the American Southwest in miniature. Rock outcroppings like the majestic Scotts Bluff National Monument offer amazing panoramic views.

FLORA AND FAUNA

As a general rule, you won't encounter life-threatening animal species in Iowa and Nebraska, even in remote areas, but you will certainly come across plenty of charming critters—from herds of Nebraska cattle to the groundhogs and pheasants that dwell in the prairies in both states.

Probably the most famous animal attraction in either state is the world's largest gathering of cranes, which occurs each spring in Nebraska's Platte River Valley, in the south-central region of the state. Some five hundred thousand sandhill cranes stop over from February through April during their migration from winter locales in Texas, New Mexico, and Mexico to summer habitats in Alaska and Canada. Almost 90 percent of the world's cranes take part in this unique Nebraska event, breathtaking to witness. Their flights en masse between the Platte River and nearby fields draw tourists from near and far. About 10 million ducks, geese, and bald eagles also use the Platte River.

Other Iowa–Nebraska animal inhabitants include plenty of fish, which populate the lakes and streams. Catfish, bass, and walleye are among the most common varieties. Cattle are the most popular four-legged beasts in Nebraska, but some bison herds have been reestablished at Fort Robinson near Crawford and Fort Niobrara Refuge near Valentine.

Iowa supports more tree species than Nebraska, and much of the countryside, as well as many small towns and larger cities, boast majestic oaks, walnuts, and pines, to name a few popular varieties. (So few native trees existed in Nebraska during the late nineteenth century that settlers often built their homes out of sod, often referred to tongue-in-cheek as "Nebraska marble.") Of course, corn and soybean crops are plentiful, but natural wetlands also dot the landscape of both states, offering visitors the chance to explore a diverse ecosystem that dominated the region before farmers settled it and state boundaries were declared.

HISTORY

The histories of Iowa and Nebraska began long before they became states (the former in 1846, the latter in 1867).

Agate Fossil Bed National Monument in Nebraska displays fossils that are 20 million years old, preserving a geological timeline that stretches back to pre–Ice Age days.

The area that is now Iowa and Nebraska has been inhabited by humans for about 12 thousand years. The first known settlers were Native American tribes who raised crops and hunted then-plentiful herds of buffalo. About 17 different Native American groups called Iowa home. Tribes in the region included the Omaha, Pawnee, and Potawatomie—names that have become important place names in present-day Iowa and Nebraska. "Nebraska" itself comes from a Native American word meaning "flat water," in reference to the Platte River. "Iowa" means "the land between two rivers"—that is, between the Missouri and the Mississippi. Native American tribes are believed to have begun agriculture in the region, near the Mississippi, sometime shortly after the fifth century B.C.

The 1804 Lewis and Clark expedition was an all-important step in the transition from the Iowa and Nebraska of old to the modern states we know today. By opening up the region to widespread settlement from the East, the infamous pair of explorers paved the way for all those who came to live off Iowa's fertile soil or, further west, set up residence on Nebraska's more rugged landscape. Riverbanks were popular sights for establishing new towns in the nineteenth century, and today's map still bears that out. (Waterways, of course, provided transportation.) Many former military forts in the two states also evolved into communities.

Groups who stopped through on their westward trek left their mark on the area; among these were the Mormons, who rested a while near Omaha before moving on to Utah. The Germans who settled the Amana Colonies in Iowa found religious freedom and therefore remained; the Amanas still thrive today, their settlement-era traditions and lifestyle preserved both for their own cultural interest and to attract tourists.

If the Missouri and Mississippi were obviously important transportation routes that helped the fledgling states grow and develop, the railroads became just as important in the nineteenth and early twentieth centuries, if not more so.

By 1867, the Union Pacific reached across the entire width of Nebraska, part of the nation's first transcontinental railroad. Several more lines were added around the state over the next couple of decades. Nebraska remains a powerful railroad state, more so than Iowa.

In the twentieth century, both Nebraska and Iowa solidified their status as agricultural leaders feeding America and the world. Omaha's stockyards boomed as the railroads transported thousands of cattle into the city. Horse-drawn power gave way to motorized tractors in the fields, increasing the scale of agriculture in a progression that continues today in the corporate farms and livestock operations that have increasingly popped up.

Today, agriculture still thrives in Iowa and Nebraska, even as cities grow and suburbs encroach on farmland. Politicians seeking the nation's highest office still woo Iowa in advance of the rest of the country, thanks to the state's pole position in the caucus-primary schedule. And Nebraska is still the only state to have one legislative body, the Nebraska Unicameral, in its state government.

CULTURES

German, Irish, and Swedish roots run deep in both Iowa and Nebraska. Ethnic heritage reveals itself in many ways, from name patterns (Dutch surnames often begin with "Van" or "Ver," for example) to particular towns' traditions. The town of Pella, Iowa for instance, holds a Tulip Festival each May. Another small Iowa town, Decorah, thrives on its Norwegian ties. In the southwest part of the state, Elk Horn celebrates its Danish past, down to an actual windmill that was moved from the homeland and reassembled.

THE ARTS

Iowa and Nebraska together have a long list of not-to-miss arts attractions in the larger cities that stand up to the offerings in other regions of the country. The Joslyn Art Museum in Omaha is an internationally respected museum that holds a fine collection of American and European works and hosts a full schedule of music and other performing arts programs. Its counterpart in Iowa, the Des Moines Art Center, is that state's most respected arts institution. The Sioux City Art Center in Iowa also impresses with the distinct, glass-filled architecture of its building and the quality of its exhibits.

But plenty of less urban locales throughout both states feature distinctive

OMAHA SKYLINE

Greater Omaha Convention and Visitors Bureau

arts offerings well worth a tourist's study. The Amana Colonies in east-central Iowa, for example, display the time-honored arts and crafts that have made this religious Germanic settlement thrive; art sales and tourism have been economic mainstays of the Amana Colonies for years.

In north-central Iowa, the Surf Ballroom in Clear Lake is an oasis of live music, dancing, and nostalgia. Similarly, the Val Air Ballroom in West Des Moines preserves the atmosphere of an earlier era entertained by such performers as Glenn Miller.

Thanks to its status as a university town, Lincoln, Nebraska, boasts not only museums but performance venues, such as the Lied Center, that host a impressive calendar of distinguished artists and top-drawer productions. The same can be said of Iowa City, home to the University of Iowa. Both Iowa City and Des Moines also celebrate the work of local and regional artisans who craft jewelry, paintings, sculptures, and other visual delights.

Culture thrives in rural Iowa and Nebraska, too. It seems that every small community celebrates an annual festival of some kind that not only brings the community together and promotes tourism but also showcases native art of all kinds.

CUISINE

Hearty family-style dining is definitely the dominant cuisine of these two states. If you don't have a relative in the region who can cook you up a classic down-home meal, you'll find plenty of restaurants ready to serve you the meat-and-potatoes fare the rural Midwest is famous for.

German food (give me a second helping of sauerkraut, please), for instance, is on the menu at the fine Ox Yoke Inn in the historic Amana Colonies of east-central Iowa. The Iowa Machine Shed is a veritable temple of family-style dining; the original restaurant is in Davenport, another is located in suburban West Des Moines, next to Living History Farms, appropriately enough. Breitbach's Country Dining, in the small town of Balltown, Iowa, near the Mississippi, is not only the state's oldest operating bar and restaurant, it's also one of its best. A carnivore's paradise, Ole's Big Game Steak House & Lounge, just off I-80 in Paxton, Nebraska, serves thick slabs of Nebraska-produced beef in a decor punctuated by some two hundred stuffed, mounted animals.

If your taste extends beyond meat and potatoes, rest assured that other cuisine is available throughout Iowa and Nebraska. The larger cities offer most of the fine dining options. Des Moines, for example, is famous for its excellent Italian restaurants, while Omaha boasts exceptional steakhouses. You'll find great Vietnamese and Thai options in Des Moines and an excellent Indian restaurant in

Iowa City. So, while German, Italian, and Irish cuisine dominate most menus in Iowa and Nebraska, culinary options are growing in the larger cities.

OUTDOOR ACTIVITIES

Cross-country skiers and ice fishers can certainly enjoy the winter months in Iowa and Nebraska, but warm weather offers the best slate of outdoor recreation opportunities.

Two of the country's most powerful rivers—the Missouri and the Mississippi—flow through this landlocked region. River cruises and scenic riverside trails are highly recommended. Water sports are popular at the states' lakes and man-made basins. Okoboji in northwest Iowa, Red Rock Lake in central Iowa, and Lake McConaughy in west-central Nebraska are three of the larger water destinations.

Biking and hiking trails are numerous throughout both states. Many old railroad lines have been converted into scenic, tree-lined trails. In addition to trails, both states host annual bike rides that traverse the width of the state: BRAN, the Bike Ride Across Nebraska, and RAGBRAI, the Register's Annual Great Bike Ride Across Iowa.

Nebraska's Sandhills, a desert region dotted by tufts of grass, is a recreation destination favored for its flocks of migratory birds and the simple beauty of the rolling landscape.

All the usual outdoor sports activities, from golf to tennis to swimming, also await you at public and private facilities throughout both states. Prefer to remain a spectator? Take yourself out to the ballgame—at Rosenblatt Stadium in Omaha (home of the Omaha Royals) or Sec Taylor Stadium in Des Moines (home of the Iowa Cubs)—or cheer on a football team (the Nebraska Cornhuskers or the Iowa Hawkeyes).

PLANNING YOUR TRIP

Before you set out on your trip, you'll need to do some planning. Use this chapter in conjunction with the tools in the appendix to answer some basic questions. First of all, when are you going? You may already have specific dates in mind; if not, various factors will probably influence your timing. Either way, you'll want to know about local events and other seasonal considerations. This chapter discusses all of that.

How much should you expect to spend on your trip? This chapter addresses various regional factors you'll want to consider in estimating your travel expenses. How will you get around? Check out the section on orientation and transportation. If you decide to travel by car, the Planning Map and Mileage Chart in the appendix can help you figure out exact routes and driving times, while the Special Interest Tours provide several focused itineraries. The chapter concludes with some reading recommendations, both fiction and nonfiction, to give you various perspectives on the region. If you want more specifics, use the Resources guide in the appendix.

WHEN TO GO

Plan your Iowa and Nebraska vacation in January or February and you'll likely find some great cross-country skiing...or hunting...or snowmobiling...or ice-fishing...or ice-skating. But the weather will chill you to the bone, especially if you're not used to such a cold climate. (A week or two of sub-zero temperatures is a common-enough Iowa winter weather occurance.) Traveling conditions are at their most oppresive in the dead of an Iowa-Nebraska winter, too, and can turn dangerous and even deadly within a matter of minutes—freezing rain or white-out snowfall often crops up with little warning. No geographic boundaries like mountains stand in the way of a stormfront on the Great Plains, after all. Snowstorms can even hit as late as April, though, so trying to avoid snow won't always be possible. Drive a car (whether a rental or your own) with plenty of traction and power in case you should experience bad weather during your trip; a 4 x 4 SUV isn't necessary, but lightweight, small-engine cars might not provide the safest winter transportation. (If you don't like the weather in Iowa, an old saying goes, wait 10 minutes—it'll change.)

The months of May and September are generally the most temperate in the region. As agricultural states, you'll find that most of the community festivals and events that help give Iowa and Nebraska their folksy charm take place in the late summer and fall, coinciding with the growth and especially the harvest of crops—predominantly corn and soybeans, and especialy in Iowa. (Nebraska is better known as a cattle ranching state.) For instance, the Midwest Old Threshers Reunion in Mount Pleasant, Iowa, directly celebrates the harvest of the late nineteenth and early twentieth centuries by recreating it; antique threshing machines and horse-powered equipment perform their age-old tasks, entertaining and educating new generations of grocery store–fed festival-goers. The Kass Kounty King Korn Karnival in Plattsmouth, Nebraska, is another example of these states' harvest-time traditions. Even in the twenty-first century, food will remain a focal point for both industry and fun.

If you can stand the heat, the summertime months of June, July, and August will give you plenty to do in both states. Consider touring in the middle of August so you can catch the Iowa State Fair in Des Moines, one of the region's truly signature, celebrated events. Or the Okoboji area, with its clustered lakes and Arnolds Park amusement park, is the perfect summer destination, where many Iowans as well as non-Iowans relocate for an entire summer, not just a week or two of vacation. Most communities will have some sort of warm-weather celebration to attract you. In early May, Pella celebrates its Dutch heritage with Tulip Time, which attracts tens of thousands of visitors annually. Sioux City hosts River-Cade in July, which includes a variety of events on the Missouri River. The Register's Great Annual Bike Ride Across Iowa, in late July, even includes the entire state in a summertime celebration; a different route is picked each year that crosses the state lengthwise, and thousands of bikers then traverse that route within seven (sometimes grueling) days.

HOW MUCH WILL IT COST?

Unlike a large, urban tourist destination in America, an Iowa-Nebraska vacation won't break your budget. Only the top-drawer restaurants and lodgings in Des Moines and Omaha will remind you of similar spots in Los Angeles, Chicago, and New York.

An upscale hotel room in one of Iowa or Nebraska's major cities will cost around $100; the best accommodations in smaller cities and towns could cost as little as $50 or $60. Aside from sleeping in your car, camping is generally the cheapest alternative, with a $5 or $10 fee per night. Whether in a rural or urban area, bed-and-breakfast inns can vary anywhere from $40 to $120 per night, the cheaper rooms offering just a bed, TV, and shared bathroom, the more expensive suites featuring their own whirpool tubs or even balconies.

The best meals you'll find can cost $50 or more per person without wine, but plenty of great restaurants will offer tasty entrees for $15 or $20 each. And lots of establishments that serve hearty family-style food in the rural reaches of the region will cost even less but taste just as good, if not better.

Sightseeing attractions will cost anywhere from a few dollars for a rural museum to $10 or more for popular, high-traffic stops like Living History Farms near Des Moines (in the suburb of Urbandale). But there's not a real rule of thumb for price in this area, even city versus rural. Many worthwhile attractions don't cost a thing, even the highly recommended Des Moines Art Center.

ORIENTATION AND TRANSPORTATION

If you're flying into the region, Omaha's Eppley Airfield is the largest airport in the two states and probably your best point of entry and exit for cheap, convenient air travel. (Hence this book's use of Omaha/Council Bluffs as a logical starting point.) Des Moines International Airport, the next largest choice, lacks the volume and variety of choice of Eppley, despite efforts in the late '90s to refashion and expand. Nebraska has more than 100 airports within its borders, but Eppley will probably be the only one you will use in your travels.

Iowa and Nebraska are both cut in half lengthwise by Interstate 80, the nation's longest and most-traveled stretch of freeway. Interstate 29 runs north–south in Iowa, in the valley between the Missouri River and the Loess Hills. Interstate 35 cuts Iowa in half widthwise, connecting Des Moines with the Twin Cities to the north and Kansas City to the south.

Knowledge of the region's roads is important because you'll travel mostly by car. Mass transit has yet to take a firm hold between cities and within major cities themselves. Sure, you can catch a Greyhound bus between Omaha and Des Moines or use a city bus during the day in either city, but the frequency and convenience aren't up to par for the traveler. Even taxis must be called in Des Moines, unless you're at the airport.

While traveling around Nebraska, or across its 387-mile diameter (including the panhandle), you'll see lots of freight trains, but passenger rail service is comparatively scarce in both states. Union Pacific provides passenger service to five Nebraska cities, and an Amtrak line cuts through the south section of Iowa, connecting with Chicago.

So auto travel it is. Interstate speed limits are 65 miles per hour; rest stops are conveniently spaced. You'll need to travel by major two-lane highways around much of the region, but though a sacrifice in terms of speed and time, they're generally in good repair. Driving through Nebraska's Sandhills will require planning for fueling stops between the sparse gas stations, but that is the most remote territory you'll come across in the the two states. The region is full of well-tended farms and ranches, not vast wilderness.

And you won't come across any wild, mountainous terrain that's difficult to traverse by car. (Driving up the highly recommended Scotts Bluff National Monument in the Nebraska Panhandle will probably be your steepest driving experience.) Nebraska, for instance, has its lowest point (840 feet above sea level) in the southeast corner of the state and only rises to about 5,400 feet above sea level near the western border.

A transportation center to look for: Just west of the Quad Cities in Iowa, the I-80 Truck Stop in Walcott is the nation's largest truck stop. It's a veritable megaplex that includes a Hardees, a video game room, convenience store, gas station, gift shop, showers, sleeping quarters, and mini- movie theaters.

In fact, Nebraska's and especially Iowa's major cities are spread fairly well around the region. The latter state has Des Moines as its center, with Council Bluffs (and Omaha, Nebraska) on the west central border and the Quad Cities (shared with Illinois) on the east-central border. Iowa's second largest single city, Cedar Rapids, is in the northeastern part of the state. The fourth largest city is in northwest Iowa, Sioux City.

Nebraska's major cities are more aligned along I-80. The biggest city Omaha is on the east border, with Lincoln in second place just a short hour to the west and Grand Island just beyond that.

RECOMMENDED READING

Iowa
A novel that tells a story of small-town life from the emotionally charged perspectives of several characters, *The Book of Famous Iowans: A Novel* (Henry

Holt & Company, Inc.), by Douglas Bauer, has left many readers pondering over the characters' lives.

Buildings of Iowa (Oxford University Press), by David Gebhard and Gerald Mansheim, is a thorough, fascinating study of the state's architecturally relevant structures and their history.

Novelist Peter Hedges produced a couple of great Iowa-related novels in the '90s. *What's Eating Gilbert Grape* (Pocket Books), went on to become a celebrated Johnny Depp–Juliette Lewis–Leonardo DiCaprio movie that was filmed in Texas despite its Iowa setting. Most recently, Hedges published *An Ocean in Iowa* (Simon & Schuster, 1998).

For Iowa stories you might not hear elsewhere except around a campfire at night, *Ghostly Tales of Iowa* (Iowa State University Press), by Ruth D. Hein and Vicky L. Hinsenbrock, will put some spook in your travels.

The story that inspired Kevin Costner's *Field of Dreams* movie is W.P. Kinsella's *Shoeless Joe* (Mariner Books). A man who loves baseball hears voices, builds a baseball diamond in his cornfield, and the players come. It's simple yet sublime. Kinsella has published other books, too, including *Shoeless Joe Jackson Comes to Iowa* (Southern Methodist University Press, 1993).

One of the nation's funniest, most caustic political satirists is cartoonist Tom Tomorrow, who sprang from Iowa City. You can find his strips in newspapers around the country, and he has published several books' worth of his work. *Greetings from This Modern World* (1992) is one of the earlier collections, while 1998's *Penguin Soup for the Soul* represents some of Tomorrow's more recent witty words and images.

The Bridges of Madison County (Warner Books), by Robert James Waller, tells the now-familiar fictional tale of the romance between photographer Robert Kincaid and farm wife Francesca Johnson. The 1994 Clint Eastwood–Meryl Streep movie of this 1992 novel immortalized Madison County and fully secured Waller's financial future. Waller was an author and college professor for many years before his big success. *Iowa: Perspectives on Today and Tomorrow* (Iowa State University Press) is a less romantic Waller selection, published in 1991.

An excellent 1997 analysis of the cultural impact of one of the most famous Iowa natives is *John Wayne's America* (Touchstone/Simon & Schuster), by Garry Wills.

Nebraska

Nebraska Cornhusker football fans will no doubt find a must-buy in *Go Big Red: The Complete Fan's Guide to Nebraska Football* (Griffin Trade Paperback), a 1998 tome by Michael and Mike Babcock.

One of the region's most famous writers, Willa Cather, is best represented by her classic book *My Antonia*. It's a story of childhood on a Nebraska farm. The University of Nebraska Press 1994 scholarly edition is a cut above the rest.

The Gate City: A History of Omaha (University of Nebraska Press), by Lawrence H. Larsen and Barbara J. Cottrell, was originally published in 1982 but was updated in 1997 with an enlarged edition. The book's sweeping look at the region's largest city offers an impressive and authoritative read.

For a literary companion to your Nebraska travels, seek out *Guide to Nebraska Authors* (Dageford Publishing), a 1998 volume by Gerry Cox.

Those with a sense of humor can pick up *I Hate Nebraska—303 Reasons Why You Should, Too* (Crane Hill Publishing), a jokey 1996 work by Paul Finebaum.

No More Free Markets or Free Beer: The Progressive Era in Nebraska 1900–1924 (Lexington Books) is a 1999 historical work by Burton W. Folsom.

The Nebraska Sand Hills: The Human Landscape (University of Nebraska Press) makes for a good companion to your tours of central Nebraska's hilly, grassy desert. It's a 1996 book by Charles Barron McIntosh.

Those truly serious about the frontier history of the Midwest should pay the money for *The Journals of the Lewis & Clark Expedition, June 10–September 26, 1806/A Project of the Center for Great Plains Studies, University of Nebraska–Lincoln* (University of Nebraska Press). A 1993 edition, it presents as fully and accurately as possible the journals of Meriwether Lewis and William Clark. Gary E. Moulton edited this edition. The set, comprised of 11 volumes, can be purchased for $75 per volume.

In *Goodnight, Nebraska* (Vintage), Tom McNeal offers up a first novel that explores the life and acquaintances of character Randall Hunsacker, a resident of the town of Goodnight, Nebraska.

History of Nebraska (University of Nebraska Press) is a respected 1966 work by James C. Olson.

Those looking for a fun, fictional puzzler should turn to *Drive-By: A Nebraska Mystery* (Ex Mac Hina Publishing Co.), a 1995 book by William J. Reynolds.

Buffalo Soldiers, Braves and the Brass: The Story of Fort Robinson, Nebraska (White Mane), by Frank N. Schubert and published in 1993, chronicles the history of a frontier military fort and the nearby community (Crawford, Nebraska) that it existed with in an intimate symbiosis. The interaction of soldiers and civilians, the evolving race relations, the impact of the lucrative saloon and prostitution industries—frontier life is revealed in interesting, scholarly detail.

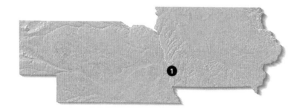

1
OMAHA AND COUNCIL BLUFFS

These neighboring cities are the perfect starting point for your Iowa-Nebraska trip, providing a taste of both states.

Once known as the hub of the meatpacking industry, Omaha, the site of the Union Stockyards, has since gone high tech. Now a business center for the telemarketing and data processing industries, the greater metro area has a population of more than 660 thousand; the city itself grew by more than 40 thousand in the last decade alone. Con Agra Corporation has funded extensive redevelopment of the downtown riverfront, where people stroll across green lawns and sit on park benches; Omaha has also expanded to the west, its suburbs reaching out into the prairie and toward Lincoln, Nebraska's state capital.

Simply put, Omaha is the most cosmopolitan stop on your Iowa-Nebraska trip, full of urban sights, restaurants, and accommodations. Relax in a café courtyard among the brick buildings and cobblestone streets of the Historic Old Market and enjoy a decidedly European ambience along with your breakfast, lunch, or dinner. Drive along one of the city's main east–west thoroughfares, Dodge Street, to glimpse what this city has to offer, from quirky restaurants to parks, major shopping malls, and the renowned Joslyn Art Museum.

Council Bluffs is the smaller of the two cities, but there are fine things to see and do here, too. Originally settled by Mormons in 1846, Council Bluffs was called Kanesville, now the name of a major street. The city became

Council Bluffs in 1853, so named to honor explorers Lewis and Clark, who held a council with the local Native American tribes among the area's beautiful bluffs.

Today, reminders of Council Bluffs' past include the Historic General Dodge House, while the casinos near the banks of the Missouri River represent new development—and draw many Omahans into Iowa for a night on the town.

A PERFECT DAY IN OMAHA AND COUNCIL BLUFFS

Start your morning at the Western Historic Trails Center in Council Bluffs, where you'll get a sense of the area's importance as a major gateway during the era of westward expansion. The Historic General Dodge House, generally regarded as Council Bluffs' finest sight, salutes one of the most important figures from that exciting, formative time in the city's history.

Then cross the river and take a stroll around Omaha's Old Market as the shops are just opening up. Stop at the Omaha History Center and Coffee Lounge, where a cup of coffee and knowledge of local history are both on the menu. Be sure to take time to visit the Antiquarium, a voluminous used bookstore, music store, and art gallery where some of the nicest, most interesting folk stock some of the most interesting reading and listening material in the area. Have lunch at one of several fine restaurants in the Old Market.

Next stop: Omaha's Henry Doorly Zoo, a vast, well-tended facility where the animals live in carefully reconstructed habitats.

Treat yourself to a gourmet dinner at the Flatiron Grill in the Old Market. Then drive out to the Lewis & Clark Monument and Scenic Overlook to watch the golden sun drop below the expanse of prairie laid out before you. Return to the Old Market for some nightlife—such as live Irish folk music at the charming Dubliner Pub—or take in a baseball game at Rosenblatt Stadium, a must if you're lucky enough to be in Omaha during a home game. *Free. (15 minutes–1 hour)*

OMAHA SIGHTSEEING HIGHLIGHTS

★★★★ THE ANTIQUARIUM
1215 Harney St., 402/341-8077

Tom Rudloff and his sister opened a secondhand bookshop in their home in 1969, and by March 1975 the Antiquarium had moved to its Old Market location and acquired four full levels of books,

GREATER OMAHA

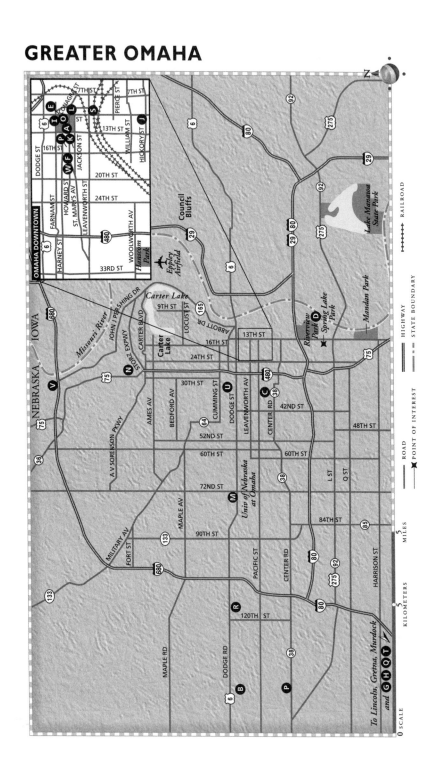

OMAHA DOWNTOWN

7TH ST
7TH ST
PIERCE ST
E
I
P
A
O
L
S
W
F
K
13TH ST
WILLIAM ST
HICKORY ST
J
DOUGLAS ST
16TH ST
JACKSON ST
20TH ST
DODGE ST
FARNAM ST
HARNEY ST
HOWARD ST
ST. MARY'S AV
24TH ST
LEAVENWORTH ST
WOOLWORTH AV
6
480
WOOLWORTH AV
33RD ST
Hanscom Park

IOWA
NEBRASKA

92
275
80
6
29
92
80
275
Lake Manawa State Park
Council Bluffs
29
6
Mandan Park
Eppley Airfield
Carter Lake
9TH ST
LOCUST ST
165
ABBOTT DR
Riverview Park
D
Spring Lake Park
13TH ST
16TH ST
75
680
Missouri River
JOHN J PERSHING DR
CARTER BLVD
Carter Lake
24TH ST
STORZ EXPWY
N
V
75
30TH ST
CUMMING ST
DODGE ST
U
480
LEAVENWORTH AV
42ND ST
C
38
CENTER RD
AMES AV
BEDFORD AV
64
52ND ST
48TH ST
A V SORENSON PKWY
60TH ST
60TH ST
36
75
72ND ST
L ST
Q ST
MAPLE AV
Univ of Nebraska at Omaha
M
38
MILITARY AV
FORT ST
90TH ST
84TH ST
85
133
PACIFIC ST
CENTER RD
80
275
92
HARRISON ST
680
R
120TH ST
80
133
MAPLE RD
DODGE RD
38
B
P
MAPLE RD
To Lincoln, Gretna, Murdock and G H Q T

0 SCALE
KILOMETERS   5
MILES   5

RAILROAD
HIGHWAY
STATE BOUNDARY
ROAD
POINT OF INTEREST

magazines, records, and an art gallery—about 14,400 square feet in all. It's by far one of the most intriguing shops in the two-state region, both for the scope of its wares—today it stocks nearly one hundred thousand books alone—and for the frequent, intelligent conversations between the owners and their customers. Blotch the cat roams the aisles. You can play chess on one of the boards at the back of the shop. The art gallery often exhibits the sculptures and drawings of local artist Bill Farmer, 74, whom Rudloff calls "one of the greatest artists of the twentieth century—as yet undiscovered."

Details: *Open year-round daily 11:30–10. Free. (1–3 hours)*

★★★★ **HENRY DOORLY ZOO**
3701 S. 10th St., 402/733-8401

With more than 4,500 animals, the world's largest indoor rainforest (the Leid Jungle), and the six-story Lozier IMAX Theater (put your eyes back in their sockets after the film), Henry Doorly is one of the Midwest's premier zoos for good reason. Sit on a bench and watch polar bears swim gracefully in their immense glass water tank. Thrill to threatening fish in the zoo's popular shark center, the Scott Aquarium, which is viewed by walking through a

As the onetime gateway between the settled East and the wild, wild West, Omaha and Council Bluffs represented the last stronghold of "civilization" for westward travelers.

SIGHTS

- Ⓐ The Antiquarium
- Ⓑ Boys Town
- Ⓒ Gerald R. Ford Birthsite & Gardens
- Ⓓ Henry Doorly Zoo
- Ⓔ Historic Old Market
- Ⓕ Joslyn Art Museum
- Ⓖ Lee G. Simmons Conservation Park & Wildlife Safari
- Ⓗ Strategic Air Command Museum

FOOD

- Ⓘ Butsy Le Doux's
- Ⓙ Cascio's Steak House
- Ⓚ Dazy Maze
- Ⓛ Indian Oven
- Ⓜ Jams
- Ⓝ Mister C's Steak House
- Ⓞ Vivace
- Ⓟ Zio's Pizzeria (3 locations)

LODGING

- Ⓠ Bundy's Bed & Breakfast
- Ⓡ Candlewood Hotel
- Ⓢ Embassy Suites
- Ⓣ Farmhouse Bed & Breakfast
- Ⓤ Offut House Bed & Breakfast
- Ⓥ Riverview Garden Bed & Breakfast
- Ⓦ Westin Aquila Hotel

tunnel, with the water all around you. Try to spot monkeys as they scurry and swing among the trees. The Cat Complex packs in lions, tigers, and leopards. A steam train can tote you around the Henry Doorly grounds for a quick overview.

Details: *Take I-80 Exit 454. Open year-round daily 9:30–5. $7.25 adults, $3.75 ages 5–11, free under 5. (1–4 hours)*

★★★★ **HISTORIC OLD MARKET**
Farnam St. to Jackson St. and 10th St. to 13th St.,
402/341-7151 or 402/346-4445

Along with the Antiquarium, the Old Market encompasses more than one hundred businesses, including music stores (Homer's), bars (Dubliner Pub), fine restaurants (Vivace), and specialty clothing shops (Bangkok Import). Omaha's most urban and vivid gathering spot, the Old Market is an old warehouse district—cobblestone streets and historic brick buildings lend the area a nineteenth-century charm. Here, life slows down to the pace of pedestrian traffic, with all ages and stripes mingling contentedly. The greatest number of folks gather on weekends, when it's not uncommon to catch a ride in a horse and buggy or listen to street musicians. A farmer's market occupies a

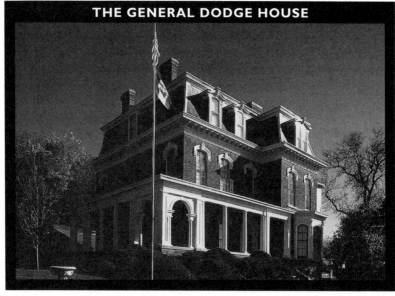

THE GENERAL DODGE HOUSE

Council Bluffs Convention and Visitors Bureau

FREE MUSIC JAMS

If it's a Saturday afternoon, check out the free music jam sessions at the **Acorn Supply Company** in Council Bluffs—a bunch of local musicians have loads of fun playing folk and country tunes in a feed store, as they have for 16 years. This will likely be one of the most memorable highlights of your trip.

---

parking lot on Saturday mornings from May through October in the southeast part of the district.

    Details: *Individual business hours vary. Free. (1–4 hours)*

★★★★ JOSLYN ART MUSEUM
2200 Dodge St., 402/342-3300, www.joslyn.org

Truly one of Omaha's treasures, the Joslyn is a world-class museum, with an emphasis on nineteenth- and twentieth-century American and European art. It holds great works and hosts great events. Degas, Monet, Segal, and Pollack are some of the marquee artists with works on display. The Joslyn is also renowned for its collection of American West art and for the Missouri River–themed watercolors and prints of Swiss artist Karl Bodmer. The museum, opened in 1931, is housed in an Art Deco structure built using 38 kinds of marble from seven different countries. In 1994, a $16 million addition was opened to house late twentieth-century works. The first Sunday of each month a longstanding concert series, Bagels & Bach, is staged in the fountain court, while on Thursday evenings in July and August, Jazz on the Green takes place outdoors.

    Details: *Free parking in east and north lots. Handicapped access via the atrium entrance. Open year-round Tue–Sat 10–4, Sun noon–4. $5 adults, $3 seniors and college students, $2.50 ages 5–17, free under 5, free to all Sat 10–noon. (1–3 hours)*

★★★★ STRATEGIC AIR COMMAND MUSEUM
28210 W. Park Hwy., I-80 Exit 426, 800/358-5029
www.sacmuseum.org

Standing beneath a 175,000-pound Boeing B-52B Heavy Bomber

---

humbles you. Its sheer scale is impressive. You're dwarfed. And when you consider the history of the metal beast, the places it has flown, and set it next to several other massive planes, you appreciate the wonder of the SAC Museum. A tribute to the aircraft of the Strategic Air Command and housed in a new facility since 1998, the museum displays its full-scale, decommissioned airplanes inside two enormous hangars. Seen from the outside, the museum indeed looks like some mysterious, massive military facility. You don't get to climb inside the planes (or fly them), but the experience is still a flight of fancy. The Apollo 9 Command Space Module is also on view, as is a Vela Satellite, which orbited 70,000 miles above the earth to detect nuclear detonations in the atmosphere.

Details: Located just north of I-80 at 2820 West Park Hwy. Open year-round daily 9–5. $6 adults, $5 seniors and active military, $3 ages 5–12, free under 5. (1–3 hours)

★★★ LEE G. SIMMONS CONSERVATION PARK & WILDLIFE SAFARI
I-80 Exit 426, 402/944-WILD

Drive through this park and you might think you have traveled back in time—or at least to some remote, forgotten region of the Great Plains. Here, you'll enjoy close views of bison, deer, wolves, waterfowl, and other animals. Covering more than two hundred acres, the park gives native Nebraska animals plenty of room to roam, and half of the park is off-limits to all but certain exotic species and their caretakers.

The Baright Visitors Center at the park entrance features gardens, indoor and outdoor exhibits, a gift shop, and a concession stand. For those who don't wish to take their car through the park, trams are available.

Details: Open Apr–Oct Mon–Fri 9–5, Sat–Sun 9:30–6. $5 per car. (1 hour)

★ BOYS TOWN (FATHER FLANAGAN'S BOYS HOME)
137th St. and W. Dodge Rd., 800/625-1400 or 402/498-1140

With his Oscar-winning portrayal of Father Flanagan in the 1938 film *Boys Town*, Spencer Tracy helped bring national recognition to this Omaha center that helps troubled young men—and women—rebuild their lives. A National Historic Landmark, Boys Town features the Hall of History, Father Flanagan's House, and All-American Rose

Garden, as well as the Oscar statuette that Tracy turned over to Flanagan.

Details: Open May–Aug 8–5:30; Sep–Apr 8–4:30. Tours 8–4:30. Free. (1–2 hours)

★ **GERALD R. FORD BIRTHSITE & GARDENS**
32nd St. and Woolworth Ave., 402/444-5955

Only hard-core Fordophiles will need to stop here. A kiosk displaying Ford memorabilia marks the site where the birth home of the 38th president once stood, and a serene garden features walkways and stone pillars. Hanscom Park's rolling green landscape is in view just across Woolworth Avenue, inviting a picnic.

Details: Open year-round daily 7:30–9. Free. (15 minutes)

COUNCIL BLUFFS
SIGHTSEEING HIGHLIGHTS

★★★ **HISTORIC GENERAL DODGE HOUSE**
605 Third St., 712/322-2406

Both Omaha and Council Bluffs are rich in railroad heritage, thanks in large part to General Grenville M. Dodge, chief construction engineer of the Union Pacific Railway. His 14-room, 3-story mansion—built in 1869 for the then-lavish sum of $35,000—overlooks the Missouri Valley. Inside, the Dodge House has undergone a restoration process since 1964 to recreate as closely as possible its original condition. Touring this house, considered sumptuous and ultra-modern in its day, offers a tactile way to mark the passing of a century. Beautiful woodwork, furniture, and stories fill each room.

Details: Take I-80 Exit 3. Open Feb–Dec Tue–Sat 10–5, Sun 1–5. $3 adults, $1.50 ages 6–16, free under 6. (1 hour)

★★ **WESTERN HISTORIC TRAILS CENTER**
S. 24th St., 712/325-4900

Opened in the fall of 1997, this informative center is reached via a narrow, blacktop road that winds through a field—hardly a hardship compared to how the pioneers traveled across this land. The Trails Center's multimedia exhibits trace the paths of those pioneers as they followed trails from St. Louis to the Pacific Ocean. State-of-the-art audio and video elements combine with more conventional displays to brilliantly

COUNCIL BLUFFS

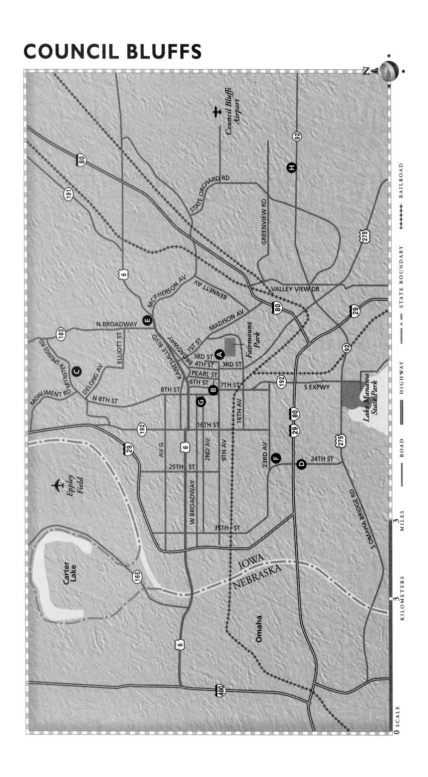

bring to life the travelers of yesteryear. You can also view a 15-minute film and stock up on books, maps, and souvenirs from the gift shop. Outdoor hiking trails lead to the Missouri River, where you can stroll along an old railroad line for a taste of nature within the metro area.

Details: *Just south of I-80, off Exit 1B, across from Bluffs Run Casino. Open year-round daily 9–5. Free. (30 minutes–1 hour)*

★ **HISTORIC POTTAWATTAMIE COUNTY "SQUIRREL CAGE" JAIL AND MUSEUM**
226 Pearl St., 712/323-2509
Listed on the National Register of Historic Places, the "Squirrel Cage" refers to the jail's unique revolving interior, designed so that just one or two jailers could be responsible for all the prisoners. It's also referred to as a "human rotary jail," which means that all the cells are housed in a large metal cylinder that can spin on an axis. All the cells' doors open to the outside of the cylinder. The cylinder is surrounded by a concrete wall as a sheath, with one opening in the wall that allows outside access to one cell door at a time. Hence a limited number of prison guards can manage a large number of prisoners. Built in 1885, its express purpose, according to Indianapolis, Indiana, inventors William H. Brown and Benjamin F. Haugh, was to "produce a jail in which prisoners can be controlled without the necessity of personal contact between them and the jailer."

Details: *Open Apr–May 15 and Sep 16–Oct Sat 10–4, Sun noon–4; May 16–Sep 15 Wed–Sat 10–4, Sun noon–4. $3 adults, $2.50 seniors, $1.25 ages 6–12, free under 6. (30 minutes–1 hour)*

SIGHTS
Ⓐ Historic General Dodge House
Ⓑ Historic Pottawattamie County "Squirrel Cage" Jail and Museum
Ⓒ Lewis & Clark Monument and Scenic Overlook
Ⓓ Western Historic Trails Center

FOOD
Ⓔ Pizza King

LODGING
Ⓕ Best Western Crossroads of the Bluffs
Ⓖ Lion's Den Bed & Breakfast
Ⓗ Terra Jane Bed & Breakfast

★ LEWIS & CLARK MONUMENT AND SCENIC OVERLOOK

Rainbow Point, N. Eighth St., 712/328-4650

Honoring the 1804 expedition of Meriwether Lewis and William Clark and their meeting in August of that year with the chiefs of the Oto and Missouri Indian tribes, the original monument was completed in 1935 by an organization known as the Colonial Dames. Modern restorations were finished in 1993. On a clear day, you can see far to the west, across the prairie and into Omaha. Good picnic site.

Details: Just north of Big Lake Park. Open year-round daily 6–10.

FITNESS AND RECREATION

Remnants of the Council Bluffs–Omaha area's industrial past and its natural history have been transformed into recreation opportunities, from abandoned railroad lines that have been turned into beautiful biking and hiking trails, to riverside development and Iowa's scenic Loess Hills.

This isn't Minnesota, but water sports are available as well. **Chalco Hills Recreation Area at Wehrspann Lake**, 8901 S. 154th St., Omaha, 402/444-6222, a day-use-only facility open from 6 a.m. to 10 p.m., features a 245-acre lake stocked with bass, walleye, pan fish, and catfish. Picnic shelters, nature trails, and soccer fields dot the landscape around the lake.

If you prefer woods to water, **Fontenelle Forest**, 1111 N. Bellevue Blvd., Bellevue, 402/731-3140, is a well-known Omaha-area forest as well as a National Historic Landmark. Its 1,300 acres include 17 miles of hiking and walking trails as well as a nature center. Tucked into the bend of the Missouri River, the forest offers scenic spots as well. It's not the best biking choice, though.

In any weather, tennis is on tap at **Hanscom-Brandeis Indoor Tennis Courts**, 3220 Ed Creighton Ave., Omaha, 402/444-5584, which has eight indoor hard courts that you can rent for a minimal hourly fee (which varies according to the day and time).

A superb crushed-limestone trail for hiking or biking, **Wabash Trace Nature Trail** runs more than 60 miles from Council Bluffs southeast to Blanchard, Iowa, on the Iowa-Missouri border. Its rural scenery lets you glimpse authentic, scenic slices of Iowa landscape and farmsteads as you travel through a series of small towns and beneath thick stretches of tree canopy. The grade is pretty much flat throughout. Call Endless Trail Bike Shop, 712/322-9760, or True Wheel, 712/328-0767, both in Council Bluffs, with Wabash-related questions; both stores also supply maps, updates on trail conditions, and passes ($1 daily), which are encouraged but not strictly enforced.

FOOD

You'll want to do most of your dining in Omaha, where choices range from old-fashioned Midwestern meat and potatoes to some of the two states' best gourmet restaurants.

Restaurant variety abounds in the Old Market district. Not just a vegan hangout, **Dazy Maze**, 521 S. 13th St., Omaha, 402/346-9342, is a cozy and funky "veggie lounge" in the Old Market district with menu items like a garden vegetable burger and black bean combinations to delight any palate. And they serve organic beer. You can order to go and, in warm weather, dine on an outdoor patio. Poetry readings are sometimes held here.

Also in the Old Market, fine dining in both the Italian and Mediterranean traditions is the specialty at **Vivace**, 1108 Howard St., 402/342-2050, where fresh breads, an extensive wine list, and tasty pasta and meat combinations draw a full house most nights. **Indian Oven**, 1010 Howard St., 402/342-4856, features, as you might guess, fine Indian food. And to add a zing to your evening fine dining in the Old Market, **Butsy Le Doux's**, 104 Howard St., 402/346-5100, features spicy Creole cooking in a casual atmosphere.

A fixture on the Omaha dining scene, **Mister C's Steak House**, 5319 N. 30th St., 402/451-1998, is the place to go to eat the kinds of animals that once flooded the city's stockyards. Another fine, beefy choice is **Cascio's Steak House**, 1620 S. 10th St., 402/345-8313, where you can feel comfortable in casual or formal attire as you enjoy the signature steaks.

In west Omaha, **Jams**, 7814 W. Dodge Rd., 402/399-8300, is a popular bar and grill with a Southwestern flair to its menu. The sandwiches feature unusual ingredients but aren't expensive, while the admirable wine list and more expensive, elaborate entrées of meat, seafood, and pasta provide fine evening dining.

If you'd like a simple and inexpensive yet tasty lunch, **Zio's Pizzeria** is traditionally regarded as Omaha's best source for pizza. Hand-stretched New York–style pizza is just one of their specialties. There are three locations: 1213 Howard St., 402/344-2222; 7924 W. Dodge Rd., 402/391-1881; and 13463 W. Center Rd., 402/330-1444.

In Council Bluffs, **Pizza King**, 1101 N. Broadway, 712/323-4911, is a locally owned Italian restaurant that cooks up fine steaks, seafood, and pasta dishes with friendly service in a large but warm dining room. The portions are hearty and generous. It's the kind of dining place that has served generations—the owners circulate around the room greeting regular customers.

LODGING

Boasting a laundry list of standard amenities (CD player, VCR, full kitchen, two-line phone with a data port, free parking) but not the expensive price tag to match, **Candlewood Hotel**, 360 S. 108th Ave., Omaha, 800/946-6200 or 402/758-2848, could be your best choice for luxury on a budget. It's situated in the west part of the city. You should be able to get a room for less than $100.

In the Old Market, **Embassy Suites**, 555 S. 10th St., Omaha, 800/EM-BASSY or 402/346-9000, offers spacious and more expensive two-room suites that include a free breakfast. Also downtown and closer to Eppley Airfield, the **Westin Aquila Hotel**, 1615 Howard St., Omaha, 800/937-8461 or 402/342-2222, likes to promote that it offers the kinds of flourishes usually cornered by bed-and-breakfasts, even though it has nearly 150 rooms and hosts many business travelers.

A bed-and-breakfast conveniently located near the Old Market, **Offutt House Bed & Breakfast**, 140 N. 39th St., 402/553-0951, is housed in a century-old building yet features central air-conditioning. Overlooking the Missouri River, **Riverview Garden Bed & Breakfast**, 9641 N. 29th St., Omaha, 800/240-3773 or 402/455-4623, is located in a quiet residential neighborhood you can reach by taking Exit 13 off I-680.

Maybe you'd prefer a more rural stay that's still comfortably close to the metro area. The first bed-and-breakfast in Nebraska was **Bundy's Bed & Breakfast**, 16906 S. 255th St., Gretna, 402/332-3616, located on a farm just southwest of Omaha (take I-80 Exit 432, then go four miles west on Highway 6). A little farther west, **Farmhouse Bed & Breakfast**, 32617 Church Rd., Murdock, 402/867-2062, was built in 1896 and now features a front porch swing, handmade quilts, antiques, and queen-size beds. Take I-80 Exit 440, go 14 miles south on Highway 50, and then drive 3.5 miles west on Church Road.

The Iowa side of the metro area also has worthwhile accommodations. For an affordable and comfortable stay, **Best Western Crossroads of the Bluffs**, located at I-80 and South 24th Street, Council Bluffs, 800/528-1234 or 712/322-3150, has what you're looking for, plus a fitness center and game room.

In downtown Council Bluffs, **Lion's Den Bed & Breakfast**, 136 S. Seventh St., 712/322-7162 or 888/48-LIONS, has a private five-room suite, a library, and rose garden.

Terra Jane Bed & Breakfast, 24814 Greenview Rd., 712/322-4200, features a converted cattle barn that can be rented for business gatherings or parties, complete with a stage, dance floor, and bar. You can also play horse-shoes or sand volleyball during your stay. The inn itself features five different rooms.

Prices hover around $100 for both bed-and-breakfasts.

CAMPING
You'll probably want to stay in a hotel or bed-and-breakfast, since this area is the two-state region's most urban spot, but there are plenty of campgrounds if you prefer to pitch a tent.

Lake Manawa State Park, I-80 Exit 3, Council Bluffs, 712/366-0220, has more than 1,500 acres with 35 electric and 33 primitive campsites, a trailer dump station, picnic shelters, trails, and, of course, the nearby lake. Golfers will be interested to know that a driving range is nearby, plus a down-home-style café or two.

North of Council Bluffs near DeSoto, the 577-acre **Wilson Island State Recreation Area**, I-29 and Hwy. 30, 712/642-2060, features 65 electric and 73 primitive campsites, a trailer dump station, trails, cabins for rent, and fishing.

Just south of the Omaha metro area, **Walnut Creek Lake and Recreation Area**, one mile south of Papillion, south of Hwy. 370 and west of 96th St., 402/444-6222, is the area's newest outdoor spot. A hundred-acre man-made lake built to control flooding, the 1,250-foot-long dam was con-structed in 1996 and the camping facilities were built in 1998.

NIGHTLIFE
With lots of pedestrians, quirky shops, and hangouts, the Old Market is the natural, easy choice for a night out in the Council Bluffs–Omaha area. You can move from a rowdy, smoke-filled live music spot to an elegant wine bar in a matter of a block or two.

Featuring an atmosphere beyond that of your run-of-the-mill coffeeshop, the **Omaha History Center & Coffee Lounge**, 512 S. 13th St., Old Market, 402/345-9135, hosts everything from screenings of silent horror flicks to forums on Omaha history. The history events are made more appropriate by the café's large collection of reference books about Omaha and an inte-rior stocked with antique furniture, which is usually for sale. Groups congre-gate in the evening, java junkies dart in during the day.

You step below street level to enter the **Dubliner Pub**, 1205 Harney St., 402/342-5887, located in the Old Market and possibly the most

OMAHA COMMUNITY PLAYHOUSE

Proud to be the "largest community theater in the nation," **Omaha Community Playhouse**, 6915 Cass St., Omaha, 888/782-4338, www.omahaplayhouse.com, has a 600-seat Mainstage auditorium and a smaller 225-seat theater that both host musicals, comedies, and dramas throughout the year. The Nebraska Theatre Caravan produces most of the productions.

authentic Irish bar experience you'll find in Nebraska or Iowa. The beer menu is wide-ranging, and, on weekends, there's usually an Irish folk group playing to a packed house of twenty-somethings.

Upstream Brewing Company, 514 S. 11th St., 402/344-0200, is a restaurant and brew pub owned by the Denver-based Wynkoop chain that also owns the Raccoon River Brewing Company in Des Moines. But Wynkoop specializes in tailoring their pubs to fit the flavor of each city they enter, and Upstream reflects an upscale urban atmosphere without being too stuffy. It's a fine place for chatting with friends or playing billiards. You can reserve a whole room for a large dinner group.

The local home of the neo-swing craze is **The Stork Club**, 10th St. and Mason St., Omaha, 402/345-8525, which serves both lunch and dinner (often an all-you-can-eat affair with prime rib and such) and energizes the dance floor to the tune of national and local swing bands. Hipster duds are optional.

Outside of the Old Market: If you like your live music with a side of beef, **The Hickory**, 2405 Hickory St., Omaha, 402/449-9103, specializes in "smoked meats, better than BBQ," as well as a steady calendar of local blues talent. For those looking for live music outside of the usual bar setting, **McFoster's Natural Kind Cafe**, 38th St. and Farnam St., Omaha, 402/345-7477, hosts folk and pop musicians on weekends in its smoke-free venue. It's also a restaurant open daily for lunch and dinner that serves vegetarian cuisine plus seafood and free-range chicken.

The Funny Bone, 705 N. 114th St., Omaha, 402/493-8036, is a local stop for many touring comedians. It's reliable for a few laughs, though the comedy scene in general is not as strong as it was a decade ago.

Yes, it's a full-fledged bowling alley, but **Ranch Bowl**, 1600 S. 72nd St., Omaha, 402/393-0900, is also a staple of the city's live music scene for rock bands. One bar hosts the live music, while a second, quieter lounge features sports on a wide-screen TV. In the summer, concerts are held in the Ranch Bowl's outdoor sand volleyball pits. From Ani DiFranco to GWAR, they've all played here.

Omaha's best home of the blues is the **18th Amendment Saloon**, 96th St. and L St., 402/339-7170, which even stages early concerts during happy hour on Thursdays as a concession to the folks who have to get up early Friday morning and go to work. Along with the Zoo Bar in Lincoln and the Grand in Des Moines, the Eighteenth Amendment draws the kind of veteran, national blues talent (like harpist James Harman, for instance) that you can still happily catch in small clubs.

If the blues aren't your bag, baseball might be. **Rosenblatt Stadium**, I-80 Exit 454, 13th Street S., 402/444-4750, offers a great night out at the ballpark, cheering on the Omaha Royals.

One of the most unusual hangouts in either city is an animal feed store—seriously. Not just for the farmer set, **Acorn Supply Company**, 329 16th Ave., Council Bluffs, 712/325-9282, plays host to local musicians who gather around 1 or 2 p.m. Saturdays to jam country and folk music and have fun. Regulars come from all around Iowa and Nebraska. Bring your own fiddle, or just grab a free donut. This is a rare example of the slice of Americana that unfamiliar outsiders expect to find everywhere in Iowa and Nebraska.

Among the night spots in Council Bluffs, **Scott Street Pub**, 25 Scott St., 712/328-7275, is the best choice. It's spacious, offers a large beer selection, and features TVs for sports fans and a decent jukebox for music lovers. It's a large, square room with a high ceiling and booths and tables, and a good place to meet friends for conversation.

Scenic Route: Loess Hills

The Loess Hills (pronounced "luss") stretch two hundred miles from Sioux City all the way down to St. Joseph, Missouri. Varying in width from 1 to 15 miles, these geological formations aren't rocky. This unbroken stretch of attractive green hills runs parallel to Iowa's western border, their fertile soils growing an abundance of grasses, trees, and other vegetation.

These hills were formed as the result of winds that deposited fine soil along the eastern edge of the Missouri River Valley starting about 18 thousand years ago; eventually, the accumulated soil became the Loess Hills. Homesteads dot the hills, but efforts are underway to turn the area into a national park.

If you want to tackle the whole route, start your scenic tour in the town of Akron, driving south on Highway 12. At Westfield you can take the 12-mile Ridge Road Loop if you wish, which will take you closer to the hills and afford scenic views of the surrounding countryside. Watch for blue and white Loess Hills Scenic Byway signs throughout the drive that will indicate such loops. The main part of the byway, called "the spine," is completely paved, but some of the loops are gravel.

In Sioux City you'll merge for a time with I-29, but near Sergeant Bluff you'll head east on County Road D38, then hook up with Highway 982, heading south to Smithland. Then you'll go south on various roads, through towns like Moorhead, Pisgah,

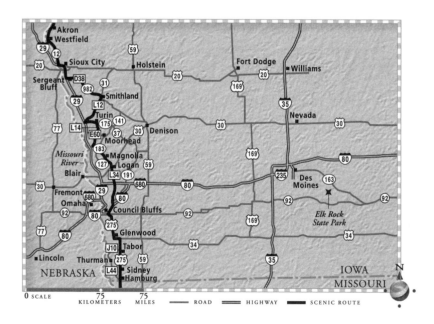

and Logan. Take Highway 191 into Council Bluffs, then Highway 275 south out of the city. Staying on Highway 275 will carry you through Glenwood and all the way down to Tabor. Just south of Tabor go southwest on J10, switching to L44 at Thurman. This will take you to Hamburg and the end of the Iowa route.

You can call the Loess Hills Hospitality Association at 712/886-5441.

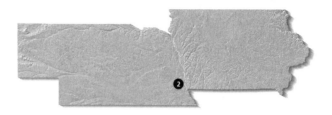

2
LINCOLN AND
SOUTHEAST NEBRASKA

The city that is ground zero for die-hard Big Red football fans is also home to some of Nebraska's best museums, nightlife, and the sort of youthful buzz that comes from a large university population. To think of Lincoln only in terms of the 100 green yards that the Nebraska Cornhuskers routinely dominate each autumn is plain unfair.

The Historic Haymarket downtown area of Lincoln preserves the warehouses and cobblestone streets in the style of the early 1900s, while the University of Nebraska–Lincoln campus is a blend of old and new. Many shops and businesses are clustered along O Street, a major east–west artery for the city.

The blend of frontier heritage and college-driven activity, both academic and social, serves Lincoln well. Travelers with all kinds of interests can find many reasons for an extended stay.

A PERFECT DAY IN LINCOLN

Get an early start in the morning with a hearty breakfast of pancakes, sausage, and hash browns at Kuhl's Restaurant on O Street, right in the middle of downtown Lincoln. If weather permits, afterward you can stroll the surrounding streets and perhaps buy a coffee drink at The Mill in the historic Haymarket district.

From there, tour the Museum of Nebraska History, allowing plenty of time to explore its detailed, fascinating exhibits. Next, a trip to the Nebraska State Capitol and its nearby neighborhood provides two important perspectives: a panoramic view of the modern city from the capitol's tower, and, displayed in the Thomas P. Kennard House, a panoramic view of 1870s Lincoln captured in an oversized vintage photo.

On the University of Nebraska's campus, make sure to duck into Morrill Hall to wonder at the scale of the skeletal remains of mammoths and mastodons in the Elephant Hall display. At the Nebraska Bookstore, also in the downtown district, you may choose from a large selection of Big Red apparel and merchandise to purchase for friends and relatives—and for yourself.

End your day by soaking in live music at the Zoo Bar, Lincoln's venue for blues nearly seven nights a week. If that's not your style, plenty of other nightlife options await you. At the first-class facility that is the Lied Center for the Performing Arts you can enjoy world-famous musical entertainment. Or you can take it easy and relax at The Coffee House.

LINCOLN SIGHTSEEING HIGHLIGHTS

★★★★ THE MUSEUM OF NEBRASKA HISTORY
131 Centennial Mall N. (15th and P Sts.), 800/833-6747 or 402/471-4754, www.nebraskahistory.org/sites/mnh
Exhaustively chronicling Nebraska's past, The Museum of Nebraska History has more than half a million artifacts that are attractively and logically displayed on three floors. Moon rocks from both the Apollo 11 and Apollo 17 missions, a full-size replica of a 1940s small-town–Nebraska general store, a hands-on History Adventure Center designed for curious kids, and a well-stocked gift shop are all part of this well-rounded museum experience.
Details: Open Mon–Fri 9–4:30, Sat 9–5, Sun 1:30–5. Free. (1–3 hours)

★★★ HISTORIC HAYMARKET
Vicinity of 9th and P Sts., 402/435-7496 or 402/434-6900
A little upscale, this is a classy but varied warehouse business district on par with Omaha's Old Market and Iowa City's Ped Mall in its ability to satisfy you with distinct food, shopping, and nightlife in one general location. The Star City Visitors Center, 201 N. Seventh St., is

LINCOLN

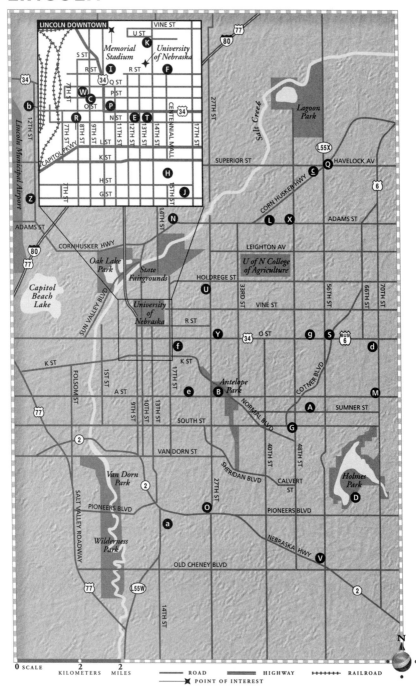

located inside Lincoln Station, a historic railway station. Fine restaurants in the district include The Oven, serving Indian cuisine, and there are appealing coffeehouses, cigar shops, and secondhand clothing stores as well.

Details: *Individual business hours vary. Free. (30 minutes–3 hours)*

★★★ NEBRASKA STATE CAPITOL
15th and K Sts., 402/471-0448

The third capitol built on this site (construction began in 1922 and ended in 1932), the structure features an impressive 400-foot dome that contains an observation deck on the 14th floor, essential to visit on clear days. A cafeteria and the "Spirit of the Prairie Gift Shop" are also inside. Lee Lawrie and Hildreth Meiers decorated the building with sculptures and mosaics that represent the state's natural, social, and political history.

Details: *Open year-round Mon–Fri 8–5, Sat 10–5, Sun 1–5. Tours begin on the hour. Free. (30 minutes–1 hour)*

SIGHTS

- ⓐ Fairview, The Bryan Museum
- ⓑ Folsom Children's Zoo & Botanical Gardens
- ⓒ Historic Haymarket
- ⓓ Hyde Memorial Observatory
- ⓔ Lincoln Children's Museum
- ⓕ The Museum of Nebraska History
- ⓖ National Museum of Rollerskating
- ⓗ Nebraska State Capitol
- ⓘ Sheldon Memorial Art Gallery & Sculpture Garden
- ⓙ Thomas P. Kennard House
- ⓚ University of Nebraska State Museum (Morrill Hall)

FOOD

- ⓛ Charlie's Seafood & Grill
- ⓜ Grandmother's
- ⓝ Harvest Moon Cafe & Bakery
- ⓞ Jax Restaurant & Lounge
- ⓟ Kuhl's Restaurant

FOOD (continued)

- ⓠ Norma's Place
- ⓡ The Oven
- ⓢ Patty's Pub
- ⓣ The Renaissance
- ⓤ T&R's Garden
- ⓥ Taj Mahal Cuisine of India
- ⓦ Vincenzo's Ristorante

LODGING

- ⓣ The Cornhusker
- ⓧ Cornhusker Super 8
- ⓨ Great Plains Motel
- ⓩ Hampton Inn
- ⓐ Harvester Motel
- ⓑ Holiday Inn Express Airport
- ⓒ Quality Inn Northeast
- ⓓ The Residence Inn
- ⓔ Rogers House
- ⓕ Town House Motel
- ⓖ Villager Motor Inn

Note: Items with the same letter are located in the same area.

★★★ UNIVERSITY OF NEBRASKA STATE MUSEUM (MORRILL HALL)
14th and U Sts., 402/472-6302, www.museum.unl.edu.

If the full skeleton of the imperial mammoth doesn't humble you with its immense scale (the living creature could punt you as if you were a football into nearby Memorial Stadium), then you don't fully appreciate how this museum's Elephant Hall brings Nebraska's natural history to life. The museum's third floor includes a life-sized re-creation of an allosaurus in the Jurassic Dinosaurs exhibit. Ralph Mueller Planetarium offers astronomy and laser shows on weekends during the school year and on Tuesday through Saturday during the summer.

*Pages from the original Nebraska State Constitution are located at **The Museum of Nebraska History**, as is an 1867 United States flag with 37 stars, sewn just after Nebraska won its statehood.*

Details: *Open year-round Mon–Sat 9:30–4:30, Sun 1:30–4:30. $2 suggested donation age 2 and older. (1–2 hours)*

★★ FAIRVIEW, THE BRYAN MUSEUM
49th and Sumner Sts., 402/483-8303

This is the home of William Jennings Bryan, the three-time Democratic nominee (in 1896, 1900, and 1908) for president of the United States. He was also the lawyer in the famed 1925 creation-vs.-evolution "Scopes Monkey Trial"—he argued in favor of creationism. His Lincoln home became a National Historic Landmark in 1964 and was extensively renovated in 1994. The museum is housed on the first floor, while the William Jennings Bryan Institute occupies the second and third floors.

Details: *Open year-round Tue–Fri 1–4. Free. (30 minutes)*

★★ FOLSOM CHILDREN'S ZOO & BOTANICAL GARDENS
1222 S. 27th St., 402/475-6741

More than three hundred animals inhabit this children's zoo, including leopards, seals, camels, baboons, and New Guinea singing dogs, identifiable by the odd yelps they emit. Extensive gardens and trees contribute to the animals' habitats. A Critter Encounter Area encourages the playful meeting of different species—as in child and goat. For more than 30 years Folsom has delighted kids and adults alike.

> *Details: Open Apr–Labor Day daily 10–5. $5 adults, $3.50 senior citizens, $3 ages 2–11, free under 2. (1–2 hours)*

★★ HYDE MEMORIAL OBSERVATORY
Holmes Park (70th St. and Normal Blvd.), 402/441-7895

The City of Lincoln owns and operates this astronomical attraction, which features three telescopes for curious stargazers. Close in on the Big Dipper, follow the line of Orion's belt, or peer at another planet.

> *Details: Open Oct–Mar Sat 7 p.m.–10 p.m.; Apr–Sep sundown–11. Free. (15 minutes–2 hours)*

★★ LINCOLN CHILDREN'S MUSEUM
121 S. 13th St., 402/477-0128

If there's something thrilling in the adult world, chances are that the Lincoln Children's Museum has a smaller version of it. This 13,500-square-foot interactive museum lets young, curious folks crawl inside a Lunar Lander (to make one small step for kids), run for a touchdown in the Little Husker Stadium, and gaze at the wonders of static electricity as demonstrated by the "shocking" Plasmasphere.

Lincoln had a population of only 30 and was still named Lancaster when it was chosen to become Nebraska's state capital in 1867, but today's city (named in honor of President Abraham Lincoln) is around two hundred thousand strong.

> *Details: Open year-round Sun–Mon 1–5, Tue–Sat 10–5. $3 age 2 and older, free under 2. Children younger than 12 must be accompanied by an adult (age 16 and older). One hour of free parking available at Center Park (12th and N Sts.) or Rampark (130 N. 12th St.). (1 hour)*

★★ SHELDON MEMORIAL ART GALLERY & SCULPTURE GARDEN
12th and R Sts., 402/472-2461, www.sheldon.unl.edu

The Sheldon Memorial Art Gallery was designed by world-renowned architect, Philip Johnson. With its emphasis on twentieth-century American art, the Sheldon displays permanent works by Andy Warhol

(*Myths: Mickey Mouse* and *Vegetarian Vegetable*), Georgia O'Keeffe, and many other well-known artists. Temporary exhibits from the University of Nebraska and elsewhere are also regularly featured.

The sculpture garden extends around the UNL campus and includes 33 works—it's a nice complement to a stroll around the attractive, sprawling campus.

Details: *Open year-round Tue–Sat 10–5, Thu–Sat 7 p.m.–9 p.m., Sun 2–9. Donations suggested. (30 minutes–1 hour)*

★★ THOMAS P. KENNARD HOUSE
1627 H St., 402/471-4764

The oldest house in Lincoln is the 1869 mansion of Nebraska's first secretary of state, one of three men who picked the site of the state's capitol. A photo of Lincoln circa 1870, when the city's population was about three thousand, is a stunning contrast to the modern city. Fine period furnishings abound.

Details: *Open Memorial Day–Labor Day Tue–Fri 9–noon and 1–4:30, Sat–Sun 1–5. $1 adults, free under 18 with adult. (15–30 minutes)*

★ NATIONAL MUSEUM OF ROLLERSKATING
4730 South St., 402/483-7551,
www.rollerskatingmuseum.com

Learn everything you wanted to know but were afraid to ask (or never thought to ask) about the 250-year history of roller-skating. Exhibits include "Evolution of the Wheel 1860–1998" and "Orchestras, Organs & Disco: Music in the Rink." Roller hockey, roller polo, roller basketball—it's roller-skating heaven, as long as you care deeply for the sport. Offices of the national roller-skating organization are also in the building.

Details: *Parking in back of building. Open year-round Mon–Fri 9–5. Free. (15–30 minutes)*

SOUTHEAST NEBRASKA
SIGHTSEEING HIGHLIGHTS

★★★ THE SPIRIT OF BROWNVILLE MISSOURI
RIVERBOAT CRUISES
Brownville, 402/825-6441 or 402/274-4011

See the sights of the Missouri River from the deck of this historic riverboat. As the giant paddlewheel powers you down the river, watch the greenery of the shoreline roll by. Dinner, dancing, and live entertainment are offered.

Details: *Cruises Jun–Aug Thu–Sun at 3 and 6, Sat at 8 p.m. $5.50 general admission. (2–3 hours)*

★★ ARBOR DAY FARM
100 Arbor Ave., Nebraska City, 402/873-8710

The National Arbor Day Foundation runs this 260-acre National Historic Landmark that encompasses extensive orchards, research fields, and the Lied Conference Center. Apple harvesting and cider making can be seen in the fall.

Details: *Open Nov–Aug Mon–Sat 9–5, Sun noon–5; Sep–Oct Mon–Sat 9–5, Sun 9–5. Free. (1–2 hours)*

★★ ARBOR LODGE STATE HISTORICAL PARK AND ARBORETUM
2nd and Centennial Aves., Nebraska City, 402/873-7222

The Victorian mansion of Arbor Day founder J. Sterling Morton, secretary of agriculture during President Grover Cleveland's term, has 52 rooms on view. Morton's son, Joy, built the Morton Salt fortune and completed renovations on the mansion. The 65-acre grounds also include various gardens and scenic walking trails.

Details: *Open Memorial Day–Labor Day 9–5; Sep–Oct 11–5; Nov–Dec 1–4. $3 adults, $1 ages 6–15, free under 6. Grounds open Memorial Day–Labor Day 8–8; rest of the year 9–sunset. Park entry permit required. Annual permit $14, daily $2.50. (Vendors might add 25 cents to the price to cover the cost of getting the permits themselves.) (1 hour)*

★★ HOMESTEAD NATIONAL MONUMENT OF AMERICA
Hwy. 4, Beatrice, 402/223-3514

The Homestead Act of 1862 resulted in early settlers claiming up to 160 acres of Nebraska land as their own. This monument commemorates the claim of Daniel Freeman, one of the region's first settlers. A restored tallgrass prairie, the site of Freeman's original cabin, a visitors center, and trails are among the features of this outdoor attraction located 40 miles south of Lincoln and 4.5 miles west of Beatrice.

SOUTHEAST NEBRASKA

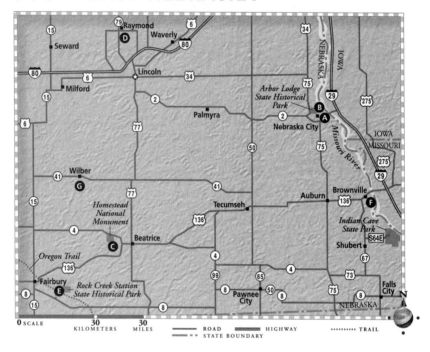

SIGHTS
- **A** Arbor Day Farm
- **B** Arbor Lodge State Historical Park and Arboretum
- **C** Homestead National Monument of America
- **D** James Arthur Vineyards
- **E** Rock Creek Station State Historical Park
- **F** The Spirit of Brownville Missouri Riverboat Cruises

LODGING
- **G** Hotel Wilber Bed & Breakfast Inn & Restaurant

Details: *Open fall–spring daily 8:30–5; summer daily 8–6. Free. (1–3 hours)*

★★ JAMES ARTHUR VINEYARDS
2001 W. Raymond Rd., 402/783-5255

This 2,500-square-foot winery has a tasting room, gift shop, and production facilities, not to mention thousands of grapevines in the surrounding countryside. It was established in 1996 among 400 picturesque acres of rolling hills just north of Lincoln. Wine varieties include barrel-aged dry reds, crisp whites, and dessert wines.

Details: *Go seven miles north of Lincoln on 14th St., then 2.5 miles west on Raymond Rd. Open Mar–Oct Mon–Thu 10–6, Fri–Sat noon–9, Sun noon–6; Nov–Feb Mon–Fri 10–5, Sat noon–9, Sun noon–6. Free. (1 hour)*

★★ ROCK CREEK STATION STATE HISTORICAL PARK
Hwy. 8, Fairbury, 402/729-5777

This the site where "Wild Bill" Hickok gunned down David McCanles, beginning his gunslinging career. It includes the Burlington Northern Foundation Visitor Center, with exhibits and a movie theater. Covered wagon rides are also available on weekends from Memorial Day through Labor Day.

Details: *Open year-round Mon–Thu 9–5, Fri–Sun 9–8. Free. (30 minutes–2 hours)*

FITNESS AND RECREATION

Lincoln's largest park, **Wilderness Park**, S. First St. and Van Dorn St., encompasses more than 1,445 acres and 11 miles of hiking and biking trails. On the southwest edge of the city is **Pioneers Park Nature Center**, 3201 S. Coddington St., 402/441-7895, where you can find the start of five miles' worth of trails through prairie grasses, woods, and wetlands.

If your children (or the child inside you) are looking for space-age recreation, visit **Laser Quest Lincoln**, 6802A P St., 402/465-5522, www.laserquest.com, a multilevel maze within which competitors battle it out with lasers until only the victor is left standing.

In the far southeast corner of the state, **Indian Cave State Park**, RR 1, Shubert, 402/883-2575, has a large sandstone cave and the Missouri River as its eastern border. Horseback riding trails, biking trails, more than 20 miles of hiking trails, and the reconstructed nineteenth-century riverside settlement of St. Deroin are all contained on the park's 3,050-plus acres.

FOOD

Open at 6 a.m. for breakfast, which is served throughout the day, **Kuhl's Restaurant**, 1038 O St., 402/476-1311, will leave you full and satisfied (and with a full wallet). Another meat-and-potatoes–type place for early risers is **T&R's Garden**, 48th St. and Cornhusker Ave., 402/464-5343. **Grandmother's**, 70th St. and A St., 402/483-7855, is open from 11 a.m. to midnight daily, serving everything from salads to steaks at a reasonable price. The family-owned **Norma's Place**, 6105 Havelock Ave., 402/466-9893, has a 26-year history of tasty breakfasts and lunches (but no dinners). Opens at 5 a.m. daily except Sunday, when it's closed.

Lincoln's reigning king of fine dining is **The Renaissance**, 333 S. 13th St., 402/479-8200, in The Cornhusker hotel. It's elegant and expensive.

Lincoln has a couple of fine Indian restaurants: **Taj Mahal Cuisine of India**, 5500 Old Cheney (56th St. and Hwy. 2), Suite 4, 402/420-1133, and **The Oven**, 201 N. Eighth St. (in the Haymarket), 402/475-6118, where there's live music on Sundays.

HOMESTEAD NATIONAL MONUMENT OF AMERICA

Department of Economic Development, Nebraska Division of Tourism

Vincenzo's Ristorante, 808 P St., 402/435-3889, offers authentic Italian dinners seven days of the week. The flavor is more Northern Italian, with a little French influence incorporated. A chicken risotto dish featuring a four-ounce breast sauteed in white wine is just one specialty among dozens of chicken, steak, and pasta dishes.

Seafood is the specialty at **Charlie's Seafood & Grill**, 3940 Village Dr., 402/420-7200, which opens daily at 4 p.m.; swordfish is on the menu. You can also find swordfish, other seafood, pasta, and meat entrées at **Harvest Moon Cafe & Bakery**, 1501 Center Park Rd., Suite 100, 402/420-6414. Fresh baked breads, as the name implies, are also a specialty.

Jax Restaurant & Lounge, 27th St. and Woods Blvd., 402/423-0166, offers both a daily lunch buffet and daily dinner special.

Patty's Pub, with two locations at 838 N. 27th St., 402/474-7832, and 311 N. Cotner St., 402/467-4471, is the friendly, affordable eating spot for casual fare such as sandwiches and homemade pizzas; bar games form the backdrop.

LODGING

When budget is no concern, choose **The Cornhusker**, 333 S. 13th St., Lincoln, 402/474-7474. Easily Lincoln's most elegant hotel, it offers 290 guest rooms and suites, plus fine eateries like The Renaissance and The Cafe. Its Executive Level classification denotes the best rooms and service available.

A cheaper option for downtown-area lodging is the **Town House Motel**, 1744 M St., Lincoln, 800/279-1744 or 402/475-3000, which offers a shorter list of amenities, but still plenty of comfort—you can hook your laptop up to the Internet and bring your small pet, too.

Rogers House, 2145 B St., Lincoln, 402/476-6961, is a classy and well-presented bed-and-breakfast in the middle of Lincoln. With 12 rooms spread between a couple of buildings, it offers a delightful yet not too expensive night's stay. Both the lounge and breakfast room are big, bright, and cheery.

Located 35 miles southwest of Lincoln, in the "Czech Capital of the United States," **Hotel Wilber Bed & Breakfast Inn & Restaurant**, 203 S. Wilson St., Wilber, 402/821-2020 or 888/332-1937, has 11 distinctly different rooms for rent on its second floor. Its acclaimed restaurant seats up to 65 for weekend dining.

The east part of the city has affordable accommodation choices, too. The **Great Plains Motel**, 2732 O St., Lincoln, 800/288-8499 or 402/476-3253, rents more than 40 rooms and serves a continental breakfast. The **Villager**

LIED CENTER FOR THE PERFORMING ARTS
Lied Center for the Performing Arts, 2500 S. 56th St., 402/472-4747, is that unique, striking building with all the windows that stands at the south edge of the UNL campus. The entertainment it hosts on its stage is beautiful as well. This is the sort of refined space where national theater companies and world-famous music groups like the Chieftans perform.

Motor Inn, 5200 O St., Lincoln, 800/356-4321 or 402/464-9111, has more than two hundred rooms with a wide range of options, from basic sleep needs to Jacuzzi suites. An outdoor pool, restaurant, and lounge are also part of the inn. **The Residence Inn**, 200 S. 68th St., Lincoln, 800/331-3131 or 402/483-4900, is smaller than the Villager (120 rooms), but similar to it as far as amenities go, with only a few less perks—such as room service.

Near the airport, **Hampton Inn**, 1301 W. Bond St., 402/474-2080, is part of the chain that is well known for its comfortable but affordable accommodations. It has more than one hundred rooms, a game room, an outdoor pool, and a great continental breakfast. The **Holiday Inn Express Airport**, 1010 W. Bond St., Lincoln, 402/474-1417, is similar in quality to the Hampton Inn, but this Holiday Inn location offers an indoor pool and rooms with refrigerators and microwaves.

Cornhusker Super 8, 2545 Cornhusker Hwy., Lincoln, 800/800-8000 or 402/467-4488, is an affordable motel with more than 130 rooms available. **Quality Inn Northeast**, 5250 Cornhusker Hwy., Lincoln, 800/411-3961 or 402/464-3171, has an indoor pool, hot tub and sauna, restaurant and lounge, game room, kitchenette rooms, and pet accommodations.

On Lincoln's south side is **Harvester Motel**, 1511 Center Park Rd., Lincoln, 800/500-1366 or 402/423-3131, an 80-room establishment with good rooms plus an outdoor pool, restaurant, and lounge.

NIGHTLIFE
Lincoln's undisputed home of live blues music is the **Zoo Bar**, 136 N. 14th St., 402/435-8754, members.aol.com/frgtrs/zoo, where top-notch national talent like harpist James Harman or guitarist Deborah Connor can be heard

nearly every night of the week. Pictures of past performers adorn the walls of this long, narrow club.

Sort of a neo-hippie hangout, **Bodega's Alley**, 1418 O St., 402/477-9550, features a few interesting brews on tap, Phish and Widespread Panic playing on the sound system, indoor sofa seating, and an outdoor patio. More upscale is **Libations**, 317 S. 11th St., 402/477-3880, a cigar and martini bar that features endless varieties of vodka, scotch, and other liquors.

Knickerbockers, 901 O St., 402/476-6865, is a corner bar and music venue with a distinct, edgy charm. The drinks aren't impressive, but many of the bands it hosts are. **Duffy's Tavern**, 1412 O St., 402/474-3543, alternates between live music, comedy, and karaoke. Country music fans should head to **Guitars and Cadillacs**, 5400 O St., 402/464-1100.

The Coffee House, 1324 P St., Lincoln, 402/477-6611, doesn't serve just jolts of java, it also displays artwork. And it's open until midnight daily, courting nightlife.

3
NEBRASKA'S
I-80 TRIANGLE

If you're looking for a cluster of communities offering both small-town charm and urban attractions, look no further than central Nebraska's trio of Kearney, Grand Island, and Hastings, all just a quick hop off I-80. Visitors and residents alike enjoy such area diversions as the IMAX Theater and Pioneer, one of the state's most popular stops.

Hastings is the birthplace of Kool-Aid, one of childhood's favorite means to a sugar rush. Hastings also hosts flocks of migrating Sandhill cranes each spring; as the graceful creatures land and alight, they form a rippling mass of feathers that is wonderful to behold. Grand Island—Nebraska's fourth largest city, with more than 40 thousand residents—was founded in 1866 when the Union Pacific Railroad reached the area, although Germans from Davenport, Iowa, originally settled nearby a decade earlier. The three towns together form an impressive urban oasis in the middle of Nebraska.

In spring of 2000, the Great Platte River Road Archway Monument, I-80 Exit 272, Kearney, will be completed. Eight stories high, the length of a football field, 50 feet wide, and stretching across I-80, it is no timid tribute to Nebraska's pioneer past, but rather a proud commemoration of the state's important role in the westward expansion of the nation. Two levels inside the monument depict pioneer days via traditional exhibits and state-of-the-art re-creations of covered wagons and more.

A PERFECT DAY IN THE I-80 TRIANGLE

Why not begin your time in the I-80 triangle at one of the state's popular attractions, Pioneer Village? It opens early, at 7 a.m., so if you don't care to stay very long—the sheer amount on display can be a little overwhelming—you'll still have most of the day ahead of you.

You won't be disappointed on this part of your trip if you focus on a few great museums spread among the towns. The distinguished Museum of Nebraska Art (MONA) shouldn't be missed. Stroll its peaceful galleries and learn a little about the native Nebraska artists who have given so much to the state's artistic heritage. Stuhr Museum of the Prairie Pioneer is the other standout museum that you shouldn't miss. If MONA chronicles Nebraska's past through interpretations by its artists, Stuhr chronicles the same past through the less elegant but no less important artifacts that were the tools of daily life, the art of the everyday.

In the evening, take in a show at the IMAX Theater in the Hastings Museum. In this era of superstores, megamalls, and the like, the massive IMAX movies are actually part of the oversize hype that's worth buying into.

SIGHTSEEING HIGHLIGHTS

★★★★ THE MUSEUM OF NEBRASKA ART
2401 Central Ave., Kearney, 308/865-8559,
monet.unk.edu/mona

The Museum of Nebraska Art holds the state's official collection of native visual art. There's reason to take pride in the pool of home-grown talent, based on its collection. MONA is a relatively young museum, founded in 1986, but the interior is bright and airy, and the visitor will be rewarded with an hour or two of tranquil viewing. Cozad native and oil painter Robert Henri is just one of the more prominent Nebraskan artists featured; his *Girl in a Wedding Gown* is one of the captivating paintings on display. The landscape and peoples of the Great Plains are also depicted in full force in MONA. A gift shop is located on the main floor.

Details: *Open year-round Tue–Sat 11–5, Sun 1–5. Free, donations suggested. (1–2 hours)*

★★★ HAROLD WARP PIONEER VILLAGE
Hwys. 6/34 and 10, Minden (just south of Kearney),
800/445-4447 or 308/832-1181

I-80 TRIANGLE/KEARNEY

N

INSET MAP (KEARNEY):

AV C

RAILROAD ST

11TH ST

CENTRAL AV

OLD N STATE HWY

E

2ND AV

H

44

KEARNEY

I

19TH ST

G

25TH ST

30

22ND ST

3RD AV

6TH AV

8TH ST

4TH ST

TALMADGE ST

L

K

44

MAIN MAP:

92

Osceola

81

34

York

81

Geneva

39

34

6

80

Central City

14

J

14

A Aurora

14

14

92

30

34

Grand Island

F

281

34

D Hastings

281

St. Paul

6

92

2

Wood River

30

Platte River

Oregon Trail

25 MILES

Ravenna

31 Minden

10

10

C

92

10

6

2

50A

B

44

Kearney (SEE INSET)

Fort Kearny State Historic Park

25 KILOMETERS

0 SCALE

POINT OF INTEREST

TRAIL

HIGHWAY

ROAD

If you're driving south on Highway 10 to reach Pioneer Village, there's no chance of missing it—the roadside is littered with billboards during the last several miles. It's billed as "Nebraska's #1 Attraction," and Pioneer Village certainly is massive in scale (thousands of antiques displayed in 24 buildings) and scope (covering 1830 to the present). Viewing curiosities from full-scale airplanes and tractors to the rarest, most fragile china collections, you stroll through the Village's meticulously arranged rows and rows of exhibits, feeling overwhelmed at the sheer number of objects. It's probably best to take the time to completely explore this site, because trying to rush through it could leave you with a nagging, unsatisfied feeling.

Details: Open year-round daily 7–sundown. $6 adults, $3 ages 6–15, free under 6. (2–4 hours)

★★★ STUHR MUSEUM OF THE PRAIRIE PIONEER
3133 W. Hwy. 34, Grand Island, 308/385-5316, www.stuhrmuseum.org

The first visual detail that strikes you as you approach the Stuhr Museum is that there's a moat around the main building. Maybe it's a reminder of the gulf of time that separates modern Nebraska from what you find inside the Stuhr: The main building itself has exhibits on everything from how sauerkraut was made in the 1860–1910 era to other artifacts of pioneer life. Outside, in full-scale exhibits that are open during the warmer months, a Railyard Exhibit, Railroad Town,

---

SIGHTS
- Ⓐ Edgerton Explorit Center
- Ⓑ Fort Kearny State Historical Park
- Ⓒ Harold Warp Pioneer Village
- Ⓓ Hastings Museum
- Ⓔ The Museum of Nebraska Art
- Ⓐ Plainsman Museum
- Ⓕ Stuhr Museum of the Prairie Pioneer

FOOD
- Ⓖ The Captain's Table
- Ⓗ Grandpa's Steak House and Gallery Lounge

FOOD (continued)
- Ⓓ LoRayne's Restaurant
- Ⓘ Whiskey Creek Steakhouse
- Ⓙ Woody's Restaurant & Lounge

LODGING
- Ⓓ Comfort Inn
- Ⓚ Country Inn & Suites
- Ⓓ Grandma's Victorian Inn
- Ⓛ Hampton Inn

Note: Items with the same letter are located in the same area.

---

and even the actual Grand Island cottage that was the birthplace of late actor Henry Fonda stand as quasi-communities saluting the past.

Details: Open May–Oct 15 9–5; Oct 16–Apr Mon–Sat 9–5, Sun 1–5. $4.25 adults, $2.15 ages 7–16, free under 7. (1–4 hours)

★★ EDGERTON EXPLORIT CENTER
208 16th St., Aurora (I-80 Exit 332), 402/694-4032
www.edgerton.org

Next door to the Plainsman Museum, this hands-on museum is a tribute to the late scientist, inventor, and Aurora native Dr. Harold E. "Doc" Edgerton, a one-time professor at the Massachusetts Institute of Technology. He occasionally worked with sea explorer Jacques Cousteau, but Edgerton is most famous for developing the strobe light and, along with it, high-speed photography. As a result, much of the hands-on portion of this museum involves fun tricks with strobe lights and other wonders of sight.

A spot central to both Nebraska and the continental United States, Kearney was once considered as a site for the state capital. (Lincoln won out.)

Details: Open year-round Mon–Sat 9–5, Sun 1–5. $3 adults, $2 students (4–18 years), free under 4. (30 minutes–1 hour)

★★ FORT KEARNY STATE HISTORICAL PARK
RR 4, Kearney, 308/865-5306

The first fort built to protect travelers on the Oregon Trail, Fort Kearny—the town of Kearney gained the second "e" in its name only after several years and for reasons shrouded in the past—today offers the tourist a replica of a stockade and a rebuilt sod blacksmith shop. A visitors center contains artifacts, exhibits, and a slide show. You can also take a self-guided tour of the 40-acre grounds.

Details: Two miles south on RR 4 from I-80, then four miles east on Road 50A. Open Memorial Day–Labor Day daily 9–5. $2 per car. (1–2 hours)

★★ HASTINGS MUSEUM
1330 N. Burlington Ave., Hastings, 800/508-4629

The Lied IMAX Theater is the high-profile, crowd-pleasing component of this historical museum. Aside from the five-stories-tall IMAX, three levels of the museum proper house extensive exhibits on the peoples, plants, and animals of Nebraska—there are especially a lot of stuffed birds. The basement, or "Collector's Level," has horse-drawn buggies and cars, firearms, and household objects. The J. M. McDonald Planetarium is also on-site.

Details: *Open year-round Mon–Sat 9–5, Sun 11–5. IMAX open Tue–Sat evenings. $3–$5 general admission for museum/planetarium, $5.50–$7 general admission for IMAX. (30 minutes–2 hours)*

★★ PLAINSMAN MUSEUM
210 16th St., Aurora, 402/694-6531

Many of its exhibits use hand-drawn signs for the explanatory text, but the Plainsman Museum is stuffed with lots of interesting objects and full-scale pieces from vintage area buildings—like the bank teller's window from the old Farmers Merchant Bank, originally located in McCool Junction. In a separate building, the Plainsman Agricultural Museum houses vintage implements plus a full-scale farm homestead.

Details: *Take I-80 Exit 332. Open April–Oct Mon–Sat 9–5, Sun 1–5; Nov–Mar 1–5. $4 adults, $3 seniors, $2 students. (1–2 hours)*

HAROLD WARP PIONEER VILLAGE

Department of Economic Development, Nebraska Division of Tourism

FITNESS AND RECREATION

Located along the banks of the Platte River and featuring some of the best bird watching in the region, **Crane Meadows Nature Center**, six miles west of Grand Island at I-80 Exit 305, 308/382-1820, has seven miles of hiking trails, as well as exhibits and gifts in its interpretive center. Adult admission costs just $2. It's open year-round.

Champions Sport & Recreation, 1220 W. Eighth St., Hastings, 402/462-6220, www.championsport.com, is a family-centered recreation destination with lots of big, indoor equipment—water slides, a treadwall, golf and batting cages, tennis courts, a Wee Village, and much more. Outside, Champions has an 18-hole mini-golf course and a go-cart track. Open weekdays 5:30 a.m. to 11 p.m., Saturday 8 a.m. to 11 p.m., and Sunday 10 a.m. to 11 p.m.

Island Oasis Water Park, I-80 Exit 312, north of Fonner Park, Grand Island, 308/385-5381, has a wave machine, water slides, sand volleyball courts, and a full bath house. It's open in the summer seven days a week from noon to 10 p.m.

FOOD

An institution since 1952, **Grandpa's Steak House and Gallery Lounge**, South Hwy. 44, Kearney, 308/237-2882 or 308/237-9938, is open for dinner every night except Sunday, when it's instead open for a lunch buffet. All manner of meat and seafood entrées are available. Another steak center is **Whiskey Creek Steakhouse**, 407 Second Ave., Kearney, 308/237-4300, which cooks wood-fired steaks and features 44 different margaritas.

At **Woody's Restaurant & Lounge**, if your name is Woody, you dine free—seriously.

Another locally owned steak-seafood-chicken restaurant is **The Captain's Table**, 110 S. Second Ave., Kearney, 308/237-5971, which is located in the Kearney Convention Center and open for breakfast, lunch, and dinner.

Billed as a "Seattle-style espresso bar," **Cafe Geno**, 3412 W. State St., Grand Island, 308/382-5856, serves coffee drinks, sandwiches, homemade baked goods, and desserts starting at 6:30 a.m. (except on Sunday, when it opens at noon).

Another fine café and eatery, **Cimino's Coffee & Cream Company**, 313 W. Third St., Grand Island, 308/382-3800, has a menu of more than 30

GRAND ISLAND

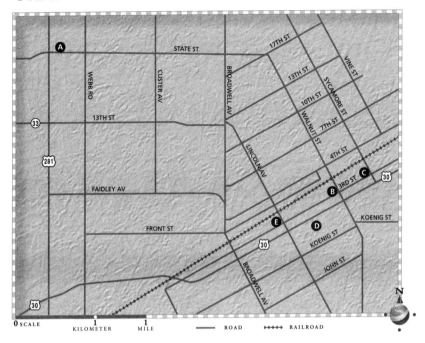

FOOD

Ⓐ Cafe Geno
Ⓑ Cimino's Coffee &
   Cream Company
Ⓒ Coney Island Cafe
Ⓓ Nonna's Palazzo

LODGING

Ⓔ Kirschke House Bed
   & Breakfast

---

different specialty coffees, bagels, and oven-roasted meats. Open at 7:30 a.m., **Coney Island Cafe**, 104 E. Third St., 308/382-7155, is famous for New York–style items like its Coney Island dog slathered in chili sauce.

Dining is elegant at **Nonna's Palazzo**, 820 W. Second St., Grand Island, 308/384-3029, serving authentic Italian food inside a historic mansion. It's open Thursday, Friday, and Saturday from 5 p.m. to 9 p.m., or by reservation.

Woody's Restaurant & Lounge, W. Hwy. 30, Central City, 308/946-2998, proudly displays its retro decor, straight out of the fifties. Its menu

---

features daily lunch buffet specials and prime rib specials on Friday and Saturday night, and it is open seven days a week.

LoRayne's Restaurant, 1216 W. J St., Hastings, 402/463-2784, has great barbecue ribs and extra-chunky chicken salad.

LODGING

Sensible rates, complimentary breakfast, and an indoor pool are the norm at **Country Inn & Suites**, I-80 Exit 272, Kearney, 800/456-4000 or 308/236-7500. Another reliable area hotel that's part of a national chain is **Hampton Inn**, 118 Third Ave., Kearney, 800/426-7866, also with an indoor pool and a complimentary breakfast.

Comfort Inn, 2903 Osborne Dr. W., Hastings, 800/228-5150 or 402/463-5252, includes a free continental breakfast and newspaper with a night's stay. There's also an outdoor pool and Jacuzzi. **Grandma's Victorian Inn**, 1826 W. Third St., Hastings, 402/462-2013, is a five-room bed-and-breakfast managed by Tim and Robin Sassman. The Victorian home is located in a quiet neighborhood, and the average room price is $60.

The **Kirschke House Bed & Breakfast**, 1124 W. Third St., Grand Island, 800/381-6851 or 308/381-6851, www.gionline.net/k.htm, is a 1902 two-story brick home with rooms for rent, plus a separate old carriage house and bridal suite available in the backyard garden. Rooms range in price from $55 to $145.

CAMPING

Hastings KOA, 302 E. 26th St., Hastings, 800/KOA-2171 or 402/462-5621, is near major town attractions like the Convention Center and the IMAX Theater. It features campsites, car rentals, hot tubs, and a video arcade.

"GLOW IN THE DARK" BOWLING

Big Apple Fun Center, 500 W. Fourth St., Kearney, 308/234-4545, features "Glow in the Dark" bowling on weekend nights. Bumper cars, a video arcade, pool tables, a sports bar, and 36 lanes of bowling are also available for a night of fun.

Wood River Motel & Campground, I-80 Exit 300, 11774 S. Hwy. 11, Wood River, 800/967-9661, is just west of Grand Island and has electric hookups, showers, a trailer dump station, and fishing.

NIGHTLIFE

In a cluster of small college towns, you'll have no problem finding a menu of nightlife from which to choose.

Dad's Tavern, 1910 Central Ave., Kearney, 308/237-2673, run by Gale and Ollie Dady, is a friendly neighborhood bar in the middle of Kearney's attractive downtown. **Coffee Central**, 1212 W. 24th St., Kearney, 402/237-5434, has open mike night every Tuesday, poetry readings on the first Wednesday of each month, and folkish live music on weekend nights.

Lear Jet's Nightclub, 2703 W. Villa Dr., Kearney, 402/237-2097, is a popular hangout for the local college crowd Wednesday through Saturday and features a DJ-driven dance floor.

The **Phoenix Club**, 2023 First Ave., Kearney, 308/236-6773, isn't some exclusive, black-tie-required joint but a down-to-earth club that features live country music and even provides dance lessons on occasion.

If you're in the area and you just *have to* catch an evening sports match on TV, stop by **Balz Sports Bar**, 3421 W. State St., Grand Island, 308/382-9193. It boasts 11 TVs, a food menu, and sports memorabilia displays.

4
PRAIRIE LAKES COUNTRY

Whether it was Zebulon Pike or Stephen Long (both nineteenth-century explorers) who first coined the term "Great Desert" to refer to southwest Nebraska, the moniker stuck. The area didn't become worthy of the appellation "Prairie Lakes Country" until the 1930s, when a series of dams were installed to control flooding of area rivers. Now lakes and reservoirs dot what is one of the last true prairie landscapes left in the state.

The lakes offer good fishing, and the flat prairie in many communities has been molded into excellent golf courses. Large stretches of the untouched prairie are still open for hunting.

The small communities throughout the Prairie Lakes region are known for their quaint charm and historic buildings. For instance, the downtown Main Street in Grant (at the intersection of Highways 61 and 23, in Perkins County) has been designated an official Historic Site by the State Historical Society.

The largest community in the Prairie Lakes region, McCook was born and boomed thanks to railroad expansion—specifically that of the Burlington Railroad line. Major rail booms sparked new construction in the town and drew settlers, especially in the 1880s and 1920s.

The Prairie Lakes landscape still offers visitors a glimpse of the Nebraska that was, in the prairie and historic buildings, and the Nebraska of today, in the man-made lakes and reservoirs, for example. The major reservoirs, from west to east, are Enders Reservoir State Recreation Area (near Enders on Highway 6),

Swanson Reservoir State Recreation Area (near Trenton on Highway 34), Red Willow Reservoir State Recreation Area/Hugh Butler Lake State Recreation Area (north of McCook on Highway 83), and Medicine Creek State Recreation Area (near Stockville in Frontier County).

A PERFECT DAY IN PRAIRIE LAKES COUNTRY

Drive along Highway 6 in the south part of the Prairie Lakes region, beginning in Champion at the Champion Mill Historical Park to access Enders Reservoir State Recreation Area just east of Champion, or Swanson Reservoir State Recreation Area farther east, near Trenton (just south of Highway 6, on Highway 25). End your day in McCook, which features plenty of attractions, like the Museum of the High Plains, and decent restaurants and lodgings. Golfers will want to tee off at Heritage Hills Golf Course in McCook, consistently rated as one of the better public courses in the country.

SIGHTSEEING HIGHLIGHTS

★★★ CHAMPION MILL HISTORICAL PARK
7 miles southwest of Imperial via S-15A, Champion, 308/882-5444

For nearly a century, from 1888 to 1968, this water-driven mill ground flour and grain for the town's—and region's—farmers. That process continues today at the mill, which has become a historical park where visitors can watch grain and flour processed as it was in the nineteenth century; bags of the mill's flour are available for purchase. The mill building itself is an interesting sight, too, a structure of connected box shapes of varying sizes. The mill's pond even offers primitive camping facilities.

Details: Open summer daily 8–8; winter daily 9–sunset. Free. (30 minutes–1 hour)

★★ MUSEUM OF THE HIGH PLAINS
423 Norris Ave., McCook, 308/345-3661

Late nineteenth– and early twentieth–century lifestyles are preserved in this museum. Artifacts from everyday life plus full-scale recreations of rooms illuminate the lives of the prairie pioneers. Household objects—such as furniture, clothing, tools, and photos—date as far back

PRAIRIE LAKES COUNTRY

Gothenburg
Platte River
Oregon Trail
80
47
47
23
Elwood
283
283
Arapahoe D
6 34
Cambridge H
Bartley
34
Medicine Creek
Medicine Creek State Recreation Area
Curtis
Stockville
Maywood
23
Wellfleet
E
83
McCook C
6
83
Red Willow Reservoir State Recreation Area
Republican River
Hayes Center
25
Trenton B
Swanson Reservoir State Recreation Area
G
25
6
Wallace
25
23
34
Madrid
Enders
61
Benkelman
Grant
61
Enders F
6
Enders Reservoir State Recreation Area
Imperial
S 15A
Champion A
Rock Creek State Recreation Area
S 15A
Parks
23

ROAD
HIGHWAY
TRAIL
UNPAVED ROAD

0 SCALE
30 KILOMETERS
30 MILES

as the 1870s. More recent history is also documented at High Plains, with World War II–era materials from the McCook Army Air Base and the Indianola German P.O.W. Camp on display. Children and adults alike will enjoy the intricate detail of the museum's model railroad. A replica drugstore is housed in the actual building in which the sugary drink Kool-Aid was concocted.

Details: *Open year-round Tue–Sun 1–5. $2 general admission. (1 hour)*

★★ SENATOR GEORGE NORRIS HISTORICAL SITE
708 Norris Ave., McCook, 308/345-8484 or 308/345-7134

Not only did Senator George Norris serve as a legislator for our country, he also founded the Tennessee Valley Association and the Rural Electric Authority. He also penned the Twentieth Amendment to the U.S. Constitution. A senator from 1913 through 1943, Norris lived in McCook; his beautiful home and furnishings have been preserved in all their period glory. See where Norris once studied, relaxed, ate, and slept. His lifestyle was of course more refined than that of the average citizen in the early twentieth century, and it's interesting to tour this example of an earlier era's notion of luxury.

Details: *Open year-round Wed–Sat 10–noon and 1–5, Tue and Sun 1:30–5. Free. (30 minutes–1 hour)*

SIGHTS

- Ⓐ Champion Mill Historical Park
- Ⓑ Massacre Canyon Historical Marker
- Ⓒ Museum of the High Plains
- Ⓓ Our Lady of Fatima Shrine
- Ⓒ Senator George Norris Historical Site

FOOD

- Ⓔ Clubhouse Restaurant & Lounge
- Ⓒ Copper Mill
- Ⓕ M&M's Natural Jaz
- Ⓒ Sehnert's Dutch Oven Bakery
- Ⓖ Tom's Tavern

LODGING

- Ⓓ Arapahoe Court
- Ⓒ Best Western Chief Motel
- Ⓖ The Blue Colonial Bed & Breakfast
- Ⓗ Cambridge Bed & Breakfast
- Ⓒ Cedar Inn-4-Less
- Ⓑ Flying A Ranch B&B
- Ⓒ Holiday Inn Express
- Ⓒ Red Horse Motel
- Ⓓ Shady Rest Motel
- Ⓖ Trenton House

Note: Items with the same letter are located in the same area.

FURNAS COUNTY MUSEUM

Furnas County Museum, Arapahoe, 308/962-5238, holds artifacts of daily pioneer life that stretches back throughout the history of Furnas County and its generations of agriculturally focused residents. It's open May–Sep Sat 2–5. Free (but donations encouraged).

★ **MASSACRE CANYON HISTORICAL MARKER**
Hwy. 34, Trenton, 308/334-5566
Built in 1931, the Massacre Canyon Historical Marker commemorates the final August 4, 1873, battle between the Sioux and the Pawnee. The Sioux had outnumbered and overpowered the retreating Pawnee until the U.S. Calvaries appeared and forced the Sioux to disengage. The area was afterward quickly settled by ranchers arriving from the east. The pink granite marker stands 35 feet high and weighs 91 tons.
Details: Open year-round. Free. (15–30 minutes)

★ **OUR LADY OF FATIMA SHRINE**
Hwys. 6 and 34, Arapahoe, 308/962-5238
Polish chaplain Father Henry Davis, after surviving a stint in a World War II prisoner of war camp, returned to America to build this beautiful shrine. He dedicated it to the Virgin Mary and the account of her appearance before children shepherds near the city of Fatima, Portugal. St. Germanus Church in Arapahoe maintains the trees, statues, and plants that make up the shrine.
Details: Go five blocks west of Hwys. 6 and 34. Open year-round. Free. (15–30 minutes)

FITNESS AND RECREATION

Enders Reservoir State Recreation Area, 5 miles east and 4.5 miles south of Imperial, 308/882-4748, features 26 miles of shoreline surrounding 1,700 acres of water. Since it feeds irrigation systems, you'll find the water level extremely low in dry summers. Walleye, bass, and catfish swim in its waters. **Swanson Reservoir State Recreation Area**, two miles west of Trenton on Hwy. 34, 308/334-5444, is a 4,794-acre lake with nearby camping facilities (which include modern rest rooms and showers) at Spring Canyon. **Red Willow Reservoir/Hugh Butler Lake State Recreation Area**, 10 miles north of McCook on Hwy. 83, 308/367-4411, features good bass fishing and the Willow View campground. **Medicine Creek State Recreation Area**, two miles west and seven miles north of Cambridge, 308/367-4411, encompasses the large Shady Bay Campground and 1,850 acres of water.

If indoor recreation suits you better, **Willow Lanes Inc.**, N. Hwy. 83, McCook, 308/345-2700, can suit all your bowling needs. Stop for a brew at the Seat of Honor Lounge inside.

Heritage Hills Golf Course, 6000 Clubhouse Dr., McCook, 308/345-5032, has been consistently judged to be one of the better public golf courses in the country. The scenic course is a challenging par 72. A round costs $32 with a cart, $22 without.

FOOD

A popular dining spot is **Copper Mill**, N. Hwy. 83 and Coppermill St., McCook, 308/345-2296, serving prime rib, steaks, and even oysters on the half shell. The restaurant boasts one of the best wine lists in the region. **Sehnert's Dutch Oven Bakery**, 312 Norris Ave., McCook, 308/345-6500, specializes in the tasty Jiffy Burger.

M&M's Natural Jaz, 617 Broadway, Imperial, 308/882-4149, is a sandwich shop as well as a natural foods store and bakery.

Clubhouse Restaurant & Lounge, 106 N. Commercial Ave., Maywood, 308/362-4938, is proud of its prime rib in particular and its country-style cooking in general. A separate dining room is reserved for families.

Tom's Tavern, 405 Main St., Trenton, 308/334-5705, features noontime lunch and dinner specials during the week, from Mexican fare to prime rib meals.

LODGING

Holiday Inn Express, 1 Holiday Bison Dr., McCook, 308/345-4505, features a deluxe breakfast bar as well as affordable rates. **Best Western Chief Motel**, at the intersection of Hwys. 6/34 and 83, McCook, 308/345-3700, features an indoor pool and free continental breakfast and is next door to a Country Kitchen restaurant. Pets are allowed. Computer hookups are also available. The **Cedar Inn-4-Less**, 1300 E. C St., McCook, 800/352-4489 or 308/345-7091, offers fewer amenities (e.g., no pool), but still provides a comfortable night's stay, as does **Red Horse Motel**, E. Hwy. 6/34, McCook, 308/345-2800.

HUNTING

In rural states like Iowa and Nebraska, where suburbs and strip malls haven't yet paved over all the land and there's timber and open prairie tucked among the vast stretches of cornfields (Iowa) and cattle ranches (Nebraska), hunting is of course a popular sport (or necessary thinning of winter herds, or confusing barbaric practice, however you choose to think of it).

But you can't just pick up a gun and go shoot. Both states have rules and regulations that govern when, where, how, and what you hunt and kill.

In general, Iowa seasons for quail, pheasants, rabbits, deer, and such run from around October or November through January. Some animals, like the plentiful and therefore unlucky coyote, can be hunted year-round. Schedules differ from year to year, so you need to check with the proper authorities for up-to-date seasons.

Public hunting areas in Iowa are marked by the Department of Natural Resources every 1/8 mile by green and white signs. Hunting on private property, of course, requires permission of the landowner. Wildlife preserves, of course, are off limits—that's why that deer is staring at you, standing 20 feet from you, unafraid.

Nonresidents can expect to pay more than $60 for a small game hunting license (around $25 for those under 18) and even more for deer and wild turkey.

The proper authority in Iowa for hunting-related information, the DNR, is at the Wallace State Office Building, Des Moines, Iowa 50319. Call 515/281-HNTR (4687). Surf to www.state.ia.us/dnr.

The Nebraska Game and Parks Commission is the font of all hunting knowledge in Iowa's neighbor to the west. The seasons are similar to Iowa, but check with the NGPC for all the up-to-date changes and intricacies of law. Nonresidents pay around $55 for small game or wild turkey hunting and around $150 for deer.

Conservation officers are located in cities and towns around Nebraska. Locations include Lincoln, 402/471-5532; Gretna, 402/332-5026; Valentine, 402/376-5909; and Scottsbluff, 308/635-1277. As with Iowa, there's also a Web site packed with information: www.ngpc.state.ne.us.

The **Cambridge Bed & Breakfast**, 606 Parker St., Cambridge, 308/697-3220, rents five rooms, three with private baths. Gerald and Gloria Hilton are the owner-operators. **The Blue Colonial Bed & Breakfast**, HC2 Box 120, Trenton, 308/276-2533, is an attractive ranch home run by Peter and Marita Todd. They specialize in five-course formal dining. Another fine bed-and-breakfast in the area is **Flying A Ranch B & B**, 6.5 miles northwest of Trenton, 800/434-5574 or 308/334-5574.

For an affordable stay, **Shady Rest Motel**, E. Hwy. 6/34, Arapahoe, 308/962-5461, is fine for a night or two. **Arapahoe Court**, W. Hwys. 6/34 and 283, Arapahoe, 308/962-7948, offers affordable rooms that also allow pets. There's room for large truck parking, too.

For a more luxurious stay, **Trenton House**, 314 W. First St., Trenton, 308/334-5213, is a new, modern house available for rent by the night, weekend, or week. It features two bedrooms and on-site washer and dryer.

CAMPING

The hatchery facilities at **Rock Creek State Fish Hatchery and Recreation Area**, seven miles north of Parks, 308/423-2080, are open year-round daily from 8 to 4:30, and the park offers primitive campsites.

Lil Brave RV Park, Hwy. 34, Trenton, 308/334-5110, offers all the hookups you'll need if you're traveling in an RV. Fees are $15, and 18 trailer spaces and 18 tent spaces are available. Open year-round; amenities include electricity, sewer, water, showers, and laundry.

Bring your trailer to **Karrer Park**, Airport Rd. and Hwy. 6/34, McCook, 308/345-2022, which has 14 available spaces from April through November. Electricity, a trailer dumping station, rest rooms, and showers are also on hand.

With 10 trailer spaces available, **Shady Rest Camp**, 309 Chestnut St., Arapahoe, 308/962-5461, also features all the water, sewer, and laundry facilities that you'll need.

Also refer to the area lakes and reservoirs listed under Fitness and Recreation for some other camping options, like **Red Willow State Recreation Area**, which provides fine camping facilities for a minimal fee.

NIGHTLIFE

Good Times Bar, N. Main St., Wauneta, 308/394-5656, features keno for your amusement and pizza for your appetite. Friday and Saturday nights feature a sirloin steak special.

5
OGALLALA AND
NORTH PLATTE

Ogallala was the namesake of the Oglala tribe of the Dakota Sioux. With the completion of the Union Pacific Railroad in 1867, Ogallala picked up an extra "a" and "l" and became a well-known railroad town and cattle-shipping thoroughfare. Apparently because this rowdy cowboy destination offered wine, women, and song after the long, dusty miles spent on a cattle drive, Ogallala also became known for a time as the "Gomorrah of the Plains." Boot Hill Cemetery is the resting place today of some of the pioneer cowboys who didn't make it out of town alive, due to fatal blows from other, hot-headed cowboys.

Just to the east of Ogallala on I-80 lies North Platte, which is famous as the home of Colonel William "Buffalo Bill" Cody, the one-time proprietor of the big Wild West Show. The town of North Platte is also still a large railroad center. Its Bailey Yard is a large and confusing mass of iron tracks and railcars.

These days in Ogallala (still Nebraska's "Cowboy Capital") and North Platte, rowdiness and rail traffic have waned and Buffalo Bill is but a memory, but the past informs the present. The two towns are vital central Nebraska hubs of commerce and recreation; cattle and horses dot the landscape and tourists flock to the lakes for great fishing and relaxation. Nebraska's largest lake, Lake McConaughy, just north of Ogallala, can keep your recreation calendar filled for days.

A PERFECT DAY IN OGALLALA
AND NORTH PLATTE

Plan on lunch at Ole's Big Game Steakhouse & Lounge, notable both for its food and unforgettable kitsch atmosphere (stuffed and mounted animals everywhere). The rest of the day, enjoy the available water and sun in ample portions on Lake McConaughy, a blissful locale for wet fun within the land-locked state of Nebraska.

SIGHTSEEING HIGHLIGHTS

★★★★ **LAKE MCCONAUGHY STATE RECREATION AREA**
1500 Hwy. 61 N., Ogallala, 308/284-3542
Twenty-two miles in length, with as many as 35 thousand acres of water, Lake McConaughy offers plenty of water-sport activity for fishers, swimmers, skiers—anyone who wants to do anything remotely associated with water. There are 23 different public access gates on the lake, with shops, restaurants, and hotels scattered around the perimeter, too. Camp, picnic, or just hang out for an afternoon. **Van's Lakeview Fishing Camp**, South Shore Big Mac at Gate 18, #1 Lakeview, Brule, 308/284-4965, offers a marina, guide service, general store, and boat rentals. **Sportsmen's Complex**, Hwys. 61 and 92, Keystone, 308/726-2521, lives up to its name, with a full stock of fishing, hunting, and lake-related supplies.
Details: Hours vary. Prices vary. (1 hour minimum)

★★ **BUFFALO BILL RANCH STATE HISTORICAL PARK**
Rd. 21, North Platte, 308/535-8035
Another native Iowan moves to Nebraska and finds fame. Born in 1846 near LeClaire, Iowa, "Buffalo Bill" Cody became an ox-team driver at age 11, was hired on as a Pony Express rider in 1860, served the Union Army in non-battle roles, and ran a hotel in Kansas for a time with his wife, Louisa Frederici—all before becoming "Buffalo Bill." He didn't pick up the nickname until he was contracted to provide buffalo meat for Kansas Pacific Railroad workers and then won a buffalo hunting contest (near Sheridan, Kansas) by single-handedly slaying 69 of the beasts. After more military service and initial forays into Wild West–style entertainment, Cody established a cattle ranch near North Platte in 1877, also known as Scout's Rest. One of his

OGALLALA REGION

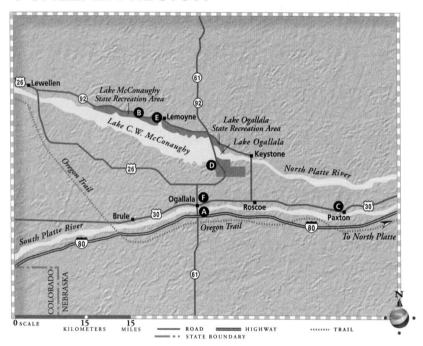

SIGHTS
- **Ⓐ** Boot Hill
- **Ⓐ** Kenfield Petrified Wood Gallery
- **Ⓑ** Lake McConaughy State Recreation Area
- **Ⓒ** Ole's Big Game Steakhouse & Lounge

FOOD
- **Ⓓ** Hill Top Inn
- **Ⓓ** Mike's Place
- **Ⓒ** Ole's Big Game Steakhouse & Lounge
- **Ⓐ** Pioneer Trails

LODGING
- **Ⓔ** Admiral's Cove Lakefront Resort
- **Ⓕ** Kingsley Lodge
- **Ⓐ** Plaza Inn

Note: Items with the same letter are located in the same area.

first celebrations there, the "Old Glory Blowout" on July 4, 1882, is generally regarded as the country's first-ever rodeo. In 1883, his first "Wild West Show" debuted in Omaha, then toured the country. Cody's ranch became a historical park in 1965, preserving the homestead and 16 acres of the original 4,000. The buildings have been restored and are preserved by the Nebraska Game and Parks Commission. Tour the house, inside and out—it still looks like it did in Cody's day. You can also tour the big barn and take horseback rides on trails around the ranch.

Details: *Open Apr–Oct daily, hours vary. Trail rides available Memorial Day–Labor Day Wed–Sun. $2.50 general admission. (1–2 hours)*

★★ CODY TRADING POST
I-80 and Hwy. 83, North Platte, 308/532-8081

Fort Cody is your shopping mecca in the Ogallala–North Platte area. Here you can buy the kinds of trinkets that children back home will love or the sort of hand-crafted jewelry and artwork that warrants a purchase as a future Christmas gift. There's even a miniature, automated Buffalo Bill Wild West Show on hand in case you miss the real thing.

Details: *Open year-round daily. Free. (15 minutes–1 hour)*

★★ LINCOLN COUNTY HISTORICAL MUSEUM AND WESTERN HERITAGE VILLAGE
2403 N. Buffalo Ave., North Platte, 308/534-5640

Celebrating the history of the peoples of the North Platte area through the years, this small but worthwhile museum also features some information on how trains influenced Lincoln County's history. From pioneer days through World War II and the present day, this is your stop to find out about the region's past.

Details: *Open May–Sep. $1.50 suggested donation. (30 minutes–1 hour)*

★★ OLE'S BIG GAME STEAKHOUSE & LOUNGE
I-80 Exit 145, Paxton, 308/239-4500,
www.olesbiggame.com

Not just an eatery but also an attraction, Ole's is the kind of place you must stop at, even just so you can talk about it with coworkers and friends after the trip. More than two hundred big game stuffed

NORTH PLATTE

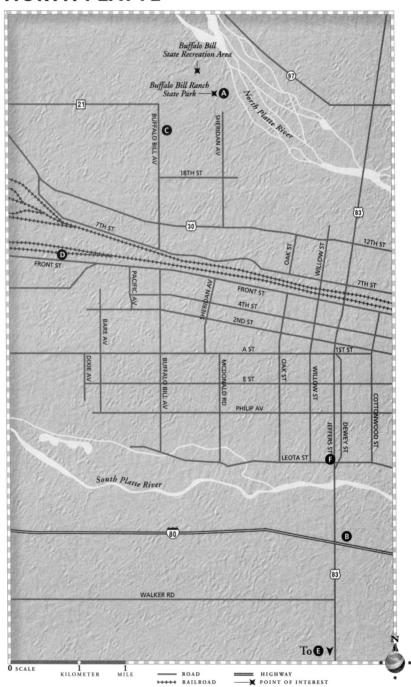

Buffalo Bill
State Recreation Area

Buffalo Bill Ranch
State Park — ✕ Ⓐ

97

North Platte River

21

BUFFALO BILL AV

Ⓒ

SHERIDAN AV

18TH ST

83

7TH ST

30

OAK ST

WILLOW ST

12TH ST

Ⓓ
FRONT ST

PACIFIC AV

SHERIDAN AV

FRONT ST

7TH ST

4TH ST

2ND ST

BARE AV

A ST

1ST ST

DIXIE AV

BUFFALO BILL AV

MCDONALD RD

E ST

OAK ST

WILLOW ST

COTTONWOOD ST

PHILIP AV

JEFFERS ST

DEWEY ST

LEOTA ST

Ⓕ

South Platte River

80

Ⓑ

83

WALKER RD

To Ⓔ ▼

N

0 SCALE
KILOMETER MILE

1   1

ROAD   HIGHWAY
RAILROAD   POINT OF INTEREST

trophies are corralled in the interior of this restaurant and bar, open for business since Prohibition was repealed. The collection reportedly started with a single deer that original owner Rosser "Ole" Herstedt himself bagged on a 1938 hunting trip. After that, Ole traveled to every continent over the next 35 years to hunt, subsequently bringing back more and more trophies. He hunted for the last time in 1973 and stepped down as the steakhouse's owner in 1988.

Details: Open year-round daily for lunch and dinner. (15 minutes– 2 hours)

★★ UNION PACIFIC BAILEY YARD
Front St., North Platte, 308/532-4966

Trains unquestionably define a large portion of Nebraska's pioneer past and transportation history up to the present. Here's the best place in the state to witness the culmination of that history—the modern click-clacking of numerous trains as they roll their way through the largest railcar classification complex in the world. Tourists can watch the action from a special observation deck. You won't forget to make this stop because as you drive around Nebraska, you'll see train after train rolling parallel to the highway. And after you visit the massive, majestic Bailey Yard, you won't soon forget the experience.

Details: Take I-80 Exit 170, go to Hwy. 83/Dewey St., then take Front St. west to Bailey Yard. Open year-round daily. Free. (15 minutes– 1 hour)

★ BOOT HILL
W. 10th and Park Hill Dr., Ogallala, 308/284-4066

SIGHTS
Ⓐ Buffalo Bill Ranch State Historical Park
Ⓑ Cody Trading Post
Ⓒ Lincoln County Historical Museum and Western Heritage Village
Ⓓ Union Pacific Bailey Yard

LODGING
Ⓔ Knoll's Country Inn
Ⓕ Stockman Inn

This pioneer cemetery was the final resting place for many a cowboy who died in the late nineteenth century in Ogallala. Some were killed by other cowboys. Some were killed by the sheriff. In July 1879, three cowhands were buried in a single day. Many who were originally buried here have long since been removed or transferred to other interment spots by relatives, but the graves of many unknown or forgotten cowboys remain. And why Boot Hill? Because most cowboys were buried still wearing their boots, of course.

If you are a non-Nebraskan zipping through the state on I-80, Ole's Big Game Steakhouse & Lounge will be one of your first reference points in the central part of the state.

Details: *Open year-round daily. Free. (15–30 minutes)*

★ **KENFIELD PETRIFIED WOOD GALLERY**
I-80 Exit 126, Ogallala, 308/284-4066
Billed as the "Museum of Ancient Wood," this unique gallery salutes art crafted by the hands of Time and Mother Nature. Local artisans have also cut and polished pieces of the wood, or fashioned them into articles like music boxes. The two-acre museum site also includes rock and flower gardens and a waterfall.
Details: *Open May–Sep Mon–Sat 9–6, Sun 1–6. Free. (30 minutes–1 hour)*

FITNESS AND RECREATION

Head to the lake for water-based recreation. If you prefer to stay dry, check out the options below.

Head-to-head competition is the name of the game at **Cody Go Karts & Bumper Boats**, I-80 and Hwy. 83, North Platte, 308/534-8277 or 308/534-3608, which features 560 feet of water slides, as well as multiple go-cart tracks, trampolines, basketball, and plenty of games for children.

FOOD

Ole's corners the market on distinct atmosphere in the Ogallala–North Platte area, but other eateries serve up fine food, too.

Hill Top Inn, Kingsley Dam, Ogallala, 308/284-4534, open for lunch and dinner Monday through Saturday, serves steaks, seafood, and drinks. **Pioneer Trails**, 55 River Rd., Ogallala, 308/284-2388, serves breakfast, lunch, and dinner, everything from prime rib to "buffalo burgers," and also sports an ice cream shop.

Mike's Place, eight miles north of Ogallala at the face of the dam, 308/284-2763, boasts about its pan-fried chicken. It opens at 6 a.m. daily for breakfast and does carry-out for the nearby boat dock.

Perhaps not the wisest choice for vegetarians, **Ole's Big Game Steakhouse & Lounge**, I-80 Exit 145, Paxton, 308/239-4500, www.olesbiggame.com, features one of the most unforgettable atmospheres of any eatery in the two-state region. For starters, a giant polar bear greets you as you walk in the door. (Don't worry, he won't bite.)

LODGING

For an extended vacation stay at Lake McConaughy, **Admiral's Cove Lakefront Resort**, Gate 6, Lemoyne, 308/355-2102, on the north shore of the lake, offers everything from cabins to a restaurant to boat rentals. **Kingsley Lodge**, 1510 N. Hwy. 61, Ogallala, 800/883-2775 or 308/284-2775, offers similar accommodations and services.

For a shorter stay and budget rates, the **Plaza Inn**, E. Hwy. 30, Ogallala, 308/284-8416, has 45 rooms and a heated pool.

If you're seeking quaint charm and a personal touch, book one of the three rooms at **Knoll's Country Inn**, 6132 W. Range Rd., North Platte, 877/378-2521 or 308/368-5634, owned by Bob and Arlene Knoll. The grounds feature a hot tub and flower gardens.

More than one hundred trains make their way through Bailey Yard every day.

The **Stockman Inn**, I-80 Exit 177, North Platte, 800/624-4643, has everything you need under one roof: a restaurant, lounge, exercise room, and outdoor pool. (Well, the outdoor pool's not under a roof, but you get the idea.) The prices are reasonable, even for families.

CAMPING

Meyer Camper Court, 120 Rd. E. 80, Ogallala, 308/284-2415, features 60 camper spaces and 40 tent sites, plus a game room, playground, and heated swimming pool. Larry and Christi Meyer are the owners.

Van's Lakeview Fishing Camp, South Shore Big Mac at Gate 18, #1 Lakeview, Brule, 308/284-4965, features campgrounds on the beach, 50 electric hookups, showers, a water slide, a general store, and fishing guides.

NIGHTLIFE

Front Street, 519 E St., Ogallala, 308/284-6000, hosts the **Crystal Palace Review & Shootout**, Nebraska's longest-running summer theater, staging productions seven nights a week. Shows start at 7:15 p.m. The **Livery Barn Cafe** features an 1800s-style saloon and a free cowboy museum.

    Cheres Grill & Lounge, Lake McConaughy, 308/726-2335, is open daily and hosts a live band every Saturday night.

6
THE NEBRASKA
PANHANDLE

The landscape of the Nebraska Panhandle is a visual introduction to the south-west United States: Great bluffs and other large rock formations are broken by long, flat stretches of land, but the scale isn't as large, nor the landscape as barren as the desert. In fact, large portions of the Panhandle are covered by the Nebraska National Forest, with its Ponderosa pine trees and jutting white cliffs.

The Panhandle today holds some of the state's choicest attractions. Scotts Bluff National Monument is a must-see, a breathtaking plateau from which you can take in miles of the surrounding countryside. Scottsbluff and Gering, the twin towns at the foot of the monument, are highly recommended places to stop and spend a night. They offer lots of great lodging, dining, and friendly people.

You'll want to explore the great outdoors in the Panhandle, whether in the aforementioned Niobrara Forest or at the Agate Fossil Beds, at Chadron State Park or on the actual Oregon Trail. And if you don't visit Carhenge while you're here, you'll regret it—and people familiar with Nebraska will doubt that you even were really in the state.

A PERFECT DAY IN THE
NEBRASKA PANHANDLE

Spend most of your day in the southern half of the Panhandle. Start at Agate Fossil Beds National Monument and work your way south. Stop at Carhenge

THE NEBRASKA PANHANDLE

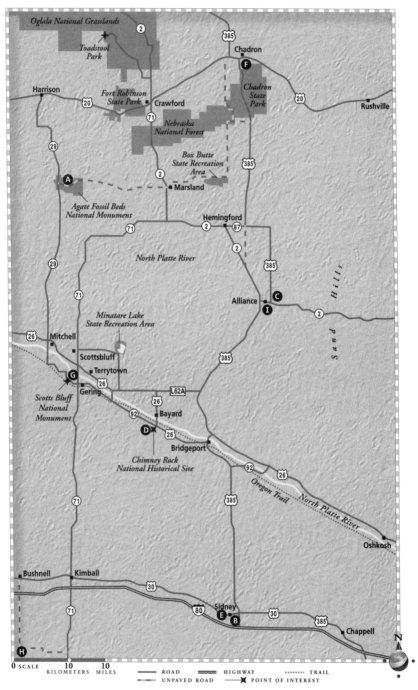

Oglala National Grasslands

Toadstool Park

Chadron

Fort Robinson State Park
Crawford

Harrison

Chadron State Park

Rushville

Nebraska National Forest

Box Butte State Recreation Area

Marsland

Agate Fossil Beds National Monument

Hemingford

North Platte River

Alliance

Sand Hills

Minatare Lake State Recreation Area

Mitchell

Scottsbluff
Terrytown

Gering

L62A

Bayard

Scotts Bluff National Monument

Bridgeport

Chimney Rock National Historical Site

Oregon Trail
North Platte River

Oshkosh

Bushnell   Kimball

Chappell

Sidney

0 SCALE   10   10
KILOMETERS   MILES

N

━━━ ROAD   ━━━ HIGHWAY   ········ TRAIL
━━━ UNPAVED ROAD   ✹ POINT OF INTEREST

to spend at least a serene half hour among the silent wrecks; take some pictures; ponder life.

Stop by Chimney Rock, then proceed on to Scottsbluff and Gering. The 18th St. Bar & Grill in Scottsbluff is both a good place for lunch or dinner and a favorite evening hangout. The best time to visit the Scotts Bluff National Monument is late afternoon, closer to sundown. The views are breathtaking.

SIGHTSEEING HIGHLIGHTS

★★★★ SCOTTS BLUFF NATIONAL MONUMENT
Hwy. 92, Gering, 308/436-4340

Die near a tall rock, and at least you get the rock named after you. Scotts Bluff National Monument was named after nineteenth-century mountaineer Hiram Scott, whose 260-pound body was discovered at the base of this 800-foot-tall bluff. Standing atop Scotts Bluff today (after driving up a winding road that can be difficult to scale in heavy traffic) will be a highlight of your Nebraska Panhandle travels. Gaze east and you feel like you're looking across the entire two states covered by this book. A telescope lets you zoom in on the town of Gering or on distant Chimney Rock. Two overlook spots lie at the end of trails; the north one affords a beautiful view of the North Platte River Valley, while the south one looks upon the

SIGHTS

- Ⓐ Agate Fossil Beds National Monument
- Ⓑ Cabela's
- Ⓒ Carhenge & Car Art Reserve
- Ⓓ Chimney Rock National Historic Site
- Ⓔ Living Memorial Gardens
- Ⓕ The Museum of the Fur Trade
- Ⓖ Scotts Bluff National Monument
- Ⓗ Sidney Historic Downtown District
- Ⓗ Tri-State Marker & Nebraska's Highest Point (Panorama Point)

FOOD

- Ⓕ Big Bat's Truck Stop and Food Court
- Ⓘ The Elms
- Ⓖ Helen's Pancake & Steak House
- Ⓘ Ken & Dale's Restaurant
- Ⓘ The Porterhouse Restaurant & Lounge

LODGING

- Ⓕ Blaine Motel
- Ⓖ Olde Main Street Inn
- Ⓘ West Way Motel & Restaurant
- Ⓕ The Westerner

Note: Items with the same letter are located in the same area.

Oregon Trail. A museum and visitors center is at the foot of the bluff, just off Highway 92.

Details: Three miles west of Gering on Hwy. 92. Museum open Memorial Day–Labor Day daily 8–8; Labor Day–Memorial Day daily 8–5. Road to the summit open summer 8–7:30, winter 8–4:30. $5 per car, $2 per motorcycle. (30 minutes–2 hours)

★★★ **AGATE FOSSIL BEDS NATIONAL MONUMENT**
301 River Rd., Harrison, 308/668-2211, www.nps.gov/agfo
The American Museum of Natural History, the Carnegie Museum, and the University of Nebraska sponsored expeditions into these hills along the Niobrara River at the turn of the twentieth century. Today, paved trails allow visitors to see the work of these expeditions, which uncovered thousands of fossils left by mammals of the Miocene era. Many age-old fossils have been left, partially uncovered, where they were found. A visitors center re-creates the landscape as it was with life-size dioramas; it also salutes "Captain" James Cook, a former Army scout and owner of the Agate Springs Ranch who hosted many Native Americans as guests and subsequently amassed a large collection of artifacts and gifts, now on display.

Details: 34 miles north of Mitchell on Hwy. 29, or 22 miles south of Harrison. Open Memorial Day–Labor Day daily 8–6; Labor Day–Memorial Day daily 8-5; trails open dawn–dusk. $2 per person or $5 per car. (1–2 hours)

★★ **CARHENGE & CAR ART RESERVE**
Hwy. 385, Alliance, 308/762-1520
Without a doubt Nebraska's most quirkily charming attraction, Carhenge is the sort of oddball tourist stop that leaves you chuckling to yourself months later. Jim Reinders built the full-scale auto sculpture in June 1987 during a family reunion. His concept was simple: Replicate England's famous Stonehenge in a roadside pasture using American cars from the 1950s and '60s, 38 in all. But Carhenge works some magical charm that turns its junkyard elements into a worthwhile, picture-snapping tourist stop. Just don't expect to see any Druids. The "Car Art Reserve" portion of the site refers to dinosaur-like steel creatures that populate some of the surrounding pasture. A roadside park and picnic area are also on-site.

Details: 2.5 miles north of Alliance on Hwy. 385. Open year-round daily. Free. (30 minutes)

★★ CHIMNEY ROCK NATIONAL HISTORIC SITE
Hwy. 92, Bayard, 308/586-2581

Chimney Rock has endured many names through the years, one of its first being "Elk Penis." (This name was bestowed upon the site by area Native Americans, who were more familiar with the anatomy of one of their food sources than with chimneys, which were used by the white settlers.) This 500-foot-high stone column towers above the landscape of the North Platte River Valley and can be seen more than 30 miles away. Travelers on the Oregon Trail used Chimney Rock as an important landmark, and its current name first came into use in 1827 as indicated by surviving journal entries. Today a modern Visitor Center Museum is located just a half mile east of Chimney Rock and its surrounding 83-acre grounds.

Before Scotts Bluff National Monument was named after Hiram Scott, local Native American tribes called it "ma-a-pa-te," or "hill that is hard to go around."

Details: *1.5 miles south of Hwy. 92, near the intersection of Hwy. 92 and Hwy. 26. Visitors center open summer daily 9–6; winter daily 9–5. $1 general admission. (30 minutes–1 hour)*

★★ THE MUSEUM OF THE FUR TRADE
6321 Hwy. 20, Chadron, 308/432-3843

Its mission to save and exhibit the "rich history of the North American fur trade," this unique museum chronicles the fur trade throughout history, from early Colonial days and including artifacts from British, Spanish, and Native American traders. The museum site itself was an American Fur Company post run by Frenchman James Bordeaux until 1872. From guns to textiles, the museum displays a wide range of items and even publishes *The Museum of the Fur Trade Quarterly* for its members.

Details: *Open Memorial Day–Labor Day daily 8–5. $2.50 adults, $1 ages 18 and older, free under 18 with parent, half price groups of 20 or greater. (1 hour)*

★★ NORTH PLATTE VALLEY MUSEUM
11th and J Sts., Gering, 308/436-5411

Tools, woodwork, clothing, and other antiques tell the story of pioneers' daily lives. Larger displays include a "bull boat" (made from buffalo hide), a sod house, a replica of an early print shop, and a log cabin. Sod House Day in Living History occurs annually on the Sunday afternoon of Memorial Day weekend and features entertainment and historical reenactments.

Details: *Open May–Sep Mon–Sat 8:30–5, Sun 1–5. $2 adults, 50 cents age 5 and younger. (30 minutes–1 hour)*

★★ RIVERSIDE ZOO
1600 S. Beltline Hwy. W., Scottsbluff, 308/630-6236

More than three hundred animals inhabit this 21-acre zoo on the banks of the North Platte River. From smaller, playful critters like otters to the humanlike chimpanzees and a powerful white tiger, Riverside has a wide variety of animals from all parts of the world. The A-Walk-Through-Flight Aviary immerses you in the habitat of the Waldrapp ibis, hammerkops, Satyrs tragopan, and other exotic birds.

Details: *Open May–Sep Mon–Fri 9:30–4:30, Sat–Sun 9:30–5:30; Oct–Apr Mon–Fri 10:30–3:30. $3.50 ages 13–64, $2.75 age 65 and older, $1.50 ages 5–12, free under 5. (1–2 hours)*

★★ SIDNEY HISTORIC DOWNTOWN DISTRICT
10th Ave. and Illinois St., Sidney, 800/421-4769

Fort Sidney was established in 1867 to protect the settlement, which was a halfway point on the Union Pacific Railroad between North Platte, Nebraska, and Cheyenne, Wyoming. It was during the days when gold was plentiful and constantly flowing in from the Dakota Territory. Popular frontier figures like Wild Bill Hickok, Calamity Jane, and Buffalo Bill regularly passed through Sidney. Dozens of historic buildings downtown, from that era and the early twentieth century, survive. Some were shops like pharmacies or meat markets, others were theaters and saloons.

Details: *Open year-round daily. Hours vary. Free. (1 hour)*

★ CABELA'S
115 Cabela Dr., Sidney, 308/254-5505

The corporate headquarters of the popular outdoors catalog and chain of stores is here, in a 73,000-square-foot showroom with more than five hundred wildlife mounts from around the world. More than 60 thousand products are for sale, a selection that no self-respecting sportsman or sportswoman can pass up while driving along I-80.

Details: *Take I-80 Exit 59. Open year-round Mon–Sat 8–8, Sun 11–5:30. Free. (30 minutes–1 hour)*

★ **LIVING MEMORIAL GARDENS**
11th St. and Toledo St., Legion Park, Sidney, 308/254-5851
Faced with a crumbling, unused public swimming pool built in the 1940s, the citizens of Sidney in 1982 turned it into a sunken garden teeming with vegetation. There's also a visitors center. The one-time wading pool is now the Pixie Garden.
Details: *Open year-round daily dawn–dusk. Free. (15–30 minutes)*

★ **TRI-STATE MARKER & NEBRASKA'S HIGHEST POINT (PANORAMA POINT)**
800/360-4712 or 308/235-3782
The marker designating where Nebraska, Wyoming, and Colorado meet has stood here since 1869. Also at this site is Panorama Point, the "top" of Nebraska, so to speak. It's 5,424 feet above sea level and wasn't identified until 1951. On clear days you can see the Rocky Mountains off in the distant southwest. Those who go to the top of Panorama Point receive a certificate.

Nebraska's state flower is the goldenrod.

Details: *Exit I-80 at Bushnell interchange 12 miles west of Kimball, go south on Rd. 17 for 10 miles, go west on Rd. 8 for 4.2 miles, turn south on Rd. 9 and go 1 mile to Rd. 6, go west for 2 miles to Rd. 5, which goes past the home of Henry Constable, on whose land the highest point is located. Past the highest point is a one-mile trail leading to Panorama Point. Open year-round daily dawn–dusk. Free. (1 hour)*

FITNESS AND RECREATION
Plenty of open spaces and changes in elevation await you in the Panhandle in your quest for outdoor recreation.

Eight miles south of Chadron on Highway 385, **Chadron State Park**, 308/432-6167, Chadron, 308/432-6167, was Nebraska's very first state park. Trails and swimming are available.

Toadstool Area, 308/432-3367, is reached via a gravel road that intersects Highway 2 about five miles north of Crawford. Sandstone slabs sit

SCOTTSBLUFF/GERING/TERRYTOWN

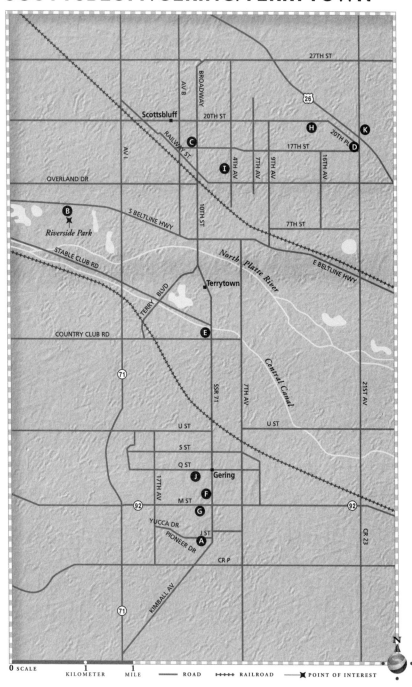

27TH ST

AV 8

BROADWAY

US 26

Scottsbluff

20TH ST

RAILWAY ST

AV 1

C

H

K

17TH ST

20TH PL

D

4TH AV

7TH AV

9TH AV

16TH AV

OVERLAND DR

I

10TH ST

B

S BELTLINE HWY

7TH ST

Riverside Park

STABLE CLUB RD

North Platte River

E BELTLINE HWY

Terrytown

TERRY BLVD

COUNTRY CLUB RD

E

Central Canal

71

SSR 71

7TH AV

21ST AV

U ST

U ST

S ST

Q ST

J

Gering

92

17TH AV

F

92

M ST

G

CR 23

YUCCA DR

PIONEER DR

J ST

A

CR P

71

KIMBALL AV

N

0	SCALE	1	1	
		KILOMETER	MILE	

ROAD ┼┼┼┼ RAILROAD ✕ POINT OF INTEREST

atop eroded stems of Brule clay (inspiring the Toadstool name). The area is full of fossils from the Cenozoic era.

Practically one-stop shopping for the outdoor fitness crowd, **Fort Robinson State Park**, three miles west of Crawford on Hwy. 20, 308/665-2900, offers you a well-rounded experience of nature and the past. You can stay in ex-cavalrymen's quarters, swim, host cookouts, fish, hike, take stagecoach rides, mountain bike, and more—all in this one park.

Lake Minatare State Recreation Area, seven miles north of Minatare, 308/783-2911, has 2,000 acres of water ready for boating, fishing, and other wet recreation. There's also a stone lighthouse on the grounds. Open January 16 through September.

Maybe the ultimate outdoor recreation available in the two-state region is the **Oregon Trail Wagon Train**, two miles south of Bayard on Oregon Trail Rd., 308/586-1850. Offered in June, July, and August by reservation, it's a four-day trek ($479 adults, under 13 $379) along the historic trail in which you live, sleep, and eat like the pioneers once did. Less-adventurous 24-hour treks are also available, for $150 for adults, under 13 $125. Groups of 20 or more can design their own treks to last from three to six days.

FOOD

If you're traveling around the Panhandle, why not dig into some hearty travel food—like pancakes?

Helen's Pancake & Steak House, 950 W. Hwy. 20, Chadron, 308/432-9958, has daily lunch and dinner specials, featuring different food styles (such as Italian and Mexican) on different days. Opens at 6 a.m. For

---

SIGHTS

- Ⓐ North Platte Valley Museum
- Ⓑ Riverside Zoo

FOOD

- Ⓒ 18th Street Bar & Grill
- Ⓓ Buffalo Steakhouse
- Ⓔ Bush's Gaslight Restaurant & Lounge
- Ⓕ Gering Bakery

FOOD (continued)

- Ⓓ Grampy's Pancake House
- Ⓖ Log Cabin Restaurant & Lounge
- Ⓗ Valentino's

LODGING

- Ⓓ Candlelight Motel
- Ⓘ Fontenelle Inn
- Ⓙ Prairie Chanticleer
- Ⓚ Scottsbluff Inn

Note: Items with the same letter are located in the same area.

---

those who crave breakfast any time of the day, **Big Bat's Truck Stop and Food Court**, 1250 W. Hwy. 20, Chadron, 308/432-4504, is the place to go.

18th Street Bar & Grill, 1722 Broadway, Scottsbluff, 308/632-6977, has two different rooms, one the restaurant and one the bar, plus a friendly serving staff and buckets of free peanuts (in the bar). **Grampy's Pancake House**, 1802 E. 20th Pl., Scottsbluff, 308/632-6906, serves not only pancakes but all kinds of great breakfast and dinner food.

Valentino's, 1508 E. 20th St., Scottsbluff, 308/635-2726, offers fine Italian entrees, from meats to pastas. **Buffalo Steakhouse**, 1901 21st Ave., Scottsbluff, 308/635-3111, is open from 6 a.m. to 2 p.m. and from 5 p.m. to 11 p.m. in the Scottsbluff Inn.

Log Cabin Restaurant & Lounge, 1205 M St., Gering, 308/436-4786, offers hearty meat-and-potatoes fare. **Gering Bakery**, 1446 10th St., Gering, 308/436-5500, is known for its cabbage burgers, which are German-Russian pocket sandwiches.

The Elms, 1015 E. Third St., Alliance, 308/762-3425, is a fine steak and seafood restaurant. **Ken & Dale's Restaurant**, 123 E. Third St., 308/762-7252, Alliance, specializes in tasty sandwiches and soups. **The Porterhouse Restaurant & Lounge**, 417 Box Butte Ave., Alliance, 308/762-2424, serves everything from sirloin to seafood and basic burgers and sandwiches. **Bush's Gaslight Restaurant & Lounge**, Terrytown, 308/632-7315, is worth the trip.

LODGING

A charming historical building that used to mark the starting point of the "Chadron to Chicago Horse Race," the **Blaine Motel**, 159 Bordeaux St., 800/788-9428 or 308/432-5568, is a locally owned and operated motel with 13 units and inexpensive rates. Another good choice in Chadron is the **Olde Main Street Inn**, 115 Main St., 308/432-3380, which has 10 rooms, 3 of which have kitchens. Innkeeper Jeanne Goetzinger is the current operator of the century-old building, which was first a YMCA and then a hotel starting in 1931. In fact, the current dining room was originally the gym—with a basket-ball court, bowling alley, and swimming pool. **The Westerner**, 300 Oak St., Chadron, 800/947-0847 or 308/432-5577, has 27 rooms with prices as low as $30 for singles or $40 for doubles.

If you're in the Alliance area for the night, the **West Way Motel & Restaurant**, 1207 W. Hwy. 385, Alliance, 308/762-4040, has 44 rooms, some with waterbeds, plus a restaurant and lounge.

Candlelight Motel, 1822 E. 20th Pl., Scottsbluff, 800/424-2305, is a fine choice for your Scottsbluff stay. There's a lounge and a total of 56 rooms. Larger, with 138 rooms, is the **Scottsbluff Inn**, 1901 21st Ave., Scottsbluff, 800/597-3111 or 308/635-3111, which has an indoor pool, its own Henry's Restaurant & Lounge, exercise facilities, and even a same-day dry cleaning service. Not long ago, the **Fontenelle Inn**, 1424 Fourth Ave., Scottsbluff, 308/632-6257, was a dilapidated hotel. Now it's a delightful, renovated bed-and-breakfast that's well worth the little bit of extra money you'll pay to stay here. Bill and Brenda Dean are the proprietors.

Prairie Chanticleer, 1155 Q St., Gering, 308/436-3713, is a three-unit bed-and-breakfast that's a little less expensive than the other choices in the area.

CAMPING

Chadron State Park, eight miles south of Chadron on Hwy. 385, 308/432-6167, has not only modern campsites but cabins available for rent April to November and during certain hunting seasons.

Free camping is available 10 miles north of Hemingford at **Box Butte County Reservoir**, 308/762-1520, which also has a beach, sanitation facilities, and picnic shelters.

RV travelers can stop at **Sunset Motel & RV Park**, 1210 E. Hwy. 2, just east of Alliance, 800/341-8000 or 308/762-8660, which has 25 units at mid-priced rates plus a showerhouse, laundry, and vending area.

NIGHTLIFE

18th Street Bar & Grill, 1722 Broadway, Scottsbluff, 308/632-6977, is where local folks congregate to chat, watch sports on TV, or toss back a few brews.

Scenic Route: Highway 20

(Route takes you through the regions in Chapters 7, 8, 9, 12, and 13)
*Say you're impatient. Say you're bad with directions. Say you'd like to just get in
your car and drive in a long, straight line, with the sights of Nebraska and Iowa
rolling easily past you. Well, you can do it. Traveling Highway 20 across Nebraska
and Iowa is the shortcut method of sampling the sights of both states, and you'll be
able to linger in plenty of the smaller communities, in the northern region that make
up much of the fabric and flavor of both states down-home cultures.*

Starting in western Nebraska, in the town of Harrison, you could visit the nearby
Agate Fossil Beds National Monument. *The next town, Crawford, features*
Fort Robinson State Historical Park *just to the south. Reaching Valentine (see
Chapter 7), you'll have the chance to stop at* **Fort Niobrara National Wildlife
Refuge,** *just northeast of town on Highway 12, overlooking the Niobrara River. Still
following Highway 20, in Northeast Nebraska (see Chapter 8), the town of O'Neill is
the state's "Irish Capital," which celebrates not only St. Patrick's Day in a big way
but summer, with Summerfest held on the second weekend in July.*

*The end of Highway 20 in Nebraska is at South Sioux City, with Sioux City,
Iowa, just across the Missouri River (see Chapter 9).*

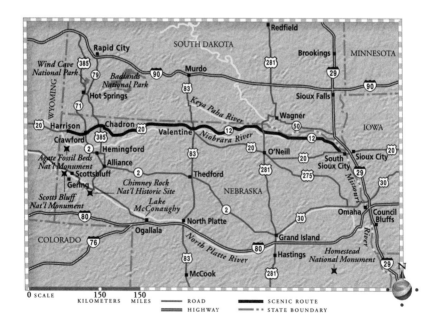

7
VALENTINE AND
THE SANDHILLS

Thanks to its name, Valentine is one of the romantic capitals of the world (along with Paris, France, and Venice, Italy). Situated in north-central Nebraska, Valentine—sometimes called Heart City—has an Iowan to thank for its name.

Edward Kimball Valentine was born in the Iowa town of Keosauqua in 1843. He settled in Omaha in 1866 after a distinguished military career, going on to become a lawyer, judge, and congressman. He was so popular among his constituency that the then-new town of Valentine was named after him.

Valentine is situated at the northeast corner of Nebraska's Sandhills—see the Sandhills side trip section, later in this chapter, for a full discussion of the largest stretch of sand dunes in the Western Hemisphere. The nearby Niobrara River is another natural feature from which Valentine benefits; the river's waterfalls and wildlife attract residents and visitors alike. The planted McKelvie National Forest, founded by President Theodore Roosevelt in 1902, thrives just to the west of Valentine.

And here's a measure of Nebraska's size: Cherry County, of which Valentine is the county seat, is larger than the state of Connecticut.

A PERFECT DAY IN VALENTINE

Valentine itself is a charming town, with a downtown main street lined with restaurants, bars, and the odd boot and western wear shop. Outside of

VALENTINE REGION

N

SOUTH DAKOTA
NEBRASKA

Rushville

Merriman

Bowring Ranch
State Historical Park

Cottonwood Lake
State Recreation Area

Nenzel
S-16F

Samuel R. McKelvie
National Forest

Niobrara River

Merritt Reservoir
State Recreation Area

Smith Falls
State Park

Fort Niobrara
National Wildlife
Refuge

Sparkes

Valentine
(SEE
INSET)

S-16B

Valentine National
Wildlife Refuge

Burton

Bassett

Ainsworth

Calamus River

North Loup River

Middle Loup River

Dismal River

Mullen

Calamus Reservoir
State Recreation
Area

Burwell

Taylor

Middle Loup River

Dunning

Brewster

Nebraska
National Forest

SCALE
0

50
MILES

50
KILOMETERS

=== STATE BOUNDARY

ROAD

RAILROAD

★ POINT OF INTEREST

VALENTINE

GREEN ST

GOVERNMENT ST

MALCOLM ST

HALL ST

MAIN ST

CHERRY ST

HELEN ST

5TH ST

7TH ST

4TH ST

3RD ST

1ST ST

C ST

A ST

C ST

Valentine are major natural attractions like Fort Niobrara National Wildlife Refuge and Valentine National Wildlife Refuge. Let these two dominate your day's visit. In the Valentine area's remoteness lies its charm. Exploring the area, from the waterfalls and wildlife of the Niobrara River to McKelvie National Forest, you'll gain an understanding of how the solitude of the area has shaped the citizens of Valentine and the surrounding rural landscape.

VALENTINE SIGHTSEEING HIGHLIGHTS

★★★★ FORT NIOBRARA NATIONAL WILDLIFE REFUGE
Four miles east of Valentine off Hwy. 12, 800/658-4024 or 402/376-3789

Established in 1912 with just a handful of buffalo, elk, and deer, this 19,000-acre preserve today is a great place to spot more than two hundred species of birds, plus other animals. Tour the grounds via vehicle along the wildlife drive to see herds of buffalo, bison (about 375), and deer elk (about 70), or hike to the Fort Falls. A visitors center features exhibits on the history of the area. Each October, buffalo and Texas longhorn steer are auctioned off to prevent overpopulation on the preserve. A scenic nature trail leads to the Fort Falls.

Details: Pastures open year-round daily dawn–dusk. Visitors center open Memorial Day–Labor Day daily 8–4:30; Labor Day–Memorial Day Mon–Fri 8–4:30. Free. (1–3 hours)

SIGHTS
- Ⓐ Bowring Ranch
- Ⓑ Centennial Hall
- Ⓒ Cherry County Historical Society Museum
- Ⓓ Fort Niobrara National Wildlife Refuge
- Ⓔ Rosebud Casino
- Ⓕ Sandhills Spirit of the West

FOOD
- Ⓖ Jordan's
- Ⓗ Peppermill Steakhouse
- Ⓘ Scotty's Ranchland Foods
- Ⓙ Snake Falls Canyon Restaurant

LODGING
- Ⓚ Comfort Inn
- Ⓛ Heartland Elk Ranch
- Ⓜ Lovejoy Ranch
- Ⓝ Motel Raine
- Ⓞ Niobrara Inn
- Ⓟ Town House Inn
- Ⓠ Trade Winds Lodge
- Ⓡ Sandhills Double R Ranch
- Ⓢ Valentine Motel & RV Park

Note: Items with the same letter are located in the same area.

★★ CENTENNIAL HALL
Third and Malcolm Sts., Valentine, 402/376-2418
Built in 1897, this two-story red brick building is the oldest standing high school building in the state. Christened Centennial Hall in 1983 as the culmination of an effort to preserve the building, it is now a museum exhibiting local artifacts. The Hallock Bells Collection is a room full of more than 1,700 bells. The Dukat Room displays antique china and housewares. There's also a Military Room, One-Room School, and a Western Heritage Room.

Details: Open May–Sep Thu, Fri, and Sat 1–5. $2 adults, $1 students in kindergarten through 8th grade, free under 5. (1 hour)

★ CHERRY COUNTY HISTORICAL SOCIETY MUSEUM
Main St. and Hwy. 20, Valentine, 402/376-2015
The settlement of the Valentine area, starting with its use as a military reservation in 1879, is chronicled in this museum's collection of pioneer artifacts and stories. The log cabin, once owned by the city's very first postmaster, is preserved with period furnishings. Items from Fort Niobrara, Sioux Indian tribes, and early cattlemen are on display. There are newspaper and microfilm records dating back to 1884.

Details: Open Memorial Day–Labor Day Wed–Sat 1–6. Donations encouraged. (30 minutes–1 hour)

★ ROSEBUD CASINO
Hwy. 83, Valentine, 800/786-ROSE,
www.rosebudcasino.com
With its own hotel, restaurant, gift shop, slot machines, card tables, and bingo games, this casino serves a large chunk of north-central Nebraska and south-central South Dakota.

Details: Nine miles north of Valentine on Hwy. 83. Open year-round daily 24 hours. (15 minutes–1 hour)

OTHER SIGHTSEEING HIGHLIGHTS

★★★ BOWRING RANCH
3 miles northeast of Merriman on Hwy. 61, 308/684-3428
This is Nebraska's only living history ranch. The late Arthur Bowring was a United States senator; the ranch's visitors center is named after his wife, Eve. You can tour the ranch home, see the herds of

---

Hereford cattle, and check out all other areas of this ranch as it preserves and demonstrates the history of ranching in the Sandhills throughout the years.

Details: *Open Memorial Day–Labor Day daily 8–5. Free with Nebraska State Park sticker. Annual permit $14, daily $2.50. (Vendors might add 25 cents to the price to cover the cost of getting the permits themselves.) (1–2 hours)*

★★★ SANDHILLS SPIRIT OF THE WEST
South of Nenzel on Road 16F, 888/690-0009 or 402/823-4009, www.sandhills–ne.com/spiritwest/

You can't say you've really been to the Sandhills until you experience them cowboy-style. This service based on Nollet Ranch in the small town of Nenzel offers just that—a meal, live entertainment from cowboy poets and musicians, a wagon ride, and songs around the campfire.

Nebraska's nickname is the Cornhusker State.

The meal alone is worth the price tag: a steak supper with baked potatoes, green beans, biscuits, and peach cobbler. A little more money gets you a more complete tour of the ranch.

Details: *Just south of Hwy. 20 on Road S16F. Open Jun–Aug Sat evenings, open to groups of 30 or more by reservation. $19.95 adults, $1 per year of age for children 10 and younger. Extended wagon tour $10 adults, 75 cents per year of age for children 10 and younger. (2 hours–1 day)*

FITNESS AND RECREATION

The calm of the flowing water, the scenic landscape on either shore, the birds flying high overhead—why not float down the Niobrara for an afternoon?

Graham Canoe Outfitters, E. Hwys. 20/83, Valentine, 800/322-3708 or 402/376-3576, run by Doug and Twyla Graham, has everything you need to canoe and camp on the Niobrara. Other canoe suppliers in town include **Brewers Canoers & Tubers**, 433 E. Hwy. 20, Valentine, 402/376-2046 or 402/376-2503; **Little Outlaw Canoes/Tubes**, 1005 W. Hwy. 20, Valentine, 800/238-1867 or 402/376-1822; **Sunny Brook Camp Outfitters**, 402/376-1887, Valentine; **Supertubes**, 310 W. Hwy. 20,

THE SANDHILLS AND CENTRAL NEBRASKA

If you think of the Sandhills as desert with sparse tufts of green grass, that's only a start. Though it may seem hard to believe, the area's climate during the last 50 years has been relatively wet in the scheme of long-term trends. As a result, vegetation has gained a little bit of a foothold.

Nearly 20 thousand square miles of sand dunes make up the Sandhills, the largest such formation in the Western Hemisphere. The dry bed of an inland sea was blown eastward about five thousand years ago to form these dunes; today some are as high as 400 feet and up to 20 miles long.

Water hides far beneath the dunes. **The Ogallala Aquifer** is a large underground reservoir that rises to the surface in certain places, creating marshes and lakes. Agriculture is still the Sandhills' primary industry, and cattle outnumber people in most areas.

If you're looking for a guided tour of this fascinating region, **Sandhills Safaris**, 402/376-1281, is a Valentine business that offers just that service.

By far the best and most hospitable accommodations you'll find in the Sandhills are at **Sandhills Guest Ranch Bed & Breakfast**, near Brewster, 308/547-2460, run by the DeGroff family (Lee and Beverly and son Ryan). The DeGroffs are local ranchers who are well-versed in the history of the Sandhills and are, very likely, Nebraska's friendliest folk. Sandhills Country Cabin and Doc's Hideout (other possible accommodations) are just northwest of Brewster, while the actual DeGroff home (where you'll join the family for a hearty, delicious breakfast), is just two miles east of the town on Highway 91.

Doc's Hideout, a luxurious cabin with three rooms and satellite TV, is named after Doc Middleton, a real-life Robin Hood–type character who once lived in and roamed about the Sandhills. The DeGroffs can sketch his life history for you.

Valentine, 402/376-2956 or 402/376-1789; **Yucca Dune**, 148 E. First St., Valentine, 402/376-3330, www.yuccadune.com; and **Rocky Ford Outfitters**, Valentine, 402/497-3479.

Valentine National Wildlife Refuge, 25 miles south of Valentine on Hwy. 83, 402/376-3789, allows hunting of ducks, deer, pheasants, and a few

If you stay at the ranch in the right season, you can help the DeGroffs with their livestock, go horseback riding, or take a guided tour of the Sandhills. Nearby rivers (Dismal, Middle Loup, North Loup, and Calamus) also provide good rafting. The rates here are more than reasonable.

Just two miles west of Brewster on Hwy. 2 is the **Nebraska National Forest**, 308/533-2257, with 90,444 acres of Sandhills—20,000 of which are covered with planted trees. Cattle graze part of the forest, but the entire area is open to your exploration. Thirty-five campsites are available, 19 of which have electricity (for an $11 fee); showers, tennis courts, a softball diamond, and a trailer dump station are also available. A group campsite can accommodate parties of 10 or more.

The town of Burwell in central Nebraska is a Sandhills community that loves rodeos. Both July and September bring several days' worth of large-scale rodeo action. **Nebraska's Big Rodeo** in particular has been a Burwell tradition since the 1920s. Call 308/346-5210 for specific rodeo times and information. Also in July, on Independence Day weekend, Burwell hosts a "pre-1865" historical festival called **Nebraska's Big Rendezvous**.

Just seven miles northwest of Burwell, 5,123-acre **Calamus Lake & Recreation Area**, 308/346-5695, is popular with folks who come here to fish, boat, and camp.

If you make it as far south as Broken Bow, **Arrow Hotel**, across from the square downtown, 308/872-6662, offers good accommodations in a historic building. **"The Lobby" Restaurant & Lounge**, in the hotel, is open for breakfast, lunch, and dinner and specializes in a prime rib buffet. Broken Bow also has other attractions, mostly of the outdoor variety. The town's tourism number is 308/872-5691.

other species in accordance with Nebraska's seasons, limits, and license requirements. Fishing is also permitted. But these 71,516 acres, established in 1935, also offer other diversions that are more peaceful. Bird-watching is best in May, September, and October. There are public-use roads in the refuge, as well as hiking trails. Some of the lakes also include picnicking facilities.

McKelvie National Forest, just southwest of Valentine on Hwy. 97, is about 115,000 acres of planted trees and open terrain preserved for regional wildlife and livestock. Camping, hunting, fishing, and other outdoor pursuits are also available.

The popular 72,900-acre **Merritt Reservoir**, 26 miles southwest of Valentine on Hwy. 97, features fishing, boating, swimming, and all manner of outdoor activities.

FOOD

In the middle of cattle country, enjoying a good steak is recommended—if not quite necessary.

Jordan's, East Hwy. 20, Valentine, 402/376-1255 or 888/244-9771, has it all—fine dining, a café, and a sports bar. Dinner is served Tuesday through Saturday nights. The café is open daily for breakfast and lunch, opening at 6 a.m. The sports bar is open Monday through Saturday starting at 4 p.m. and has pool tables, dart machines, and foosball tables.

Steak is in the name of **Peppermill Steakhouse**, Main St., Valentine, 800/669-1440 or 402/376-1440, which specializes in choice beef cuts. It opens at 6 a.m. Tuesday through Saturday, hosts live music in the summer, and features a Sweetheart Ballroom.

Southeast of Valentine, 23 miles on Hwy. 97, **Snake Falls Canyon Restaurant**, 402/376-3667, is open Wednesday through Sunday for breakfast, lunch, and dinner. Homemade is the mantra here, with everything from apple crisp to baked ham and malts and floats.

To grill your own food while camping out on the Sandhills, stop first at **Scotty's Ranchland Foods**, 127 N. Cherry St., Valentine, 402/376-3114, open daily and featuring thick cuts of beef and pork. (You're in the heart of cattle country, after all.)

LODGING

Niobrara Inn, 525 N. Main St., Valentine, 402/376-1779, has three rooms and one suite in ... you thought I was going to say a renovated Victorian home, right? Nope—an American foursquare home dating back to 1912. Bill and Stasia Stokley are the proprietors. You can lounge in the living room with a grand piano and fireplace or on the front porch. It's sensibly priced.

Advising potential guests to "sleep in the Raine," **Motel Raine**, Hwy. 20 W., Valentine, 800/999-3066 or 402/376-2030, is run by Sam and Georgia Spain and offers all the usual amenities at a budget price.

THE NATION'S LONGEST HIKING/BIKING TRAIL

The **Cowboy Trail**, First and Main Sts., Valentine, 800/658-4024, is the nation's longest hiking and biking trail, stretching 321 miles from Chadron to Norfolk. It was formerly the Chicago & Northwestern railroad line. Trailhead Park in Valentine offers entry to it, and one of the trail's best scenic spots is near town: a trestle bridge 150 above the Niobrara River.

Trade Winds Lodge, E. Hwys. 20/83, Valentine, 800/341-8000 or 402/376-1600, offers views of the Sandhills from its rooms and even fish cleaning and freezing facilities.

One of Valentine's most modern lodging options is **Comfort Inn**, 101 Main St., 800/478-3307 or 402/376-3300, which has an indoor pool, exercise room, and family suites.

With flowers planted out front and a Valentine-inspired heart incorporated into its signage, the charming **Valentine Motel & RV Park**, Hwys. 20/83, Valentine, 800/376-2450 or 402/376-2450 is a solid, economical choice for a night's stay.

Billing itself as "more than just a bed-and-breakfast," **Town House Inn**, 435 N. Main St., Valentine, 402/376-2193, is a nineteenth-century home with rooms decorated in southwest and country motifs. A sitting room features a TV and VCR.

Renting 800-square-foot log "vacation homes," **Heartland Elk Ranch**, HC 13, Valentine, 402/376-1124, is situated among pine tree–covered terrain overlooking the canyons of the Niobrara River. Breakfast is served each morning on the great room deck. Personal Sandhills tours are available, too.

Sandhills Double R Ranch, 60 miles south of Valentine on Hwy. 97, 308/546-2314, is run by Jim and Pat Bridges and has cabins for rent by the day, week, or month. Sportsmen or large groups can hunt, fish, and participate in other outdoor activities.

Offering a lovely stay, **Lovejoy Ranch**, HC 27, Box 16, Valentine, 800/672-5098 or 402/376-2668, offers two rooms and one suite run by Cherryl Lovejoy and Jody Dexter. This architecturally unique home provides elegant, yet comfortable lodging.

CAMPING

Within 190-acre **Smith Falls State Park**, three miles west and four miles south of Sparks (or 18 miles east of Valentine), 402/376-1306, you'll find campsites, rest rooms, showers, and picnic shelters. Smith Falls also contains Nebraska's highest waterfall.

Merrit Reservoir, 25 miles southwest of Valentine on Hwy. 97, is located on the Snake River and has about 240 non-pad campsites plus trailer dump stations, picnic shelters, fish cleaning stations, and other lakeside amenities.

Cottonwood State Recreation Area, off Hwy. 20 at Merriman, has 25 primitive campsites on its 240 acres plus toilets, picnic tables, and shelters.

NIGHTLIFE

The **Rosebud Casino**, nine miles north of Valentine on Hwy. 83, 800/786-ROSE, www.rosebudcasino.com, is open 24 hours daily and features the only nightlife in the area beyond the neighborhood bar scene.

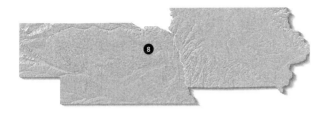

8
NORTHEAST NEBRASKA

Often called the "Land of Lewis and Clark," northeast Nebraska was once home to the Sioux and Omaha Indian tribes. In the 1860s, German settlers from Wisconsin settled in what is now Norfolk, on the north fork of the Elkhorn River, which powered the town's gristmill.

Originally spelled "Norfork," when the town applied for a post office, the national postal officials changed the name to "Norfolk" because they assumed the townsfolk had simply misspelled it.

Former TV talk show host Johnny Carson is Norfolk's most famous native son. George L. Carlson, inventor of artificial insemination, also hails from Norfolk.

Norfolk attractions include Willow Creek State Recreation Area and Ashfall Fossil Beds State Historical Park. Other, smaller communities surrounding Norfolk also offer diversions. Pierce, to the north, is home to Nebraska's first winery, Cuthills Vineyards, as well as a historical museum complex and the Willow Creek State Recreation Area.

A PERFECT DAY IN NORTHEAST NEBRASKA

If you pay attention, you'll discover a real sense of history in northeast Nebraska. Check out Ashfall Fossil Bed State Historical Park to view fossilized animal remains. The Elkhorn Valley Museum & Research Center will educate

NORTHEAST NEBRASKA

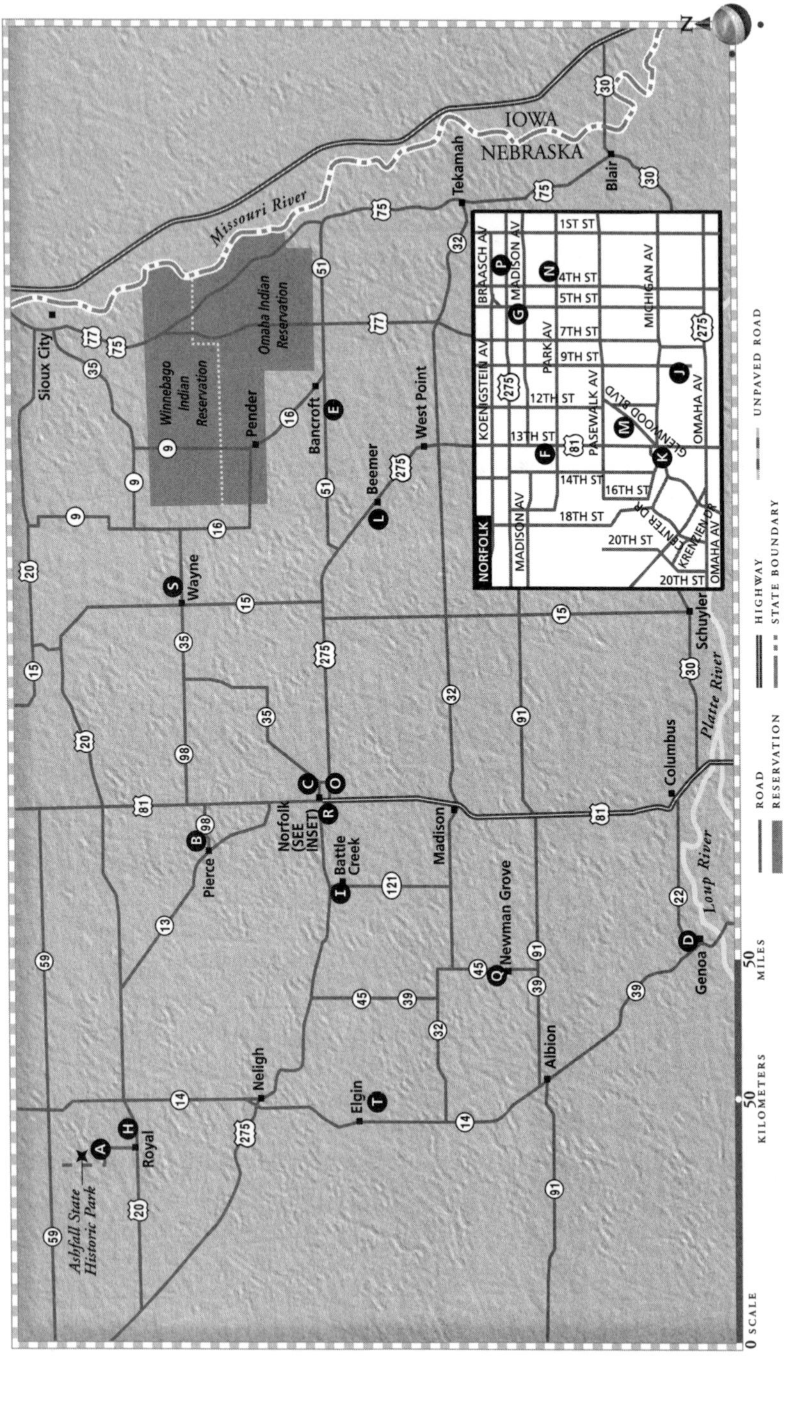

IOWA
NEBRASKA

Missouri River

Sioux City

Winnebago
Indian
Reservation

Omaha Indian
Reservation

Pender

Bancroft

West Point

Tekamah

Blair

Beemer

Wayne

Norfolk
(SEE
INSET)

Pierce

Battle
Creek

Madison

Newman Grove

Schuyler

Platte River

Columbus

Genoa

Loup River

Neligh

Albion

Royal

Ashfall State
Historic Park

Elgin

NORFOLK

1ST ST
4TH ST
5TH ST
7TH ST
9TH ST
12TH ST
13TH ST
14TH ST
16TH ST
18TH ST
20TH ST
20TH ST

BRAASCH AV
MADISON AV
MICHIGAN AV
KOENIGSTEIN AV
PARK AV
PASEWALK AV
GLENWOOD BLVD
OMAHA AV
MADISON AV
RIVERVIEW DR
KRENZIEN DR
OMAHA AV

ROAD
RESERVATION
HIGHWAY
STATE BOUNDARY
UNPAVED ROAD

0 SCALE

50 MILES

50 KILOMETERS

0 SCALE

you on the lives of early settlers, just as the Genoa Museum will teach you about the land's original inhabitants, Native Americans. The John G. Neihardt Center will inspire you through poetry and the poet's life to ponder how nature and current landscapes shape our building of the future.

This part of your trip presents a good opportunity to stay at a secluded bed-and-breakfast, such as the Taylor House Bed & Breakfast in Battle Creek, where peace and quiet await you.

SIGHTSEEING HIGHLIGHTS

★★★ ASHFALL FOSSIL BED STATE HISTORICAL PARK
Six miles north of Hwy. 20 on SR 59, Royal, 402/893-2000
Hundreds of prehistoric animal skeletons were found buried in volcanic ash here. Usually the bones of such animals are, over time, scattered far and wide by geological activity, but these animals were caught unawares by the volcanic fallout and were instantly, uncannily preserved by layers of ash. The creatures look eerily lifelike in their poses, unchanged since their deaths. The paleontologists who first explored this collection discovered much about the animals' way of life, and the fossils still speak to today's visitors.

SIGHTS
- Ⓐ Ashfall Fossil Bed State Historical Park
- Ⓑ Cuthills Vineyards
- Ⓒ Elkhorn Valley Museum & Research Center
- Ⓓ Genoa Museum
- Ⓔ John G. Neihardt Center
- Ⓕ Johnny Carson Home
- Ⓖ Norfolk Arts Center
- Ⓗ Northeast Nebraska Zoo
- Ⓘ Parks of Pride Arboretum
- Ⓑ Pierce Historical Museum Complex

FOOD
- Ⓙ Brass Lantern
- Ⓙ Granny's Bread Basket
- Ⓚ Great American Sirloin Buffet
- Ⓛ Marilyn's Tea Room & Quilt Room
- Ⓜ Ricardo's Mexican Restaurant
- Ⓚ Sirloin Stockade
- Ⓝ Tastee Treet
- Ⓞ Truck Haven Cafe of Norfolk
- Ⓟ Uptown Eating Establishment

LODGING
- Ⓠ Crystal Key Inn
- Ⓡ Eco-Lux Inn
- Ⓢ Grandma Butch's B&B
- Ⓢ K-D Inn Motel
- Ⓣ Plantation House
- Ⓢ Swanson's B&B
- Ⓣ Taylor House Bed & Breakfast
- Ⓑ Willow Rose B&B

Note: Items with the same letter are located in the same area.

Details: May Tue–Sat 10–4; Memorial Day–Labor Day Mon–Sat 9–5, Sun 11–5; Labor Day–second weekend in Oct Tue–Sat 10–4, Sun 1–4. $2.50 per car. Exhibit $1 adult, free under 7. (1–2 hours)

★★ CUTHILLS VINEYARDS
RR 2 Box 210, Pierce, 402/329-6774

Six acres of French grapes, tended by Ed and Holly Swanson, produce what are generally regarded as Nebraska's best wines. A 1920 barn houses the winery, which opened in 1994. A gift shop is also on hand, and you can take a self-guided tour of the winery and vineyards. Cuthills hosts an annual "Wine & Wings" tasting and music festival at the end of August; cooking demonstrations, winery tours, and hayrack rides are part of the celebration.

Details: Three miles west of Pierce on H&N Blvd. Open year-round Sat 9–7, Sun 1–7. Free. (30 minutes–1 hour)

★★ ELKHORN VALLEY MUSEUM & RESEARCH CENTER
515 Queen Valley Rd., Norfolk, 402/371-3886

Among this museum's permanent exhibits is a square-turn tractor, one of only three in existence. (In the old days, turning corners at the end of a crop row was problematic. Tractor manufacturers devised the square-turn tractor to try to solve the problem.) Dederman Cabin in Johnson Park is Norfolk's oldest residence, a two-room cabin built in 1868 from sing willow logs to house the Fredrick John Dederman family. Dederman himself gathered the logs from the banks of the nearby Elkhorn River.

In 1932, John G. Neihardt wrote "Black Elk Speaks."

Details: Open year-round Tue–Sat 10–4, Sun 1–4. $2.50 adults, seniors and children ages 6–12 $1.50, free under 6. (1–2 hours)

★★ GENOA MUSEUM
402 Willard Ave., Genoa, 402/993-2330

This small town on the way north as you're heading toward Norfolk and the rest of northeast Nebraska is known as the state's Pawnee capital—its museum boasts one of the largest collections of Pawnee weapons, tools, relics, and artifacts. Also featured are exhibits relating to the area's Mormon heritage, a story text, and antiques from Genoa's history.

Details: *Open year-round Fri–Sun 2–4:30. Free. (30 minutes–1 hour)*

★★ JOHN G. NEIHARDT CENTER
Elm and Washington Sts., Bancroft, 402/648-3388

Poetry fans might want to visit Bancroft, known as "The Poet's Town" after a poem by one-time poet laureate John G. Neihardt, who lived in the town from 1900 to 1920. The center preserves some of the poet's workspace and pays tribute to the culture of the Sioux Indians (which Neihardt was greatly involved in) with exhibits and a Sioux Prayer Garden.

Nebraska was the 37th state admitted to the Union.

Details: *Open year-round Mon–Sat 8–noon and 1–5, Sun 1:30–5. $1 adults, children admitted free with adults. (1 hour)*

★★ JOHNNY CARSON HOME
306 S. 13th St., Norfolk

Now a private residence, this was the childhood home of TV legend Johnny Carson, *The Tonight Show* alum and one-time Norfolk resident. Carson has maintained his ties with the city and over the years donated more than $2 million to a variety of projects like the Carson Regional Radiation Center, the Carson Theater, and the Elkhorn Valley Museum. But, don't expect to see Johnny himself.

Details: *May be viewed only from the street. (5 minutes)*

★★ PARKS OF PRIDE ARBORETUM
Battle Creek, 402/675-8185

More than 550 varieties of trees and shrubs, along with wildflowers, grow in this 55-acre park. You can stroll a mile through the arboretum on a five-foot-wide paved path that leads to an information center and gazebo. Playground equipment for children and the preserved 1875 office of Battle Creek's first doctor also stand on the grounds.

Details: *Open year-round daily. Free. (30 minutes–1 hour)*

★★ PIERCE HISTORICAL MUSEUM COMPLEX
417 S. Elm St., Gilman Park, Pierce, 402/329-4576 or 402/329-4873

Four buildings make up this historical museum. The main structure was a once a depot of the Chicago & Northwestern Railway Co. A schoolhouse dates back to the 1870s. With tools more than a century old, the blacksmith shop includes a forge and a hand-built covered wagon. The Gilman Arboretum has more than 150 different varieties of trees and shrubs on 14 acres around Bill Cox Memorial Lake; you can access the arboretum via a wood-chip walking path.

Details: *Open Memorial Day–Labor Day only Sun and holidays 1:30–4:30. Visitors can call ahead to arrange an appointment. Free. (1–2 hours)*

★ **NORFOLK ARTS CENTER**
130 S. 5th St., Norfolk, 402/371-7199
This museum's main gallery features exhibits by a list of local and regional artists that changes monthly. The Harry Jackson Western bronze collection is a permanent feature.

Details: *Open year-round Tue–Fri 9–5, Sat 1:30–4:30. Free. (1 hour)*

★ **NORTHEAST NEBRASKA ZOO**
Third and Ponca Sts., Royal, 402/893-2002
Monkeys, reptiles, birds, bobcats, lemurs, and other animals are on hand. Mountain lions are a more recent addition.

Details: *South of Hwy. 20. Open Mar–Oct Mon–Sat 9:30–5, Sun noon–5. Call for winter hours. $2.50 adults, $1.25 children. (1–2 hours)*

FITNESS AND RECREATION

Animals often offer the best outdoor relaxation. **Taylor Creek Pet Farm**, 501 W. Sixth St., Madison, 402/454-3947, is near the fairgrounds and features exotic birds, sheep, donkeys, and miniature horses.

If water and games are more to your liking, **Gillman Park**, 402/329-4873, features playgrounds and picnic areas, rest rooms, shelters, and campsites, plus a 175,000-gallon swimming pool. There's also a baseball field and lighted sand volleyball courts.

Willow Creek State Recreation Area, 15 miles north of Norfolk on Hwy. 13, then two miles west, 402/329-4053, is a 1,600-acre tract with a 700-acre lake for fishing and boating, plus a beach for swimming. There are also trails (including horse trails), an archery range, and picnic shelters.

If you don't mind traveling a little farther north, almost into South Dakota, **Kreycik Riverview**, RR I Box 30, Niobrara, 402/857-3850, is a working elk, buffalo, and cattle farm that offers tours of its grounds and full-fledged elk hunts in the fall. Kenard and Chris Kreycik own and operate the farm. Tours are offered May 15 through September on Friday, Saturday, and Sunday at 10 a.m., 2 p.m., and 4 p.m., or by appointment. Cost is a mere $5 per person.

If you don't know how to play horseshoes, you should learn. **Ta-Ha-Zouka Park**, Norfolk, 402/371-7081, has 24 horseshoe courts and is officially sanctioned by the National Horseshoe Pitchers Association.

FOOD

Northeast Nebraska is full of restaurants that almost seem like private dining rooms run by seasoned down-home cooks—at least, that's the way the food tastes.

Featuring small-town charm and prices to match, **Granny's Bread Basket**, 102 W. Main St., Pierce, 402/329-4370, serves great grains and delicious lunch fare.

A little east of Norfolk, **Marilyn's Tea Room & Quilt Room**, 417 E. Third St., Beemer, 402/528-3282, is in the Queen Anne–style home of Marilyn Schantz, whose Mennonite heritage informs her cooking. Open Tuesday through Saturday from 9 to 4 and on Sundays from 8 a.m. to I p.m.

The **Uptown Eating Establishment**, 326 Norfolk Ave., Norfolk, 402/371-7171, has been called one of the finest steak and seafood restaurants in Nebraska. A 15-year institution decorated in Art Deco style, it also has a ballroom and hosts many special events. **Ricardo's Mexican Restaurant**, 800 S. 13th St., Norfolk, 402/371-4340, is open for lunch and dinner. The restaurant is famous for its burritos, stuffed potatoes, and fried ice cream.

For steaks or a buffet-style meal, try **Great American Sirloin Buffet**, 1032 S. 13th St., Norfolk, 402/397-0522. **Brass Lantern**, 1018 S. Ninth St., Norfolk, 402/371-2500, not only has steaks but is well-known for its seafood selection. **Sirloin Stockade**, 1021 S. 13th St., 402/379-2021, cuts their steaks fresh daily and also serves fine pasta and seafood entrées. Open daily from 11 a.m. to 9 p.m.

Decidedly less formal is **Truck Haven Cafe of Norfolk**, Hwy. 275 East, Norfolk, 402/379-3828, where classic American diner food is served up speedily and with a smile.

For dessert, stop for ice cream at **Tastee Treet**, 300 S. First St., Norfolk, 402/371-3303.

LODGING

Looking for elegance in your bed-and-breakfast inns? **Crystal Key Inn**, 314 S. Fourth St., Newman Grove, 402/447-2772, will fit the bill. Breakfast is presented in full-blown Victorian style, with fine china. Four rooms and one suite are for rent, with economical pricing.

Willow Rose B&B, RR 2, Box 575, Pierce, 402/329-4114, rents six rooms and one cabin as a two-story home in the style of a 1950s Southern mansion. Michael Wichman runs this bed-and-breakfast, located near a charming creek and acres of undeveloped land; explore nearby Willow Trails.

Serving a continental breakfast, **Eco-Lux Inn**, 1909 Krenzien Dr., Norfolk, 402/371-7157, also has a spa and exercise room.

In a renovated Queen Anne–style home, **Taylor House Bed & Breakfast**, 300 S. Second St., Battle Creek, 402/675-6900, offers comfy accommodations in a small-town setting.

Grandma Butch's B&B, 502 Logan St., Wayne, 402/375-2759, is a 1907 two-story home with a wrap-around front porch. It features four inexpensive rooms, and a kennel is available for your pets. **Swanson's B&B**, RR 2, Box 148, Wayne, 402/584-2277, rents two rooms in a charming farmhouse. Flower gardens and farm animals dot the surrounding grounds. A cheaper, non-bed-and-breakfast choice in Wayne is the **K-D Inn Motel**, 311 E. Seventh St., Wayne, 402/375-1770, which was recently renovated and is conveniently close to downtown.

Five rooms are available at **Plantation House**, RR 2, Box 17, Elgin, 888/446-2287 or 402/843-2287, run by Merland and Barbara Clark.

CAMPING

Willow Creek State Recreation Area, 15 miles north of Norfolk on Hwy. 13, then two miles west, Pierce, 402/329-4053, has 80 electric campsites, a trailer dump station, and modern shower facilities. **Gillman Park**, 106 S. First St., Pierce, 402/329-4873, also has camping with electric and water hookups.

Maskenthine Lake & Recreation Area, east of Norfolk on Hwy. 275, 402/439-2046, has 25 campsites with electric hookups, showers, and hiking and biking trails, all near a 90-acre lake.

NIGHTLIFE

Step into a historic saloon setting during your visit to northeast Nebraska. **McHenry's Irish Saloon & Cafe**, 109 N. Broadway, Bloomfield, 402/373-

2625, has a century-old Brunswick cherrywood bar as its dominant decor. It serves food as well as drinks.

Recalling the glory of the historic King's Ballroom, which burned down, **King's Lounge**, 1000 Riverside Blvd., Norfolk, 402/379-3358, is a popular night spot.

Sometimes, quiet nightlife is the best cap to a day of tourist-minded hustle and bustle. **Great Plains Espresso**, Sunset Plaza, Norfolk, 402/371-2000, offers both a good caffeine jolt and a fine place to hang out.

Stebs, 2215 College St., Cedar Falls, IA, www.stebs.com, 319/277-0071, is a music club and bar in the heart of Cedar Falls' college town that hosts a wide range (from rock to jazz and reggae) of local and national bands. Those under 21 can get in, too, but just have to pay an extra $1 cover charge.

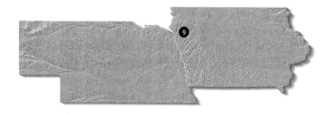

9
SIOUX CITY

Sioux City, Iowa, was brought to life by the Missouri River, the military, and miners. Founded in 1854 by surveyor John Cook, the city was flourishing by the 1870s. It had become a center for steamboat and rail traffic that received a steady influx of goods used to supply militias in the Dakotas and gold miners in Montana. Today you can stand at Dakota Point Lookout in Stone State Park and gaze down on the Missouri River Valley and three different states.

Sioux City is a charming tourist destination, boasting not only great views of the Missouri River—whether from a bluff on land or while floating on the river itself—but also intriguing museums and impressive architecture. The downtown district in particular is a hub of activity, commerce, and culture.

Tourists will find plenty to do in and around the city. The Sioux City Art Center is one of the best art spaces in the state. For folks who prefer the great outdoors, Stone State Park offers miles of multi-use trails, and Lewis & Clark Park hosts Sioux City Explorers baseball games. The annual Saturday in the Park festival (held in early July at the Bandshell in Grandview Park) consistently draws top national music acts.

A PERFECT DAY IN SIOUX CITY
Spend the morning at the Sioux City Art Center, a fascinating building both inside and out. Head downtown to grab lunch and stroll Historic Fourth

Street, lined with specialty shops, pubs, restaurants, and other attractions. The district has a decidedly nineteenth-century ambiance. Wind up your day at Stone State Park, which offers the sort of nature-lover delights that downtown Sioux City cannot—a good bet on a sunny afternoon.

SIGHTSEEING HIGHLIGHTS

★★★★ SIOUX CITY ART CENTER
225 Nebraska St., 712/279-6272
www.sc-artcenter.com
Its glassy exterior curious and futuristic, the Art Center's centerpiece is its three-story, 46-foot-high atrium. Inside, the permanent collection focuses on the Upper Midwest. A Junior League Hands On! Gallery has 12 hands-on stations for children that invite them to mold, shape, and interact with art exhibits. The third-floor galleries host changing menus of exhibits.
   Details: Open year-round Tue, Wed, Fri, and Sat 10–5, Thu noon–9, Sun 1–5. Free. (1–2 hours)

★★★ HISTORIC FOURTH STREET
Fourth St. between Virginia and Iowa Sts., 712/279-4800
This concentration of nineteenth-century buildings makes up the business district of Sioux City. Many of the buildings exhibit a Richardsonian Romanesque style of architecture. (Say that three times fast.) The **Eveans' Block**, 1126 Fourth St., originally a bank, and the **Boston Block**, 1005–1013 Fourth St., originally a manufacturing building, are both listed in the National Register of Historic Places. The impressive masonry, ornate detailings, and extensive restoration of the buildings in this district make for fascinating strolling among the streets.

There are three higher learning institutions located in Sioux City: **Morningside College, Briar Cliff College,** *and* **Western Iowa Tech Community College.**

   Details: Open year-round daily. Free. (1 hour)

★★ SERGEANT FLOYD WELCOME CENTER AND MUSEUM

SIOUX CITY

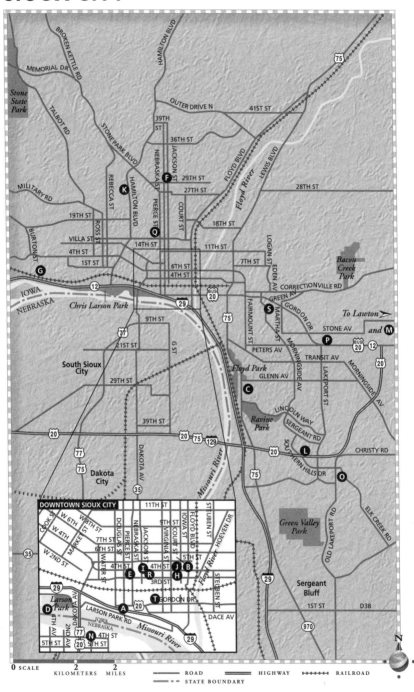

Stone State Park

MEMORIAL DR

BROKEN KETTLE RD

HAMILTON BLVD

75

OUTER DRIVE N

41ST ST

TALBOT RD

STONE PARK BLVD

39TH ST

36TH ST

NEBRASKA ST

JACKSON ST

29TH ST

27TH ST

FLOYD BLVD

LEWIS BLVD

Floyd River

28TH ST

MILITARY RD

REBECCA ST

HAMILTON BLVD

PIERCE ST

COURT ST

18TH ST

K

F

19TH ST

ROSS ST

VILLA ST

4TH ST

14TH ST

1ST ST

Q

11TH ST

6TH ST

4TH ST

7TH ST

LOGAN ST

EDEN AV

GREEN AV

CORRECTIONVILLE RD

Bacon Creek Park

BURTON ST

G

IOWA

NEBRASKA

12

Chris Larson Park

29

BUS 20

75

FAIRMOUNT ST

MARTHA ST

GORDON DR

S

To Lawton

STONE AV

and

M

P

BUS 20

12

20

77

9TH ST

21ST ST

G ST

PETERS AV

TRANSIT AV

MORNINGSIDE AV

LAKEPORT ST

MORNINGSIDE AV

South Sioux City

29TH ST

Floyd Park

GLENN AV

C

LINCOLN WAY

SERGEANT RD

20

39TH ST

DAKOTA AV

20   75   129

Ravine Park

Missouri River

20

75

SOUTHERN HILLS DR

L

CHRISTY RD

O

77

75

Dakota City

35

Green Valley Park

OLD LAKEPORT RD

ELK CREEK RD

DOWNTOWN SIOUX CITY

11TH ST

STEUBEN ST

FLOYD BLVD

HOEVEN DR

COOK ST

W 6TH ST

W 8TH ST

DOUGLAS ST

NEBRASKA ST

JACKSON ST

9TH ST

COURT ST

IOWA ST

VIRGINIA ST

35

W 4TH

MARKET ST

7TH ST

6TH ST

PIERCE ST

5TH ST

W 2ND ST

WATER ST

4TH ST

4TH ST

E   **T**   **R**   **J**   **B**

H

3RD ST

STEUBEN ST

Larson Park

D

4TH AV

IOWA BLVD

29

LARSON PARK RD

IOWA

NEBRASKA

A

20

T

GORDON DR

DACE AV

STEUBEN ST

29

Sergeant Bluff

1ST ST

D38

77

2ND AV

4TH ST

N

5TH ST

Missouri River

29

970

N

0 SCALE   2   2
KILOMETERS   MILES

ROAD   HIGHWAY   RAILROAD
STATE BOUNDARY

Hamilton Blvd. and S. Larsen Park Rd., 712/279-4840

This former Missouri River inspection ship (also known as a diesel tug) is now dry docked here and serves as a museum, gift shop, and welcome center. Its length is 138 feet. The museum portion is full of photos, models, and antiques that preserve and explain the riverboating way of life.

Details: Open May–Sep daily 8–6; Oct–Apr daily 9–5. Free. (30 minutes–1 hour)

★★ SIOUX CITY PUBLIC MUSEUM
2901 Jackson St., 712/279-6174

Antiques, documents, and other reminders of the city's history, plus various Native American artifacts, fill this museum, which is housed in a historic mansion built in 1890. The museum nicely ties together the pieces and groups of people that make up Sioux City's past. Check out the building's ornate stonework.

Details: Open year-round Tue 9–8, Wed–Sat 9–5, Sun 1–5. Free. (1 hour)

★ BELLE OF SIOUX CITY
100 Larsen Park Rd., 800/424-0080 or 712/255-0080

More than 12 thousand square feet of gaming madness (400 slots plus all kinds of card game tables) is stuffed onto this three-deck riverboat. The top deck offers open-air observation, while an attached, two-story barge houses the Full-House Buffet.

SIGHTS
- Ⓐ Belle of Sioux City
- Ⓑ Historic Fourth Street
- Ⓒ Sergeant Floyd Monument
- Ⓓ Sergeant Floyd Welcome Center and Museum
- Ⓔ Sioux City Art Center
- Ⓕ Sioux City Public Museum
- Ⓖ War Eagle Monument

FOOD
- Ⓗ Bluestem
- Ⓘ Buffalo Alice
- Ⓘ First Edition Beef & Spirits I
- Ⓙ Luciano's
- Ⓚ Minerva's Restaurant & Bar
- Ⓛ Sirloin Stockdale
- Ⓜ Theo's
- Ⓝ Waterfront Grille

LODGING
- Ⓞ Comfort Inn
- Ⓟ Economy Inn
- Ⓠ English Mansion Bed & Breakfast
- Ⓡ Hilton Inn
- Ⓞ Holiday Inn Express
- Ⓝ Marina Inn
- Ⓢ Palmer House
- Ⓣ Riverboat Inn

Note: Items with the same letter are located in the same area.

Details: Open year-round Sun–Thu 10–3, Fri–Sat 10–5. Free. Cruises run May–Oct and are separate. (15 minutes–2 hours)

★ **SERGEANT FLOYD MONUMENT**
Hwy. 75 and Glenn Ave., 712/279-4800
This 100-foot-high stone obelisk is similar in appearance to the George Washington Monument in Washington, D.C., and in 1960 was the first-ever monument in the country to be designated a Registered National Historic Landmark. It commemorates Charles Floyd, a sergeant in the United States Army who set out as part of the Lewis and Clark expedition but lasted only 90 days before dying near this site.
Details: Open year-round daily. Free. (15–30 minutes)

★ **WAR EAGLE MONUMENT**
I-29 Exit 151 and W. Fourth St., 712/279-4800
This monument is named after Wambdi Okicize, a.k.a. Indian Chief War Eagle, who was a member of either the Mdewakanton or the Isanti Dakota tribe. He died in 1851. The bluff on which the monument stands offers a clear, picturesque view of the tri-state area. Without his efforts for peaceful relations between settlers and Indians, Sioux City's history might have been far more troubled.
Details: Open year-round daily. Free. (15–30 minutes)

FITNESS AND RECREATION

Stone State Park, 5001 Talbot Rd., Sioux City, 712/255-4698, is located in the northwest corner of the city, along Highway 12. Its more than 1,069 acres are almost entirely part of the unique Loess Hills formations. This park is also an "urban wildlife sanctuary" where wild turkeys, deer, coyotes, and foxes can roam free. The Dorothy Pecaut Nature Center features a 400-gallon aquarium with native fish. Hiking, biking, skiing, and snowmobiling trails run throughout the park.

FOOD

You can rely on Sioux City–area restaurants to provide hearty dining and expect some to serve up unique atmospheres.

In the famous "exhibition kitchen" at **Minerva's Restaurant & Bar**, 2901 Hamilton Blvd., Sioux City, 712/252-1012, you can watch over the food preparation with your own eyes. Every entrée comes with a "bottomless" Italian salad. Another recommended fine dining spot is **First Edition Beef & Spirits I**, 416 Jackson St., Sioux City, 712/277-4566, which serves lunch and dinner and specializes, of course, in prime rib, steaks, and seafood. (First Edition Beef & Spirits II is located in Dakota Dunes, South Dakota.)

Built more than a century ago, **Luciano's**, 1019 Historic Fourth St., Sioux City, 712/258-5174, bakes its own bread, serves fine wines, and is open for dinner Tuesday through Saturday. Best to make reservations.

The more casual **Bluestem**, 1012 E. Fourth St., Sioux City, 712/279-8060, features contemporary American cuisine. **Buffalo Alice**, 1022 Fourth St., Sioux City, 712/255-4822, has an appropriate name, since it serves buffalo wings, along with nachos, pizza, and more than 154 kinds of beer.

If you're hungry on a Thursday night, head to **Theo's**, on Hwy. 20 between Sioux City and Lawton, 712/944-5731, for its all-you-can-eat prime rib and salad bar. Tasty beef entrees are always available. One of the more affordable eateries is **Sirloin Stockade**, 4565 Southern Hills Dr., Sioux City, 712/276-7810, which, in addition to beef, features soups, salads, and desserts in a cafeteria-style setting.

In the Marina Inn, **Waterfront Grille**, Fourth and B Sts., South Sioux City, Nebraska, 402/494-5025, boasts a fine view of the Missouri River.

LODGING

The hotels in Sioux City offer solid accommodations.

Hilton Inn, 707 Fourth St., Sioux City, 800/593-0555 or 712/277-4101, features an indoor pool, refrigerators and microwaves in the rooms, and a restaurant and lounge. Offering all that plus in-room appliances is the **Riverboat Inn**, 701 Gordon Dr., Sioux City, 800/238-6146 or 712/277-9400.

If you're looking for more modest lodging, try **Palmer House**, 3440 Gordon Dr., Sioux City, 712/276-4221. This distinct place has an outdoor pool, and allows pets.

For a cheaper stay, try **Economy Inn**, 2921 Gordon Dr., Sioux City, 712/277-4242, which has an outdoor pool. **Holiday Inn Express**, 4230 S. Lakeport St., Sioux City, 712/274-1400, also features fine accommodations at a budget price; a continental breakfast is served, too. **Comfort Inn**, 4202 South Lakeport St., Sioux City, 712/274-1300, is a budget choice with amenities like an indoor pool and continental breakfast.

For a memorable bed-and-breakfast stay, **English Mansion Bed & Breakfast**, 1525 Douglas Ave., Sioux City, 712/277-1386, is housed in a restored 1894 Richardsonian Rococo home and has seven original hand-painted ceiling murals, double whirlpool tubs, feather beds, and fireplaces. Five mid- to high-priced rooms are available. **Marina Inn**, Fourth and B Sts., South Sioux City, 800/798-7980, contains a restaurant, lounge, and an indoor and outdoor swimming pool.

CAMPING

Twelve of the 32 campsites at **Stone State Park**, 5001 Talbot Rd., Sioux City, 712/255-4698, have electric hookups. There are also picnic shelters, picnic tables, and grills. **Scenic Park Campground**, Fourth and D Sts., South Sioux City, 402/494-7535, features 53 RV spots and a wide range of recreational facilities and amenities: tennis courts, a 50-meter Olympic swimming pool, athletic fields, showers, picnic shelters, and a concession stand.

Along the Missouri River, **Cottonwood Cove Park**, 14th and Hickory St., Dakota City, 402/987-3448, features sand volleyball, shelters, boat docks, and even horseshoe pits along with its campsites.

NIGHTLIFE

Playing in the Lewis & Clark Park, the **Sioux City Explorers**, 3400 Line Dr., 712/277-9467, provide the city with fast and furious minor league baseball action. It's a fairly new stadium that seats about 3,200.

Pierce Street Coffee Works, 1920 Pierce St., Sioux City, 712/255-1226, hosts live acoustic music on the weekends. The **Blues Cellar**, 2001 Leech Ave., Sioux City, 712/277-2575, is located in the lower level of the KD Station and hosts—you guessed it—live blues bands.

If live comedy is your nightlife bag instead of live music, **Pepperoni's Comedy Club** in El Fredo Pizza, W. 19th and Center Sts., Sioux City, 712/258-0691, hosts comedians starting at 9 on Friday nights and at both 8:30 and 10:30 on Saturdays. Call ahead for ticket availability.

South Sioux City also holds a variety of nightlife options. **Dublin House**, 522 Dakota Ave., 402/494-9761, focuses on country and '50s rock music starting at 8:30 p.m. on Wednesday, Friday, and Saturday nights. **Plaza Lounge & Grill**, 2101 Cornhusker Dr., 402/494-9805, also features country and rock on weekends, but also occasionally hosts karaoke nights—you be the star, and we'll all hope your voice stays somewhat in tune.

10
OKOBOJI,
IOWA'S GREAT LAKES

Welcome to a popular summer resort destination in northwest Iowa that just might make you think you took a wrong turn and ended up a little farther north—in Minnesota, Land of 10,000 Lakes.

Okoboji is home to the Iowa Great Lakes. Spirit Lake lies the farthest north in the Okoboji cluster, while East Lake Okoboji, West Lake Okoboji, Minnewashta, Upper Gar, and Lower Gar snake chain-like to the south.

The town of Okoboji is situated in the middle of all this water, which of course makes it the perfect northwest Iowa center for fun under the sun and in the water. If you approach the area from the south, you'll first go through Arnolds Park, a community dominated by a longstanding amusement park with the Roof Garden that hosts a summer series of live music. Other small towns (Wahpeton, Millford, Orleans) are scattered around the lakes' perimeter.

Since so many people make Okoboji their summer home, inhabiting one of the many ranch-style cottages or town home complexes that dot the shore-line acres, the occasional tourist will find plenty to do in that season. The restaurants and nightclubs teem with patrons, and the water-related shops buzz with business, ready to rent you a boat for action on the lake. In addition, Arnolds Park offers rides and other attractions.

Museums and other non-lake attractions are located in and around Okoboji, but water and sun will likely dominate this portion of your trip. After all, do you go to Hawaii to stay indoors?

OKOBOJI REGION

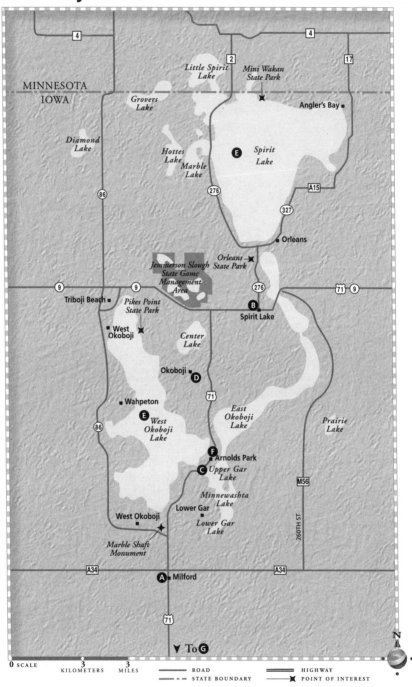

MINNESOTA
IOWA

Little Spirit Lake
Mini Wakan State Park
Grovers Lake
Angler's Bay
Diamond Lake
Hottes Lake
Marble Lake
Spirit Lake **E**
Orleans
Jemmerson Slough State Game Management Area
Orleans State Park
Triboji Beach
Pikes Point State Park
Spirit Lake **B**
West Okoboji
Center Lake
Okoboji **D**
Wahpeton
West Okoboji Lake **E**
East Okoboji Lake
Prairie Lake
Arnolds Park **F**
Upper Gar Lake **C**
Minnewashta Lake
Lower Gar
West Okoboji
Lower Gar Lake
Marble Shaft Monument
260TH ST
Milford **A**
To **G**

0 SCALE   3   3
KILOMETERS   MILES   —— ROAD   ═══ HIGHWAY
- - - STATE BOUNDARY   ✠ POINT OF INTEREST

N

A PERFECT DAY IN OKOBOJI

Your perfect day will revolve around all the activity available to you on the lakes. Even when you're not actually in the water—boating, waterskiing, swimming, or whatever—it's recommended that you dine and relax with friends in one of the many lakeside clubs and restaurants that offer patio seating in full view of the water and sky. Arnolds Park also promises abundant recreation, and it's the kind—in case you start to feel a little water-logged during your visit—where you don't have to get wet.

SIGHTSEEING HIGHLIGHTS

★★★★ IOWA GREAT LAKES
Okoboji area, 800/270-2574 or 712/332-2209

Even if you don't bring a single inner tube or swimsuit with you to Okoboji, plenty of services can ensure your enjoyment of the area's main attraction: the lakes. Spirit Lake and West Lake Okoboji are the two largest bodies of water, so most of your activity will probably be located there. **Oak Hill Marina**, Lake Minnewashta, Hwy. 71, Arnolds Park, 712/332-2701, rents all kinds of boats, from party-

SIGHTS

- Ⓐ Clark Museum of Area History/Clark's Antique Acres
- Ⓑ Dickinson County Museum
- Ⓒ Gardner State Historic Site
- Ⓓ The Higgins Museum
- Ⓒ Kabele's Trading Post
- Ⓔ Iowa Great Lakes
- Ⓕ Iowa Great Lakes Maritime Museum
- Ⓓ Lakes Art Center
- Ⓐ Oak Hill Marina
- Ⓓ Okoboji Expedition Company
- Ⓐ Triggs Bay Resort

FOOD

- Ⓐ Hollywood Grille
- Ⓒ Hey, Good Cookies!
- Ⓐ Koffee Kup Kafe

FOOD (continued)

- Ⓐ Maxwell's On the Lake
- Ⓐ Mother Natures Restaurant & Lounge
- Ⓐ Smokin' Jakes
- Ⓐ Yesterdays

LODGING

- Ⓑ Crescent Beach Lodge
- Ⓒ Oaks Motel
- Ⓑ Okoboji Avenue Inn
- Ⓖ Time Out Bed & Breakfast
- Ⓒ Village West
- Ⓐ West Oaks
- Ⓓ Wild Rose of Okoboji Bed & Breakfast Inn & Gift Shop

Note: Items with the same letter are located in the same area.

ready pontoons to the water-skiing variety. **Okoboji Expedition Company**, 1021 Hwy. 71 S., Okoboji Plaza, Okoboji, 712/332-9001, www.expeditionco.com, specializes in bicycles, roller blades for the summer months, and ice skates and cross-country skis for the winter. From this store, you can even access your e-mail and sip an espresso. **Triggs Bay Resort**, Linden Dr., Arnolds Park, 712/332-2215, not only rents boats but is one of the few shops to rent canoes. **Kabele's Trading Post**, 504 Hill Ave., Spirit Lake, 712/336-1512, is one of the bait-and-tackle shops where fishers can load up on all the necessary gear.

Spirit Lake is Iowa's largest natural lake.

Details: Hours vary. Prices vary. (1 hour minimum)

★★ **GARDNER STATE HISTORIC SITE**
34 Monument Dr., Arnolds Park, 712/332-7248
or 712/332-2643
At 13 years old, Abbie Gardner was a young survivor of "The Spirit Lake Massacre" of March 8, 1857, in which Inkpaduta, a renegade Dakota Indian, led an attack that resulted in the death of 33 locals. The rest of Gardner's family, her parents and four siblings, were among those slain; she was kidnapped with three other women and lived to tell about it. Today Gardner's cabin still stands, preserved by the State Historical Society. It contains antique artifacts, paintings by Gardner, and an information center. The grounds include Gardner's burial site, where she was laid to rest in 1921.
Details: Open year-round as an outdoor self-guided tour. Site open Memorial Day–Labor Day Mon–Fri noon–4, Sat–Sun 9–4. Free. (1 hour)

★★ **CLARK MUSEUM OF AREA HISTORY/CLARK'S ANTIQUE ACRES**
Milford, 712/338-2147
Historic photos, advertisements, and other artifacts of daily life from past residents of the Iowa Great Lakes area preserve the events and perspectives of yesteryear. Large exhibits, like horse-drawn farm implements and even a school bus, teach about life on the land and the lakes before motorized tractors plowed the fields and speedboats zipped adventurers from shore to shore.

Details: One mile west and 1.5 miles north of Milford Catholic Church. Apr–Oct Tue–Sat 10–5, Sun noon–5. Free. (30 minutes–1 hour)

★★ DICKINSON COUNTY MUSEUM
Hwys. 71/9, Spirit Lake, 712/332-2107
In the middle of lake country sits this tribute to the iron horses of the land: trains. As one of the original depots on the Chicago–Milwaukee–St. Paul Railroad, the Dickinson County Museum preserves that heritage with its fine exhibits saluting the days of steam. Other exhibits educate visitors on what brought the trains to the area in the first place: northwest Iowa's industrial and especially agricultural wealth.
Details: Open Jun–Sep daily 1–5. Free. (1 hour)

★★ IOWA GREAT LAKES MARITIME MUSEUM
Queens Ct. and Lake St., Arnolds Park, 712/332-5264
Without getting wet, you can experience decades of life on the Iowa Great Lakes by visiting this museum. Two 30-minute slide shows featuring the photography of local David Thoreson will provide you with lake views that you might otherwise miss during your visit. Exhibits of other photos, articles, and even swimsuits also tell stories about the lakes' past. Enter a completely restored boat and accompanying boathouse to feel as if you've actually stepped back in time.
Details: Open Memorial Day–Labor Day daily 10–8. $2 general admission. (1 hour)

★★ LAKES ART CENTER
2201 N. Hwy. 71, Okoboji, 712/332-7013
In the summer this museum exhibits a variety of visual art by local, national, and international artists. Both temporary and permanent collections are on display. A gift store sells the work of local artists. A summer film series hosts regular screenings.
Details: Open summer Mon–Fri 10–4, Sat–Sun 1–4; winter Tue–Fri 10–4, Sat–Sun 1–4. Free. (1 hour)

★ THE HIGGINS MUSEUM
Sanborn Ave., Okoboji, 712/332-5859
The history of banking ... revealed in all its thrilling glory! But seriously, for the right tourist, this museum makes for an interesting stop, revealing domestic banking from 1863 through 1935 via displays of old bank notes, post cards, and a research library. For fun, you can

even calculate how much interest would have accrued to date on deposits made in 1863. **Details:** *Open May–Sep Tue–Sun 11–5:30. $2 general admission. (30 minutes–1 hour)*

FITNESS AND RECREATION

If you're in Okoboji, you should be on the lake, so fitness and recreation will become second nature. Here are a few other suggestions.

Arnolds Park, Hwy. 71 and Lake St., Arnolds Park, 800/599-6995 or 712/332-2183, www.arnoldspark.com, is ground zero for amusement park fun in the Okoboji area. Also its very own town, Arnolds Park has more than 30 rides and attractions.

For further amusement, **Ranch Amusement Parks**, Hwy. 71, Okoboji, 712/332-2159, has a track where you can race "Tiger Kat Karts," steer "Water Buffalo Bumper Boats," and play "Wet Rock Mine Mini-Golf." Open from Memorial Day through Labor Day daily at 10.

In 1895 a monument was erected in Arnolds Park in commemoration of The Spirit Lake Massacre.

Iowa's largest water park is **Boji Bay**, Hwys. 71/86, one mile north of Milford, 712/338-2473. It has water slides, a wave pool, sand volleyball courts, and tube rides.

If you'd like to sail the lakes without a lot of effort, *Queen II,* Queen II Dock, Arnolds Park, 712/332-5159, cruises West Lake Okoboji daily, from Memorial Day through Labor Day and is available for exclusive charters.

FOOD

There are plenty of appealing eateries in the Okoboji area, and food always seems to taste better when enjoyed outside, when you can feel the lake breeze on your face and gaze at the burnt-orange beauty of the setting sun.

Hollywood Grille, 28 Ackley St., Arnolds Park, 712/332-9511, is decked out in starry memorabilia, while the menu features everything from sandwiches and soups to seafood. Deck seating available. Open year-round. **Maxwell's On the Lake**, Central Emporium, Arnolds Park, 712/332-7578, is open May through September and boasts a "million-dollar view" of lake scenery.

Featuring home-cooked fare, **Koffee Kup Kafe**, Hwy. 71, Arnolds Park, 712/332-7657, serves cinnamon rolls for breakfast and prepares orders to

SAILING ON LAKE OKOBOJI

go. Specializing in smoked meats, **Smokin' Jakes**, 117 Broadway, Old Town, Arnolds Park, 712/332-5152, open May through October, is the perfect place for all kinds of meat and a zesty barbecue taste.

For a dessert snack, try **Hey, Good Cookies!**, 1601 Hill Ave., Spirit Lake, 712/336-4179, which also serves coffee drinks.

Often called the best seafood restaurant in Okoboji, **Yesterdays**, two blocks west of the stoplights in Arnolds Park, 712/332-2353, is open April through December. Choose your own live Maine lobster; it will go from the water tank to the kitchen to your plate.

Mother Nature's Restaurant & Lounge, Hwy. 71, Arnolds Park, 712/332-9469, a casual restaurant across from the amusement park, specializes in black Angus steaks.

LODGING

For those who would like to make a serious commitment to an Okoboji vacation, plenty of resorts offer vacation condos and homes where you can purchase the right to live at the lake for a certain amount of time. **Village West**, 16010 Hwy. 86, Spirit Lake, 800/677-4561, ext. 1, is a temporary home to more than 3 thousand families and is affiliated with Resort Condominiums International.

West Oaks, Arnolds Park, 712/332-7711, offers two-bedroom and two-bath villas as well as a range of indoor and outdoor recreational options.

The only lakeside motel on Spirit Lake is **Oaks Motel**, Hwys. 71/9 E., Spirit Lake, 712/336-2940. The rooms feature refrigerators and microwaves. For a double, two people pay $79 plus tax on weekends in the summer and $34 plus tax during the winter.

Affordable and conveniently located, **Okoboji Avenue Inn**, Hwy. 71, Milford, 888/422-3887 or 712/338-4701, will suit you for a couple of nights.

Crescent Beach Lodge, 1620 Lakeshore Dr., Milford, 712/337-3351, has 46 rooms on a West Lake Okoboji beach. There are also paddleboats, a children's playground, tennis courts, and a restaurant with Sunday brunch.

The **Wild Rose of Okoboji Bed & Breakfast Inn & Gift Shop**, Hwy. 71, Okoboji, 712/332-9986, has 11 suites and also features a Jacuzzi, fireplace, and outdoor terrace.

Time Out Bed & Breakfast, 250 W. Maple Dr., Hartley, 712/728-2213, was built in 1927 and now features six "romantic-themed" rooms—like the Mardi's Room.

CAMPING

Arnolds Park City Campground, 151 N. Broadway St., Arnolds Park, 712/332-2341, is open May through September with 40 electric and 30 primitive sites plus a trailer dump station.

Minnewashta Campground, 7 Bascom St., Okoboji, 712/332-2341, also open May through September, has 17 electric sites plus showers, a trailer dump station, and lake access.

NIGHTLIFE

In the summer, Okoboji thrives with people and activity, on the lake during the day and on the town at night. You can stroll along the streets, ducking into one bar or restaurant after another to find droves of people and live music.

Among the more formal nightlife options is **Okoboji Summer Theatre**, Hwy. 71, Spirit Lake, 712/332-7773, which stages nine productions from June through August, from dramas to comedies and musicals.

Funny Barn Comedy Club, 1605 Hill Ave., 712/336-4888, hosts national comedians and serves what it calls Great Lakes Pizza.

And don't forget the **Roof Garden**, Arnolds Park amusement park, 800/559-6995 or 712/332-2183, which regularly hosts national music acts, generally in the oldies and classic rock vein, on its lakeside stage.

11
MASON CITY
AND CLEAR LAKE

Mason City's name is a tribute to the Masonic heritage of its settlers. Before it was named Mason City in 1854, the Masonic community had been known as Shibboleth, Masonic Grove, and Masonville. Today, some people might like to refer to this city as River City—native son Meredith Wilson used Mason City as the inspiration for the town featured in his popular musical *The Music Man*.

Clear Lake has become infamous in the annals of music history because it is the location of the Surf Ballroom. You may recall that this is where Buddy Holly, Ritchie Valens, and J. P. "The Big Bopper" Richardson played their last-ever gig, on February 2, 1959. Shortly after takeoff from the local airport, the plane carrying the three musicians crashed, killing all on board. People gather each year on the anniversary of the musicians' deaths to remember them with a concert.

Clear Lake is also known for the 3,600-acre body of water at its center that provides the focal point for the community's summer fun. The lake, de-rived from a spring, was formed more than 14 thousand years ago by glacial action. Its elevation (1,247 feet) is higher than any point in Mason City—including the tops of buildings.

These two towns—Mason City on the east side of I-80 and Clear Lake on the west side—are conveniently located about midway between Des Moines and Minnesota's Twin Cities, Minneapolis–St. Paul.

MASON CITY

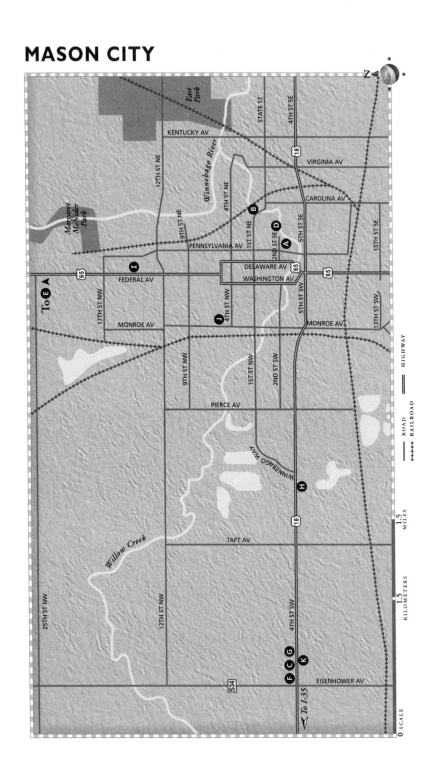

State ST
4TH ST SE
East Park
KENTUCKY AV
12TH ST NE
Winnebago River
18
VIRGINIA AV
4TH ST NE
CAROLINA AV
9TH ST NE
1ST ST NE
5TH ST SE
13TH ST SE
2ND ST SE
B
D
A
PENNSYLVANIA AV
Margaret McNider Park
I
DELAWARE AV
65
65
65
FEDERAL AV
WASHINGTON AV
To E
17TH ST NW
4TH ST NW
5TH ST SW
13TH ST SW
MONROE AV
J
MONROE AV
9TH ST NW
1ST ST NW
2ND ST SW
PIERCE AV
WINNEBAGO WAY
H
18
25TH ST NW
12TH ST NW
TAFT AV
Willow Creek
4TH ST SW
F **C** **G**
K
S34
EISENHOWER AV
To I-35

ROAD
HIGHWAY
RAILROAD

0 SCALE
1.5 KILOMETERS
1.5 MILES

A PERFECT DAY IN MASON CITY AND CLEAR LAKE

Start your day in Mason City at the Frank Lloyd Wright Stockman House. You don't even need to go inside to enjoy its beauty—the exterior is quite impressive. Stroll through the surrounding neighborhood, too. Then head to the nearby Charles H. MacNider Museum and spend plenty of time browsing through its serene galleries.

Crossing over to Clear Lake, have lunch at one of the lakeside eateries to enjoy the view. Definitely stop by the Surf Ballroom, a nostalgic spot for some and a historic stop for all. Clear Lake itself, the body of water, could easily occupy the rest of your afternoon and evening—and why not let it?

MASON CITY SIGHTSEEING HIGHLIGHTS

★★★★ CHARLES H. MACNIDER MUSEUM
303 Second St. SE, 515/421-3666

This charming museum overlooks Willow Creek (which you can see from inside the museum via the Chang Gallery) and exhibits a wide array of visual art, including a gallery devoted to the puppets and marionettes of Mason City High School graduate Bil Baird. The "World of Puppets" is full of Baird's marionettes, like those used in the movie *The Sound of Music.* A sale/rental gallery features work by regional artists. This attractive museum also holds on its two floors lithographs by Grant Wood and a portrait of George Washington by Jane Stuart.

SIGHTS
- Ⓐ Charles H. MacNider Museum
- Ⓑ Frank Lloyd Wright Stockman House
- Ⓒ Kinney Pioneer Museum
- Ⓓ Meredith Wilson Boyhood Home
- Ⓔ Van Horn's Antique Truck Museum

FOOD
- Ⓕ La Hacienda II
- Ⓖ Papa's Cafe
- Ⓗ Peachtree
- Ⓘ XTABI Supper Club

LODGING
- Ⓙ Comfort Inn
- Ⓚ Hanford Inn
- Ⓗ Holiday Inn

Note: Items with the same letter are located in the same area.

SURF BALLROOM

Kyle Munson

Details: Open year-round Tue and Thu 10–9; Wed, Fri, and Sat 10–5; Sun 1–5. Free. (1–2 hours)

★★★ FRANK LLOYD WRIGHT STOCKMAN HOUSE
530 First St. NE, 515/421-3666

Listed in the National Register of Historic Buildings, the Stockman House is a Prairie School home designed by the famous architect in 1908 when he was in Mason City working on the City National Bank and Park Inn Hotel. It's the only such Wright structure in Iowa. Recent restoration has returned it to its 1908 glory. It sits next to the Rock Glen–Rock Crest National Historic District, an area noted for beautiful, historic homes. An architecture and historical walking tour starts at 303 Second Street SE and ends at the Stockman House. Call 515/421-3666 to make reservations.

Details: Open Jun–Labor Day Thu–Sat 10–5; Labor Day–Oct Sat–Sun 10–5. $3 adults, $1 age 11 and younger. (30 minutes–1 hour)

★★★ KINNEY PIONEER MUSEUM
Municipal Airport, Hwy. 18 W., 515/423-1258 or 515/357-2980

This museum re-creates the pioneer experience, from a covered wagon journey across the prairie to everyday life in a frontier settlement—in the log cabin home, in the one-room schoolhouse, in the blacksmith shop, even in the dentist's office (a decidedly more painful experience in pioneer days). On weekends the Kinney features demonstrations of the pioneer way of life and work.

Details: Open May and Sep Wed–Fri and Sun noon–5; Jun–Aug Wed–Sun noon–5. $2.50 adults, 50 cents age 12 and younger. (1–2 hours)

★★ MEREDITH WILSON BOYHOOD HOME
314 S. Pennsylvania Ave., 515/423-3534 or 515/424-0700
This Queen Anne–style house was the home of the playwright who penned *The Music Man*, and its interior not only preserves a period look with furnishings and decoration but also salutes the life and art of Wilson.

Details: Open May–Oct Fri–Sun 1–4. $3 adults, $1 ages 6–12, free under 6. (30 minutes)

★★ VAN HORN'S ANTIQUE TRUCK MUSEUM
Two miles north of Mason City on Hwy. 65, 515/423-0550 or 515/423-9066
Do names like Mack, Sternburg, Bessemer, and Reo ring a bell? No, they're not famous prairie figures or curators of this museum, they're among the manufacturers of pre-1930 trucks that make up the exhibits here. Some vehicles on display date back to 1908. Other car-related paraphernalia—gas pumps, tools—rounds out the vintage collection.

Details: Open May 25–Sep 22 Mon–Sat 9–4, Sun 11–4. $5 adults, $1.50 children. (1–2 hours)

CLEAR LAKE SIGHTSEEING HIGHLIGHTS

★★★★ SURF BALLROOM
460 N. Shore Dr., 515/357-6151
A worthy tourist stop in its own right, the Surf Ballroom is also still an active entertainment venue. Buddy Holly, Ritchie Valens, and J. P. "The Big Bopper" Richardson played their final sets here on February 2, 1959, commonly known as "the day the music died." From the hardwood dance floor to the numerous pictures and memories on display throughout the ballroom, the Surf is sure to bring memories washing back up onto your shores.

Details: Open for tours year-round Mon–Fri 9–4. $4 general admission for a guided tour. (30 minutes–1 hour)

★★ IOWA TROLLEY PARK
3429 E. Main Ave., 515/357-RIDE
For a short tour of the Mason City–Clear Lake area, hop aboard this historic electric trolley along its one-mile route.
Details: Open Memorial Day–Labor Day weekends and holidays 12:30–4:30. $3.50 adults, $2 children. (45 minutes)

FITNESS AND RECREATION

Those who feel a need for speed—or at least to watch it—should head out to the **I-35 Speedway**, North Iowa Fairgrounds, Hwy. 18 W., Mason City, 515/423-3811 or 515/424-6515, from April through September. On Sunday evenings from 6 to 10:30, IMCA stock cars, modified cars, cruisers, and street stock cars race on this half-mile track. Admission costs $7 for adults, $2 for children.

If cars aren't your sports passion, maybe hockey is. If you're visiting during the winter, catch a **North Iowa Huskies** game at the North Iowa Fairgrounds, Hwy. 18 W., Mason City, 515/424-2929. This U.S. Hockey League team occupies the fairgrounds in the winter months. Games start at 7:05 p.m. Admission costs $6 for reserved seats and less for general admission.

For a more natural recreation spot in Mason City, try **Lime Creek Nature Center**, 3501 Lime Creek Rd., Mason City, 515/423-5309, a public conservation area atop the limestone bluffs overlooking the Winnebago River. Displays of birds, mammals, reptiles, and fish are featured, and there's an outdoor amphitheater. More than four miles of trails snake through the habitat. Admission is free.

If you'd prefer to be on the water, **Wind Venture**, Clear Lake, 515/357-3528 or 515/529-1172, offers both sailboat rides and lessons on Clear Lake for individuals and groups. The usual boarding location is City Dock, but other pickup points on the lake can be arranged. Docked at Clear Lake since 1987, the historic Missouri River cruiser **Lady of the Lake**, Sea Wall, downtown Clear Lake, 515/357-2243, transports passengers around the lake for scenic cruises during the summer and fall. Cost is $10 for adults and $5 for children under 12.

If golf's your bag, **All Vets Golf Club**, 2000 N. Shore Dr., Clear Lake, 515/357-4457, welcomes the public with daily rates. A golf shop and "19th hole" (a clubhouse bar) are on the premises, too.

FOOD

Clear Lake and Mason City offer not only the usual contingent of charming, family-owned restaurants serving family-style food, but the former city also has the distinction of providing lakeside dining that features peaceful shore views.

Next door to the Surf Ballroom, the **Boathouse Grill**, 468 N. Shore Dr., Clear Lake, 515/357-8688, is a family-run restaurant specializing in tasty pizzas, pastas, and steaks. Open Monday through Saturday, it has a lounge, too. Also featuring seafood, plus a view overlooking the lake, the **Ritz Club**, 15406 Crane St., Clear Lake, 515/357-2012, has served diners for 40 years. Barbecue ribs and chicken are also specialties.

If coffee's what you crave, **Java Island**, 407 Main Ave., Clear Lake, 515/357-3033, serves up not only espresso but tropical drinks and smoothies—even Jimmy Buffett T-shirts.

For a hearty breakfast spot, try **Martha's**, 305 Main Ave., Clear Lake, 515/357-8720, which also serves homemade pies and daily lunch specials.

The **Linden House Tea Room and Sandbar Restaurant & Lounge**, 211 N. Fourth St., Clear Lake, 515/357-3733, offers fine dining in a historic setting. The food is homemade, artwork and clothing are for sale, and a game room features billiards and darts.

For charming café food, stop at **Papa's Cafe**, 2960 Fourth St. SW, Mason City, 515/424-2166, located conveniently along Highway 18. Near Papa's is **La Hacienda II**, 342 Eisenhower St., Mason City, 515/424-9728, which serves up tasty Mexican fare.

A fine fine-dining spot is **XTABI Supper Club**, 1451 N. Federal St., Mason City, 515/424-0409, which, despite its confounding name, features delicious steaks and other hearty entrées. **Peachtree**, 2101 Fourth St. SW, Mason City, 515/423-1640, located in the Holiday Inn, offers a reliable menu for fine dining.

LODGING

Lodging options in the area are varied, from numerous bed-and-breakfast inns to accommodations that offer extended summer lodging near the lake.

Country Touch Bed & Breakfast, 1034 Hwy. 3, Hampton, 888/891-9467 or 515/456-4585, owned and operated by Dennis and Linda Viet, features five guest rooms that range in price from $55 to $105 per night. The newer rooms include balconies and fireplaces. Breakfast is, of course, included, and dinner costs just $10.

Mason City and Clear Lake offer a number of affordable, worthy accommodations. **Comfort Inn**, 410 Fifth Ave. SW, Mason City, 515/423-4444,

CLEAR LAKE

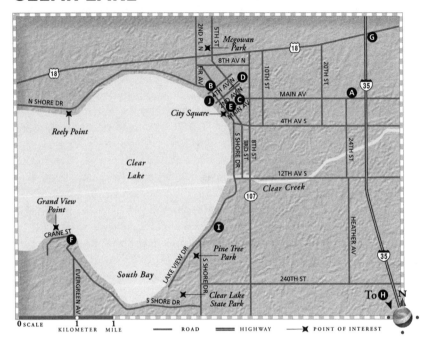

SIGHTS
- **A** Iowa Trolley Park
- **B** Surf Ballroom

FOOD
- **B** Boathouse Grill
- **C** Java Island
- **D** Linden House Tea Room and Sandbar Restaurant & Lounge
- **E** Martha's
- **F** Ritz Club

LODGING
- **G** Best Western Holiday Lodge
- **H** Country Touch Bed & Breakfast
- **I** The Loft on the South Shore
- **J** Norsk Hus By-the-Lake

Note: Items with the same letter are located in the same area.

has 60 rooms plus an indoor pool and whirlpool. The **Hanford Inn**, Hwy. 18 W., Mason City, 515/424-9494, offers 72 rooms and similar amenities (indoor pool and whirlpool), plus an indoor recreation room. **Holiday Inn**, Hwy. 18 W., Mason City, 515/423-1640, features a sauna and exercise room. It is also the biggest area hotel, with 135 guest rooms.

Norsk Hus By-the-Lake, 3611 N. Shore Dr., Clear Lake, 515/357-8368, has a name that says it all. This luxurious lakeside bed-and-breakfast inn offers just one guest room, but it comes complete with kitchen. Another fine bed-and-breakfast choice in Clear Lake is **The Loft on the South Shore**, 200 Seventh Ave. S., Clear Lake, 515/357-0160, which features a hot tub.

Hotel accommodations in Clear Lake include the **Best Western Holiday Lodge**, I-35 and Hwy. 18, Clear Lake, 515/357-5253, which has more than 140 rooms plus plenty of amenities, like free breakfast, accommodations for pets, and business facilities.

CAMPING

Clear Lake State Park, 2730 S. Lakeview Dr., Clear Lake, 515/357-4212, has 215 campsites, 95 with electric hookups. Rest rooms and showers are modern, and there's a trailer dump station. The park borders Clear Lake and encompasses three-acre Woodford Island, a mini wildlife refuge. Swimmers take full advantage of the 900-foot-long beach.

In the Mason City area, **MacNider Campgrounds**, North Birch Dr., Mason City, 515/421-3673, offers modern campsites, stream fishing, and even volleyball facilities. Rest rooms and showers are also available.

Die-hard campers stay at **Lime Creek Park**, 3501 Lime Creek Rd., Mason City, 515/423-5309, featuring not only primitive campsites but also biking, hiking, and nature trails.

NIGHTLIFE

Lu's Sports Bar & Grill, 619 Buddy Holly Pl., Clear Lake, 515/357-9011, features a rotating menu of entertainment—dance music, live comedy on Friday nights, a Saturday afternoon sports club, and Sunday teen activities. For more live music, head to **Bourbon Street Rock & Blues Club**, 1210 S. Shore Dr., Clear Lake, 515/357-0901. Along with a daily happy hour, this joint offers acoustic music on Wednesday nights and louder rock and blues on the weekends.

12
CEDAR FALLS
AND WATERLOO

The hills and valleys in and around Blackhawk County and the Cedar Falls–Waterloo area, especially as you move toward the Mississippi River, provide a rolling, serene backdrop to your travels.

William Sturgis and E. D. Adams and their families must have thought as much, anyway, in 1845 when they settled on the banks of the Cedar River, starting the first permanent settlement in Blackhawk County. First the area was named Sturgis Falls, but it eventually became Cedar Falls—the power of the Cedar River ran the town's saw- and gristmills. In the 1890s, Cedar Falls became one of the largest such mill sites in the state.

Cedar Falls' sister city of Waterloo has a similar mill-dominated past, as it was settled on the other side of the Cedar River. Today, John Deere Tractor Works is the city's major manufacturing force.

The University of Northern Iowa, located in Cedar Falls, is the focus of much of the activity in the area, from the obvious student population to the presence of many fine museums and KUNI-FM, its excellent National Public Radio–affiliated station.

And progress marches on: The $23 million Gallagher-Bluedorn Performing Arts Center recently opened on the UNI campus, with three state-of-the-art concert halls as well as academic rehearsal spaces. Its main hall seats as many as 1,600. The center is one of the state's finest performance facilities and a focal point for the arts in northern Iowa.

A PERFECT DAY IN CEDAR FALLS AND WATERLOO

In Cedar Falls, take time to tour the area in and around the University of Northern Iowa, taking in the many museums on campus as well as the shops and restaurants surrounding the university in the business district referred to as "The Hill."

In Waterloo, tour the John Deere Tractor Works—the manufacturer of the famous green beasts is surprisingly fascinating, even for the agriculturally challenged.

CEDAR FALLS SIGHTSEEING HIGHLIGHTS

★★★ UNIVERSITY OF NORTHERN IOWA MUSEUM
3219 Hudson Rd., UNI campus, 319/273-2188, www.uni.edu/museum

More than a century old, this distinguished museum serves both university students and the community, and it features the largest collection in northeast Iowa dedicated to the natural sciences (geology, biology, history, and anthropology). Special presentations, programs, and lectures are also periodically held on weekend afternoons.

Details: Open year-round Mon–Fri 9–4:30, Sat–Sun 1–4:30. Free. (1 hour)

★★ ANTIQUE ACRES
7610 Waverly Rd., 319/987-2380

This large collection of historic metal machinery tells a compelling story about the history of agriculture in Iowa. It includes steam-powered tractors, sawmilling equipment, and other farm implements. Before air-conditioned tractor cabs, before fat rubber tires, and before gigantic spraying machines that could cover huge swaths of a field, these were the iron beasts that ruled agriculture, eclipsing horse-drawn plows. Campers can take advantage of the campground, which has 70 modern campsites.

Details: Open May–Oct Mon–Fri 8–5. Free. (1 hour)

★★ HEARST CENTER FOR THE ARTS
304 W. Seerley Blvd., 319/273-8641 www.ci.cedar-falls.ia.us/human_leisure/hearst_center/

Serving as an exhibition space for local and regional artists, Hearst

CEDAR FALLS/WATERLOO

GILBERTVILLE

Evansdale

Waterloo

Cedar Falls

N ELK RUN RD

SCHENK RD

N AIRLINE HWY

DONALD ST

NEWELL ST

INDEPENDENCE AV

LAFAYETTE RD

IDAHO ST

Gates Park

E 4TH ST

FRANKLIN ST

COMMERCIAL ST

UNION RD

WASHINGTON ST

11TH ST

9TH ST

LOGAN AV

BROADWAY ST

CONGER ST

Cedar River Park

MULLEN AV

LOCUST ST

WILLISTON AV

RIDGEWAY AV

MURPHY RD

SAN MARNEN DR

FLETCHER AV

Hope Martin Park

Byrnes Park

ANSBOROUGH AV

WAGNER RD

GREENHILLS RD

BLACK HAWK RD

W 4TH ST

SERGEANT RD

Black Hawk Creek

DUNKERTON RD

Waterloo Municipal Airport

LINCOLN ST

George Wyth State Park

Cedar River

RAINBOW DR

CEDAR HEIGHTS DR

WATERLOO RD

GREENHILL RD

DEERE RD

RANCHERO RD

LONE TREE RD

MAIN ST

SEERLEY BLVD

MAIN ST

WAVERLY RD

CENTER ST

FRANKLIN ST

18TH ST

COLLEGE ST

HUDSON RD

Falls Access Park

Black Hawk Park

Birdsall Park

1ST ST

4TH ST

12TH ST

27TH ST

UNIVERSITY AV

UNION RD

SCHENK RD

0 SCALE   3 KILOMETERS   3 MILES

ROAD   HIGHWAY

Center houses one main gallery and another smaller gallery, both featuring paintings and other artwork that often depict the history and heritage of Iowa, agricultural (like the Depression-era farm crisis) and otherwise. One wall is devoted to a small permanent collection of art. Associates of artist Grant Wood have work on display here. A Wooden Sculpture Garden is also on site.

Details: *Open year-round Tue and Thu 10–9, Wed and Fri 10–5, Sat–Sun 1–4. Free. (30 minutes–1 hour)*

★★ ICE HOUSE MUSEUM
First and Clay Sts., 319/266-5149

You probably don't think of ice as a cash crop in this modern day, but the Ice House Museum will teach you how it was indeed harvested from the Cedar River in the late 1800s and early 1900s. (Before refrigeration, winter ice was stored year-round to keep food cool in "ice boxes.") Nearly 8 thousand tons of ice were

---

SIGHTS

- Ⓐ Antique Acres
- Ⓑ Hearst Center for the Arts
- Ⓒ Ice House Museum
- Ⓒ Little Red Schoolhouse
- Ⓓ University of Northern Iowa Gallery of Art
- Ⓓ University of Northern Iowa Museum
- Ⓔ Victorian Home & Carriage House Museum
- Ⓕ Bluedorn Science Imaginarium
- Ⓖ Grout Museum of History and Science
- Ⓗ John Deere Works
- Ⓘ Waterloo Museum of Art

FOOD

- Ⓙ A. J. Pickerman
- Ⓚ AJ's Midtown Bistro
- Ⓛ Bagels & More Showcase Cafe

FOOD (continued)

- Ⓜ Biemann's Blackhawk Restaurant
- Ⓔ Bob and Jerry's Steak Corral
- Ⓝ Brown Bottle Italian Ristorante
- Ⓜ Cup of Joe
- Ⓞ Danny's Diner
- Ⓟ Granny Annie's
- Ⓠ Pour Richard's Deli & Pub
- Ⓡ Toad's Bar & Grill

LODGING

- Ⓢ Best Western Midwest Lodge
- Ⓣ Carriage House Inn
- Ⓤ Daisy Wilton Inn
- Ⓥ Holiday Inn University Plaza
- Ⓦ House By the Side of the Road
- Ⓧ New Waterloo Inn
- Ⓨ River House Bed & Breakfast
- Ⓩ University Inn
- ⓐ Wellington Bed & Breakfast

Note: Items with the same letter are located in the same area.

stored annually within this space before it went out of business in 1934. It became a museum in 1975, and today you can view the various machines and tools that aided the men who had to undertake this cold work.

Details: *Open May and Sep–Oct Wed, Sat, and Sun 2–4:30; Jun–Aug Wed, Fri, Sat, and Sun 2–4:30. Free. (1 hour)*

★★ **UNIVERSITY OF NORTHERN IOWA GALLERY OF ART**
Kamerick Art Bldg., UNI campus, 319/273-6134
In this gallery devoted to UNI student exhibits (hence the name), the range of artwork is eclectic and varies depending on the time of year. An annual competition is held in April, and exhibits are also on display through the summer months.

Details: *Open year-round Mon–Thu 9–9, Fri 9–5, Sat–Sun noon–5. Free. (30 minutes–1 hour)*

★ **LITTLE RED SCHOOLHOUSE**
First and Clay Sts., 319/266-5149
This 1909 one-room schoolhouse is simple: desks, blackboard, books, bell tower, and potbelly stove. It's a stark reminder of a simpler time in education and life in general. Thumb through some of the textbooks, ring the school bell, and see if you can fit into one of those desks.

Details: *Open May and Sep–Oct Wed, Sat, and Sun 2–4:30; Jun–Aug Wed, Fri, Sat, and Sun 2–4:30. Free. (1 hour)*

★ **VICTORIAN HOME & CARRIAGE HOUSE MUSEUM**
308 W. Third St., 319/266-5149
Built in 1861, this Victorian home has been restored to its period appearance, complete with mannequins outfitted in appropriate period clothing. The Carriage House Museum holds the exhibits and documents of the historical societies for both the city and the county.

Details: *Open year-round Wed–Sun 2–4. Free. (30 minutes–1 hour)*

WATERLOO SIGHTEEING HIGHLIGHTS

★★★ **GROUT MUSEUM OF HISTORY AND SCIENCE**
503 South St., 319/234-6357, www.cedarnet.org/grout

Housed in a Victorian Italianate home, this museum has a strong focus on astronomical (as in stars, not size) matters, with its 50-seat planetarium. There's also a Children's Interactive Science Center, where physics, anthropology, and biology come to life via hands-on experiments and computer games. You can also browse exhibits that trace the advance of industry in the Waterloo and Cedar Falls area. Adults can visit a genealogical reference section.

Details: Open Sep–May Tue–Sat 1–4:30, Sun 1–4:30; Jun–Aug Tue–Sat 10–4:30, Sun 1–4:30. $2.50 general admission, free under 3. (1 hour)

★★★ JOHN DEERE WATERLOO WORKS
3500 Donald St., 319/292-7801

Even non-Midwesterners are familiar with the green-and-yellow color scheme and leaping deer logo of John Deere tractors and farm machinery. "Nothing runs like a Deere," right? Here you can tour four John Deere manufacturing plants to see for yourself how a tractor comes together from start to finish. It's a fascinating look into the inner workings of the machines that generations of Iowans have depended on to work the land. By the time you leave, you will know much more about how small pieces of metal come together in the manufacture of a machine as massive and powerful as a large John Deere tractor.

Details: Open year-round. Tractor Assembly and Component Works tours weekdays 9 a.m. and 1 p.m., Engine Works weekdays 9:30 a.m. and 1 p.m., Foundry weekdays flexible hours. Must be 12 or older. Free. (1–3 hours)

★★ BLUEDORN SCIENCE IMAGINARIUM
322 Washington St., 319/233-8708

Dive into the hands-on realm of physics—light, sound, forces. Demonstrations include "Eggs" (watch out, they break!), "Bubbles" (watch out, they pop!) and "Super Cold" (watch out, it burns!). Make your own laser show or become a human gyroscope and discover your center of gravity.

Details: Open Jun–Aug Tue–Sat 10–4:30, Sun 1–4:30; Sep–May Tue–Fri 1–4:30, Sat 10–4:30. Free. (1–2 hours)

★ WATERLOO MUSEUM OF ART
225 Commercial St., 319/291-4491

This collection of Midwestern art focuses on decorative arts and folk art, plus international works and those of Grant Wood. An interactive Junior Art Gallery and gift shop are also on site.

Details: *Open year-round Mon 10–9, Tue–Sat 10–5, Sun 1–4. Free. (30 minutes–1 hour)*

FITNESS AND RECREATION

The rolling landscape of these riverside cities will provide you with plenty of outdoor recreation among grass, trees, and water, while urban diversions like zoos and farmer's markets can be enjoyed without leaving civilization.

Hartman Reserve Nature Center, 657 Reserve Dr., Cedar Falls, 319/277-2187, www.co.black-hawk.ia.us/hartman, is a 260-acre wooded nature preserve situated along the banks of the Cedar River. The Hartman Interpretive Center holds exhibits and is connected to five miles' worth of trails, which are open from dawn to dusk.

The **Cedar Valley Arboretum and Botanic Gardens**, 1501 E. Orange Rd., Waterloo, 319/235-1167, has not only gardens but a natural prairie, fountains, ponds, trails, and greenhouses.

Sunrise Exchange Club Children's Petting Zoo, Cattle Congress Grounds, 307 Rainbow Dr., Waterloo, 319/234-4110, open during the summer, features a variety of friendly farm animals. It's a good outdoor diversion for the whole family on a summer afternoon.

FOOD

From home-style restaurants to quaint diners and corner pub food, Cedar Falls and Waterloo have plenty of flavors to satisfy every taste.

A. J. Pickerman, 127 E. 18th St., Cedar Falls, 319/266-8197, is a casual spot that serves all kinds of tasty sandwiches. There's also a location in Waterloo at 1515 E. San Marnan Dr., 319/233-7222. Heartier, home-style cooking awaits you at **Biemann's Blackhawk Restaurant**, 119 Main St., Cedar Falls, 319/277-4050, serving daily lunch and dinner specials.

For those who like to participate intimately in their own cooking, even away from home, **Bob and Jerry's Steak Corral**, 204 1/2 Main St., Cedar Falls, 319/277-4556, lets you grill your own steak for dinner. It's also known for its unlimited salad bar.

Serving up a helping of nostalgia with its meals, **Danny's Diner**, 1525 W. First St., Cedar Falls, 319/266-1462, features not only burgers, shakes, and malts in the familiar 1950s style, but a jukebox to match. **Cup of Joe**,

102 Main St., Cedar Falls, 319/277-1596, serves its coffee drinks and desserts in a 1950s-era building.

Pour Richard's Deli & Pub, 2209 College St., Cedar Falls, 319/277-0075, offers not only good sandwich-and-burger food, but a wide selection of beers and other beverages. Another establishment in the same vein is **Toad's Bar and Grill**, 204 Main St., 319/266-3507.

A reliable breakfast stop that's open early is **Granny Annie's**, 1724 W. 31st St., Cedar Falls, 319/277-4650, which specializes in rolls, muffins, and brownies. If it's breakfast bagels you crave, **Bagels & More Showcase Cafe** has locations at 6322 University Ave., Cedar Falls, 319/277-4285; 2226 College St., Cedar Falls, 319/277-3790; and 624 Sycamore St., Waterloo, 319/236-3220.

In Waterloo, **AJ's Midtown Bistro**, 3251 W. Fourth St., Waterloo, 319/236-6600, has flavorful dishes in a cozy atmosphere. **Brown Bottle Italian Ristorante** serves great pasta dishes at both of its locations: West Fifth St., Waterloo, 319/232-3014, and 1111 Center St., Cedar Falls, 319/266-2616.

LODGING

Some of the best accommodations in Cedar Falls are at **Holiday Inn University Plaza**, 5826 University Ave., Cedar Falls, 800/465-4329 or 319/277-2230, with nearly two hundred rooms, a restaurant and bar, and indoor and outdoor pools. It's also one of the more expensive choices. Usually a little less pricey, **Best Western Midwest Lodge**, 4410 University Ave., Cedar Falls, 800/728-9819 or 319/277-1550, is about half as large and has an indoor pool. **University Inn**, 4711 University Ave., Cedar Falls, 319/277-1412, www.skyport.com/uni-inn/, is a smaller, quiet motel that's family owned.

Carriage House Inn, 3030 Grand Blvd., Cedar Falls, 319/277-6724, is generally regarded as the city's most luxurious bed-and-breakfast stop, with three rooms—including a whirlpool room. **River House Bed & Breakfast**, 2818 Cottage Row Rd., Cedar Falls, 888/766-9204 or 319/266-9204, is located on the Cedar River, near a recreation trail. Three rooms are available.

A slightly more rural bed-and-breakfast choice is **House By the Side of the Road**, 6804 Ranchero Rd., Cedar Falls, 319/988-3691, near Cedar Valley Nature Trail. There's a log cabin available for rent for parties and receptions, along with two guest rooms.

Waterloo also has its share of fine lodging options. The **Daisy Wilton Inn**, 418 Walnut St., Waterloo, 319/232-0801 or 319/230-0599, is a restored

Truth be told, the green, rolling landscape of northeast Iowa lays claim to the title of "God's Country." No place else in Iowa reminds the eye so much of the English countryside. Launching from Cedar Falls and Waterloo into the smaller communities to the northeast makes perfect sense for a pleasant trip and takes you deeper and deeper into the scenic hills.

Effigy Mounds National Monument, three miles north of Marquette off Hwy. 76, 319/873-3491, is an essential stop not only for the breathtaking sight of 191 prehistoric burial mounds, many in the shapes of animals, but also because the 1,481-acre park is an important link to Iowa's past. This is a better stop in warm to cool weather, when you can enjoy hiking the miles of trails in the park and taking in the picturesque views of the flora and fauna natural to the Mississippi River Valley. A bonus you hadn't expected: You'll leave this place knowing the difference between conical, linear, and compound mounds. The park's visitors center is open daily 8 to 5.

South of Effigy Mounds, **Pikes Peak State Park**, 15316 Great River Rd., McGregor, 319/873-2341, also has effigy mounds, but it's a better spot for picnicking (which isn't allowed at Effigy Mounds National Monument) and camping (with 60 electric campsites, showers, and a trailer dump station). The park's 500-foot bluff is the highest on the Mississippi River.

Hard-core Little House on the Prairie fans might want to trek all the way north to the **Laura Ingalls Wilder Park and Museum**, 3603 236th Ave., Burr Oak, 319/735-5916, just a few miles south of the Iowa-Minnesota border. A National Historic Site, the museum is one of the childhood homes of the popular author (she lived here when she was nine years old). Her family ran the Masters Hotel in Burr Oak for a year. The park and museum are open May through September, 9 to 5.

The **Vesterheim Norwegian-American Museum**, 502 W. Water St., 319/382-9681, is the centerpiece of the town's heritage and gathers more than 21 thousand objects inside 15 buildings. The main museum (originally a hotel) features four floors of exhibits of everything from horns ("standard beer-drinking vessels") to an entire ship (TradeWind, the smallest sailboat known to have crossed the Atlantic without assistance). Fine arts are displayed in the Anna Hong Gallery. The Vesterheim is open November through April, 10 to 4. Admission is $4 for adults, $3 for seniors, $2 for ages

7 to 18. Along with the outer buildings, it is open May through October, 9 to 5, during which months admission goes up a dollar.

Have lunch next door to the Vesterheim at the **Dayton House Norwegian Cafe**. Menu items include smorbrod (open-faced sandwiches), lapskaus (beef and pork stew), and Uff Da Beer.

Also take time in Decorah to stroll the shops along Water Street and, just a couple blocks south, the **Broadway–Phelps Park Historic District**, lined with dozens of historic homes and buildings.

Just north of Decorah on North Winn Road, **Seed Savers Heritage Farm**, 3076 North Winn Rd., Decorah, 319/382-5990, is a must-see (and smell) collection of heirloom fruits, vegetables, and flowers—pure varieties (more than 18 thousand) that are in danger of disappearing from the world. The 173 acres also feature picturesque limestone bluffs and valleys with gently flowing streams. An orchard holds 700 nineteenth-century apple varieties. More than 30 White Park cattle also graze on the farm—a rare breed from the British Isles of which only 300 are in existence today. A barn holds a gift shop where you can buy some of the seeds used to grow the plants on the farm. Suggested donation for your visit is only $1. Seed Savers is open June through September from 9 a.m. to 5 p.m. daily.

South of Decorah, in the Czech village of Spillville, visit the **Bily Clocks Museum**, in the middle of town on Main Street, 319/562-3569. It not only displays the intricate, wood-carved clocks of late brothers Frank L. and Joseph C. Bily, but the building was also home, in the summer of 1893, to renowned Czech composer Dr. Antonin Dvořák ("New World Symphony").

Even if you've never heard or sung William S. Pitts' hymn "The Church in the Wildwood," it might be a good idea to drive by the subject of that song and a famous roadside attraction, the **Little Brown Church in the Vale**, 2730 Cheyenne Ave., Nashua (two miles east of Nashua on Hwy. 218), 515/435-2027.

Montauk Historic Governor's Home, one mile northeast of Clermont on Hwy. 18, 319/423-7173, was home to William Larrabee, the twelfth governor of Iowa. His family maintained this brick and limestone mansion for more than a century. Now the State Historical Society of Iowa operates Montauk, which overlooks both the Turkey River and Clermont. It's open from Memorial Day weekend until October 31.

WATERLOO FARMER'S MARKET

From 8 a.m. to noon on Saturday mornings in May through October, downtown Waterloo hosts a **Farmer's Market**, between Park Ave. and E. Fourth St., in the Homeland Bank parking lot, 319/233-7049. Usually about 50 local vendors hawk their produce, plants, baked goods, and crafts.

Victorian home decorated with antiques. On the National Register of Historic Places, **Wellington Bed & Breakfast**, 800 W. Fourth St., Waterloo, 319/234-2993, has four rooms for rent with their own refrigerators. This is a slightly higher priced option.

New Waterloo Inn, 2343 Logan Ave., Waterloo, 319/236-3238, has 50 rooms and an indoor pool. Rates here are inexpensive.

CAMPING

Antique Acres (also see Cedar Falls Sightseeing Highlights), 7610 Waverly Rd., Cedar Falls, 319/987-2380, has a modern, 70-site campground that's open May through October.

For a more rural choice, head to **Black Hawk Park**, three miles north on Hwy. 218 and one mile west on Lone Tree Rd., Cedar Falls, 319/266-6813. It has walking and biking trails, 102 electric campsites, and 23 primitive sites, plus showers and a trailer dump station.

Also outside of the urban bustle, **Hickory Hills Park**, five miles west on Road D52 then three miles south on Road V37, La Porte City, 319/342-3350, has 80 electric sites and 50 primitive sites near a 55-acre lake.

NIGHTLIFE

For a change of pace from the typical nightclub scene, in June or July, head to Overman Park, Second Street and Franklin Avenue in Cedar Falls' Historical District, where the **Cedar Falls Municipal Band** plays a free concert at 7:30 p.m. each Tuesday in the park's open-air band shell. Organized in 1891, the 45-piece Municipal Band is Iowa's oldest concert band. It even has its own museum at 203 1/2 Main Street. Call 319/266-1253 or 319/266-2922.

Cadillac Lanes, 650 LaPorte Rd., Waterloo, 319/234-6888, offers "Quarter Mania" on Monday and Thursday nights—bowling costs a mere 25 cents per game, and tap beer just a quarter per glass.

If there's a concert or dancing going on at the **Electric Park Ballroom**, 310 W. Conger Ave., Waterloo, 319/233-3050, it's well worth the price of admission to spend an evening in this historic venue.

Scenic Route: Great River Road

(Route takes you through the regions in the next three chapters)
More than 3,000 miles of road runs parallel to the majestic Mississippi River, all the way from Canada to the Gulf of Mexico. Following this motor route through the Iowa portion could easily rank as your most scenic jaunt around the state. Throughout the route and especially in northeast Iowa, the views of the Mississippi Valley from the road are high elevations from which you can take in sweeping vistas of the water and often tree-filled land below. Bring plenty of camera film.

Starting in the north, near New Albin, take Highway 26 south to Lansing, from there traveling via Road X52 to Harpers Ferry. (Always watch for the distinctive Great River Road signs, the symbol printed in the shape of a riverboat steering wheel.)

From Harpers Ferry (where the nearby Yellow River State Forest offers more than 9,000 acres of outdoor activities), continue south on Highway 364, which merges with Highway 76 before reaching the beautiful twin river towns of Marquette and McGregor. Take time to explore some of the unique shops in these charming communities, and even consider straying across the Mississippi into Prairie du Chien, Wisconsin.

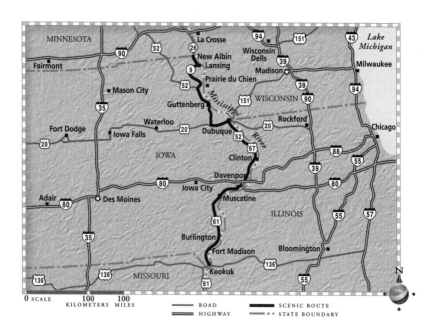

Road X56 carries you south to Guttenberg, then Highway 52 takes you to Millville. Road C9Y takes you to North Buena Vista and then Balltown. (If you're hungry when reaching this spot, you'll find dining at Breitbach's in Balltown a food feast to remember.)

Road C9Y travels on into Dubuque (see Chapter 13), where it's easy to catch up on Mississippi history and facts with the city's many river-themed attractions, then Highway 52 takes you south out of Dubuque, all the way south through St. Catherine, St. Donatus, Bellevue, Green Island, and the Mississippi island town of Sabula. Just west of Sabula you'll hook up with Highway 67 to go south into Clinton; south to the Bettendorf and Davenport, the Iowa half of the Quad Cities (see Chapter 14).

You'll actually be heading west at this point (following Iowa's border) as you drive on Highway 22 out of the Quad Cities and into Muscatine, passing through the towns of Buffalo, Montpelier, and Fairport along the way. (Check out the Mark Twain lookout in Muscatine.)

Road X61 goes south from Muscatine to Highway 99, which takes you into Toolesboro, then through Oakville and Kingston before hitting Burlington (see Chapter 15). Highway 61 goes from Burlington to Fort Madison, then on down into Keokuk, the southern tip of your Iowa Great River Road trip. Look out over Lock & Dam No. 19 and reflect on the fact that you've only toured a relatively small portion of the powerful water flow that is the Mississippi.

13
DUBUQUE

Mineral wealth is the reason Dubuque exists. In 1788, French fur trader Julien Dubuque crossed the Mississippi River into what is now Iowa in order to mine lead; in 1837, the city was founded and named in his honor.

In the late nineteenth century, Dubuque was Iowa's leading industrial center. It became known as "Key City," a moniker explained by a current exhibit in the Mississippi River Museum: "Dubuque opens and unlocks the agricultural, commercial and mineral resources of northern Iowa, Minnesota, and a large portion of the Lake Superior country to active communication with the Atlantic cities on the east and numberless large and flourishing cities of the Mississippi and the Ohio and the South." In other words, Dubuque was touted as the great gateway to all points north.

No longer the manufacturing powerhouse it once was, twenty-first-century Dubuque nevertheless remains a major Mississippi community. Vestiges of its nineteenth-century glory can be seen in the architecture of the grand Victorian homes sitting atop the bluffs and in the downtown warehouses and hotels near the river's edge.

Dubuque offers both historical and contemporary, natural and man-made attractions for the tourist. Natural wonders include Crystal Lake Cave and eagles that soar high above Lock and Dam #11. In contrast, the Dubuque Diamond Jo Casino, floating in the Ice Harbor, represents recent developments in the city's business and cultural life.

Antiques shoppers will find plenty of wares to dig through among the many independent shops. Those who prefer to view building-size antiques will delight in curiosities like the Fenelon Place Elevator (which used to carry people from the bottom to the top of a bluff) and Shot Tower, a brick chimney–like structure located downtown that produced lead shot during the Civil War.

Dubuque holds an impressive diversity of attractions, so that the Mississippi's flow seems to carry not only water but also a spirit of adventure.

A PERFECT DAY IN DUBUQUE

Begin your Dubuque day at the highly recommended Mississippi River Museum, next to the mighty river itself, in the Ice Harbor. Not only does it make sense geographically to begin here, but the river is also the metaphorical lifeblood of the city. Start with the Mississippi, then flow through the rest of Dubuque. While at the museum, check out the observation deck at the top of the tower. (If you have any Dubuque-related questions, stop at the Iowa Welcome Center located in the same warehouse building as the museum.)

Next, head downtown to take in the sights via a horse-drawn carriage; later, set out on foot to explore some of the sights up close. Stroll through the historic neighborhoods such as the 11th Street district atop the bluffs, graced with many grand homes and buildings. Locust Street and Main Street also feature historic buildings. Stop for lunch at Sfikas Restaurant downtown.

For a little afternoon shopping, Dubuque Antique Mall is a favorite destination. The Mines of Spain Recreation Area is worth a stop to experience the unadulterated nature of the Upper Mississippi River environment. The thick forests here are impressive.

Come evening, dine at Breitbach's in nearby Balltown, worth the trip and truly an Iowa institution. If you can catch a concert or musical in the century-old, 644-seat Grand Opera House Theater, 135 W. Eighth St., 319/588-4356, don't miss the chance.

DOWNTOWN DUBUQUE SIGHTSEEING HIGHLIGHTS

★★★★ MISSISSIPPI RIVER MUSEUM
Third St./Ice Harbor, 319/557-9545

A tribute to the mighty river that forms Iowa's eastern border, this museum located on its banks launches its tours with a showing of *River of Dreams*, a brief but informative documentary rich in sound

DOWNTOWN DUBUQUE

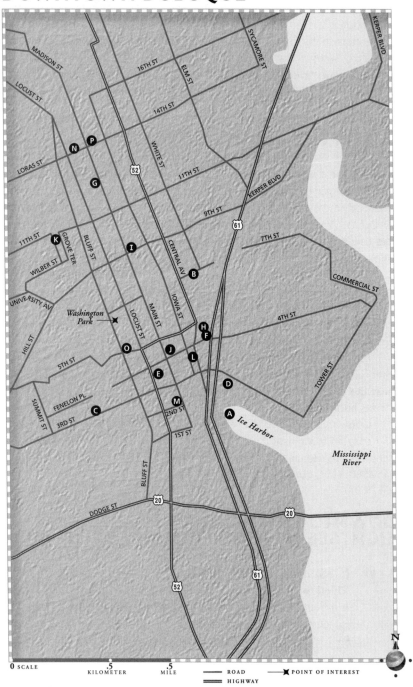

MADISON ST

LOCUST ST

SYCAMORE ST

KERPER BLVD

16TH ST

ELM ST

14TH ST

WHITE ST

LORAS ST

N **P**

52

G

11TH ST

9TH ST

KERPER BLVD

61

11TH ST

K

GROVE TER

BLUFF ST

WILBER ST

7TH ST

COMMERCIAL ST

I

CENTRAL AV

B

UNIVERSITY AV

HILL ST

Washington Park

LOCUST ST

MAIN ST

IOWA ST

H
F

4TH ST

TOWER ST

O

J

L

5TH ST

E

D

SUMMIT ST

FENELON PL

C

3RD ST

M

2ND ST

A Ice Harbor

1ST ST

Mississippi River

BLUFF ST

DODGE ST

20

20

52

61

0 SCALE   .5 KILOMETER   .5 MILE   —— ROAD   ✛ POINT OF INTEREST

=== HIGHWAY

N

effects and narrated by Garrison Keillor, noted writer and host of the radio series "A Prairie Home Companion." Afterward, you're free to explore exhibits that illustrate the lives of people on the Mississippi and throughout Dubuque's history. Included with admission, the Woodward Riverboat Museum next door holds additional exhibits, such as "Steamboat Accidents & Disasters."

Details: Open year-round daily 10–5:30. $4 general admission. (2–3 hours)

★★★ DUBUQUE MUSEUM OF ART
Locust St. and Washington Park, 319/557-1851
Relocated in 1999 from its old digs at Eighth and Central to this brand new building, the Dubuque Museum of Art remains unchanged in spirit: It's a living, breathing institution that fosters and exhibits the work of artists both local and national. In the past, children artists have painted murals for the museum, and specific exhibitions have featured dozens of Iowans. The museum's focus is twentieth-century art, but within that category, the museum courts a wide stylistic range of work.

Details: Open year-round Tue–Fri 10–5, Sat–Sun 1–5. Suggested donation $2 adults, $1 children. (1–2 hours)

★★★ FENELON PLACE ELEVATOR (FOURTH STREET ELEVATOR)
512 Fenelon Pl., 319/582-6496
This 296-foot stretch is the world's shortest, steepest railway, and one of only three in the nation. Think of it roughly as a ski lift on a rail that goes straight up. Built in 1882 by a banker who wanted a fast method of transportation to and from home during his lunch hour, modern riders can embark at Fourth Street and ride 189 feet up to

---

SIGHTS
- Ⓐ Diamond Jo Casino
- Ⓑ Dubuque Museum of Art
- Ⓒ Fenelon Place Elevator (Fourth Street Elevator)
- Ⓓ Mississippi River Museum

FOOD
- Ⓔ The Bridge Restaurant & Lounge
- Ⓕ Dottie's Cafe
- Ⓖ Mario's Italian Restaurant & Lounge
- Ⓗ Sfikas Restaurant/ Grandma's Pastry
- Ⓘ Yen Ching

LODGING
- Ⓙ Holiday Inn-Dubuque Five Flags
- Ⓚ Hancock House
- Ⓛ Hotel Canfield
- Ⓜ Julien Inn
- Ⓝ Mandolin Inn
- Ⓞ Redstone Inn
- Ⓟ Richards House

GALENA, ILLINOIS

An important mining town for lead in the 1800s, **Galena** underwent a re-naissance in the 1960s, when merchants began to transform the downtown Main Street, which had bluffs towering above it on one side and the Galena River rolling gently by on the other. Now it's several blocks' worth of unique shops that sell everything from antiques to wine, soaps, and rural real es-tate in the English countryside–like landscape that surrounds the town—all rolling hills and green pastures containing herds of grazing animals.

Galena also gave the Union Army no fewer than nine generals during the Civil War, the most famous being Ulysses S. Grant, who of course went on to become President of the United States. The **Ulysses S. Grant State Historic Site**, 500 Bouthillier St., Galena, 815/777-3310 or 815/777-0248, was the home Grant and his family lived in after the Civil War, and many of the original furnishings are still on view for today's tourists. Grant's children donated the home to the city in 1904, and it's currently operated by the Illinois Historic Preservation Agency. From parlor to kitchen, a tour of the home is a revealing look not only into the life of Grant, but also a glance into the style of life for wealthy citizens in the nineteenth century. Tours, available daily, last about a half hour and cost only $2 by way of a sug-gested donation.

The major Galena attraction, of course, is the dozens and dozens of unique shops along Main Street. Depending on your taste for antiques or

Fenelon Place. During the trip, you can enjoy a scenic view of the surrounding countryside.

Details: Open Apr–Nov daily 8–10. Round-trip $1.50 adults, 50 cents children; one-way 75 cents adults, 25 cents children; $1 bike and rider; free under 5. (30 minutes)

★ DIAMOND JO CASINO
Third St./Ice Harbor, 800/582-5956 or 319/583-7005

Press your luck with more than 640 slot machines and game ta-bles—featuring blackjack, craps, roulette, Caribbean stud, and poker—at this riverboat casino docked in Dubuque. It infrequently leaves shore, usually just for one early morning cruise Monday through Friday. (Gambling is legal on and off shore for those age 21

homemade, locally produced products, you could spend hours or a whole day or two wandering among the wares.

***Galena Cellars Winery**, 515 S. Main St., Galena, 800/397-WINE or 815/777-3330, www.galenacellars.com, will be one of the first shops you happen upon if you start at the south end of Main Street. It's family owned and housed in an 1840s granary. Stop in for samples, buy a few bottles, or dine in the restaurant on the second floor. **Rocky Mountain Chocolate Factory**, 207 S. Main St., Galena, 815/777-3200 or 815/777-3037, www.rockymtchoc.com, will satisfy your craving for chocolate with hand-crafted fudge, truffles and other sugary delights. **The Great Galena Peddlery**, 116 N. Main St., Galena, 815/777-2307, features many fine teas, herbs, and various accessories. **World Class Imports**, 117 S. Main St., Galena, 815/777-6308 or 815/777-6309, offers a dazzling array of special gifts from Amish furniture to Waterford crystal.*

*Also plan to dine in Galena, because the **Eldorado Grill**, 219 N. Main St., Galena, 815/777-1224, is one of the absolute best fine dining establishments you'll find in the Midwest. Call ahead to make a reservation, and budget for plenty of money. All prices are justified once you taste an entrée from the changing menu of game, fresh fish, and produce, all "naturally raised." The authentic margaritas are amazing, too, as well as the wine list. Dinner starts at 5 p.m. The Eldorado is closed on Tuesdays and Wednesdays.*

and older in several locations around Iowa.) Diamond Jo also houses a Dining Emporium.

Details: *Next to the Mississippi River Museum. Open year-round Mon–Tue 8 a.m.–2a.m., Wed–Thu 8 a.m.–4 a.m., Fri–Sat 24 hours, Sun closed at 2 a.m. (30 minutes–1 hour)*

OTHER DUBUQUE
SIGHTSEEING HIGHLIGHTS

★★★ EAGLE POINT PARK
West on Shiras Ave., off Rhomberg Ave., 319/589-4263
Simply one of the most scenic parks in all of Iowa and Nebraska,

DUBUQUE BY CARRIAGE

Horse-drawn carriages take you on a tour of downtown Dubuque. **Dubuque by Carriage**, Fourth St. and Bluff St., 319/580-0558, starts at the Diamond Jo Casino, Third St., Ice Harbor. Not only do you see the sights at a leisurely pace, but the drivers also inform you about the history of the area and many of the sights (Victorian homes, shops, restaurants, and landmarks) along the route. Tours are available April through October Sunday through Thursday from 10 to 5, Friday through Saturday 7 p.m. to 10 p.m. Christmas tours operate weekends November through December. Evening reservations available Monday through Thursday. $25 for a half-hour ride for two adults, $45 for a 45-minute ride for two adults.

Eagle Point overlooks a breathtaking sweep of the Mississippi River. Set just above River Lock and Dam #11, you can watch cargo-carrying river barges float their way through the narrow system of gates. This stop will likely be your most relaxing in Dubuque. The Mississippi side of the park is also dotted with permanent viewing towers at key outcroppings so you can better explore the opposite shore, the river itself, and the trains that run along both sides of the river.

The park was founded in 1908 under the direction of Judge Oliver Shiras and assumed much of its present form in the 1930s under the influence of Park Superintendent Alfred Caldwell (a big Frank Lloyd Wright fan, which you'll be able to discern from the park's buildings) and with the help of the Works Progress Administration. A wading pool, rock garden, and fish pond are on site. **Riverfront Pavilion**, built in 1910, is the park's oldest structure. But the most impressive shelter on the grounds is arguably the **Log Cabin Pavilion**; its picnic tables and huge brick ovens overlook a view of Dubuque. There are no camping facilities, unfortunately, but everything else about Eagle Point makes it a perfect choice for an attraction, not just an outdoor experience.

Details: *Open May–Oct daily 7–10. $1 per car. (1–3 hours)*

★★ CRYSTAL LAKE CAVE
7699 Crystal Lake Cave Dr., 319/556-6451 or 319/872-4111
Escape to a different, alien-looking world beneath the surface in this natural cave with stalagmites and stalactites galore. It's officially classified as a Great American Show Cave. Picnic grounds and gift shop are also on the site.
Details: Three miles south of Dubuque on Hwy. 52. Open Memorial Day–Labor Day daily 9–6; May and Oct weekends 9–5. $8 adults, $4 ages 5–11, free under 5. (1 hour)

★★ DUBUQUE ARBORETUM AND BOTANICAL GARDENS
3800 Arboretum Dr., 319/556-2100
See acres of annual and perennial flowers, wildflowers, grasses, cacti, ornamentals, trees, shrubs, and more flourishing varieties of flora, all on display (in season) at these award-winning gardens. There's also a garden gift shop, viewing porch, and specialized sections like Walters' dwarf conifer collection. Free concerts by local musicians and groups are staged here in the summer.
Details: Just off West 32nd St., in Marshall Park. Tours May–Nov. Call for information. Free. (1–2 hours)

★★ MATHIAS HAM HOUSE
2241 Lincoln Ave., 319/557-9545
This 1856 Italian-style villa preserves and displays the luxurious home life that mining magnate Mathias Ham enjoyed in pre–Civil War Dubuque. Its furnishings were shipped upstream on the Mississippi from New Orleans and St. Louis. A two-room log cabin, moved to its present site in 1915 from Eagle Point Park, stands on the mansion's grounds.
Details: On the corner of Shiras and Lincoln Aves., below Eagle Point Park. Open May–Oct 10–4:30. $10 family, $3.50 adults, $1.50 children (6–15), free under 6. (1–2 hours)

★ DUBUQUE GREYHOUND PARK & CASINO
1855 Greyhound Park Dr., 800/373-3647 or 319/582-3647, www.dgpc.com
Slot machines, live greyhound racing, and simulcast racing are all available at this track and casino.
Details: Casino open year-round Sun–Thu 9 a.m.–2 a.m., Fri–Sat 24 hours, live greyhound racing May–Oct. (30 minutes–1 hour)

FITNESS AND RECREATION

The 26-mile, all-season **Heritage Trail**, 319/556-6745, stretches from Dyersville to three miles north of Dubuque at Highway 52 and Rupp Hollow Road, next to Heritage Pond. The surface is crushed compacted limestone, and bicyclists and hikers are welcome for a $1.10 daily fee. You can rent a bike at **Banzai Spoke-N-Ski**, Asbury Square, 319/583-6449, or at **The Bike Shack**, 2600 Dodge St., 319/582-4381. The **Mines of Spain Recreation Area**, 8999 Bellevue Heights, 319/556-0620, is 1,380 acres of woods and rugged terrain on Dubuque's southeastern edge. Its unique sights (rock shelters, endangered plant species and wildlife, pristine forests) and many trails are open year-round, with daily hours from 4 a.m. to 10:30 p.m. Watch for bald eagles in the early morning hours.

Bunker Hill Golf Course, 2200 Bunker Hill Rd., 319/589-4261, has 18 holes, while **Dubuque Family Golf & Recreation Center**, 13075 Derby Grange Rd., 319/556-4653, has both an outdoor driving range and mini-golf course.

You don't need good weather to knock down pins at **Riverside Bowl**, 1860 Hawthorne Blvd., 319/583-5768, or to let the good times roll at **Skate Country**, 5630 Saratoga Rd., 319/556-4224.

It's not the Colorado Rockies, but **Sundown Mountain**, 17017 Asbury Rd., 319/556-6676, offers some of Iowa's best skiing, with more than 20 trails cutting through a cedar forest.

FOOD

Tucked among the hills of Davenport and the surrounding country are some great, distinct dining experiences.

Breitbach's Country Dining, 563 Balltown Rd., Balltown, 319/552-2220, offers some of the area's best food, served in a friendly rural atmosphere. Iowa's oldest operating bar and restaurant, this locale has been owned by six generations of the Breitbach family since 1852. It's located just northwest of Dubuque on the scenic Great River Road. The seafood dishes are especially good.

Dubuque Family Restaurant, 2600 Dodge St., 319/557-8800, offers casual country dining within the city limits. It's no Breitbach's, but it's a fine choice.

Located on the same street, **Dottie's Cafe**, 504 Central Ave., 319/556-9617, and **Sfikas Restaurant/Grandma's Pastry**, 401 Central Ave., 319/582-8140, both serve great home-style food. **The Bridge Restaurant & Lounge**, 31 Locust St., 319/557-7280, is another locally owned downtown spot that specializes in casual dining.

Yen Ching, 926 Main St., 319/556-2574, serves up tasty Mandarin food from a large menu. A pair of silent gold lions guards the entrance to the dining room. Lunch is served daily except on Sunday. Boasting the "finest dining by a dam site," the **Tollbridge Inn**, 2800 Rhomberg Ave., 319/556-5566, was built on the original foundation of the Iowa–Wisconsin tollbridge. This three-floored restaurant owned by Mike and Debby Noel overlooks the Mississippi and, of course, a dam. Lunch and dinner are served seven days a week, and a pianist performs in the bar every Friday, Saturday, and Sunday night. The scenic view makes this food stop a sightseeing highlight, too.

The **Moracco**, 1413 Rockdale Rd., 319/582-2947, offers casual dining with a non-Western flair. For good Italian food, dine at **Mario's Italian Restaurant & Lounge**, 1298 Main St., 319/582-0904.

LODGING

For a picturesque view of downtown Dubuque and the Mississippi, the **Julien Inn**, Second and Main Sts., 800/798-7098 or 319/556-4200, is a perfect choice. This 150-year-old hotel features 50 rooms, the German-style Alte Glocke Restaurant, and a charming piano bar. Less fancy but still boasting a fine riverside view, **Hotel Canfield**, 36 W. Fourth St., 319/556-4331, has 60 rooms and reasonable rates. It's also a historic structure, dating back to 1890.

For a more modern stay downtown, **Holiday Inn–Dubuque Five Flags**, 450 Main St., 888/800-3043 or 319/556-200, www.holiday-inn.com/hotels/dbqia/, offers amenity-rich accommodations with prices that still often stay below $100. If you're not charmed by historic buildings, choose this fine hotel.

Self-billed as a "small, elegant hotel," the **Redstone Inn**, 504 Bluff St., 319/582-1894, is a 15-room Victorian mansion catering to the upscale traveler.

ANTIQUES

Dubuque Antique Mall, 401 Locust St., 319/584-2288, is the area's antiques haven. This mall is made up of 64 different showcases that sell everything from cute country crafts to handmade furniture and archaic farm tools. It's handily located between Five Flags Center and Cable Car Square. Open daily 10 to 5.

DUBUQUE

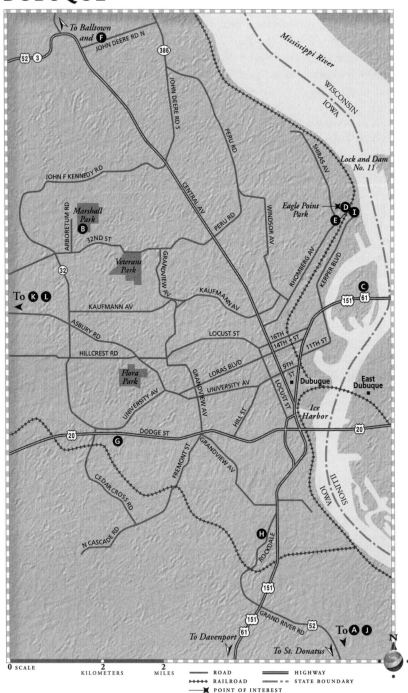

To Balltown and **F**

JOHN DEERE RD N

52 **3**

386

JOHN DEERE RD S

PERU RD

Mississippi River

WISCONSIN

IOWA

SHIRAS AV

Lock and Dam No. 11

JOHN F KENNEDY RD

CENTRAL AV

WINDSOR AV

Eagle Point Park **D** **I**

E

ARBORETUM RD

Marshall Park **B**

32ND ST

RHOMBERG AV

KERPER BLVD

Veterans Park

GRANDVIEW AV

32

C

To **K** **L**

KAUFMANN AV

KAUFMANN AV

151 **61**

ASBURY RD

LOCUST ST

16TH ST

14TH ST

11TH ST

HILLCREST RD

LORAS BLVD

9TH ST

Flora Park

UNIVERSITY AV

UNIVERSITY AV

LOCUST ST

■ Dubuque

East Dubuque ■

HILL ST

Ice Harbor

GRANDVIEW AV

20

DODGE ST

20

G

FREMONT ST

GRANDVIEW AV

ILLINOIS

CEDAR CROSS RD

IOWA

N CASCADE RD

H

ROCKDALE

151

151

GRAND RIVER RD

52

To **A** **J**

151

61

To Davenport

To St. Donatus

N

0 SCALE	2 KILOMETERS	2 MILES

——— ROAD   ═══ HIGHWAY

+++++ RAILROAD   ─ ·· ─ STATE BOUNDARY

✕ POINT OF INTEREST

The marble fireplaces aid relaxation, the fax machines and modem hookups help guests do business (if they must). Afternoon tea and a continental breakfast are included in the rate.

Dubuque boasts more than its share of bed-and-breakfast inns. The **Hancock House**, 1105 Grove Terr., 319/557-8989, is a Queen Anne–style mansion with nine guest rooms and an antique decor. Mississippi River views, whirlpools, and a separate cottage are available. A four-story Victorian mansion with more than 80 stained-glass windows, the **Richards House**, 1492 Locust St., 319/557-1492, has fireplaces and private baths in its rooms. Named for the image of a stringed instrument in a leaded and painted window on the first landing of its grand staircase, the **Mandolin Inn**, 199 Loras Blvd., 319/556-0069, is also known for its dining room with a floor-to-ceiling china cabinet and hand-painted wall scenes. A 1940 Scotch cottage, **Juniper Hill Farm**, 15325 Budd Rd., 800/572-1449 or 319/582-4405, is situated on a 40-acre estate eight miles northwest of downtown Dubuque. The three guest suites all feature private baths and handmade quilts. A year-round outdoor hot tub is also available. Rates for couples range from $75 to $140 per night. Dubuque's only lighthouse is also a bed-and-breakfast inn: **Lighthouse Valleyview**, 15937 Lore Mound Rd., 800/407-7023 or 319/583-7327, features a tri-state view, theme rooms, and gathering areas.

Just 20 minutes southeast of Dubuque on Highway 52 (the Great River Road), **Gehlen House Bed & Breakfast**, 101 N. Main St., St. Donatus, 800/280-1177 or 319/773-8200, calls itself "Little Luxembourg." It was built 150 years ago by Luxembourg immigrant Peter Gehlen and, in the years before becoming a bed-and-breakfast in 1996, served as a post office, tavern, and doll museum.

CAMPING

Camping facilities in the area include the **Dubuque Yacht Basin RV Park**, 1630 E. 16th St., 319/556-7708, with 12 acres that include hiking and biking

SIGHTS
- Ⓐ Crystal Lake Cave
- Ⓑ Dubuque Arboretum and Botanical Gardens
- Ⓒ Dubuque Greyhound Park & Casino
- Ⓓ Eagle Point Park
- Ⓔ Mathias Ham House

FOOD
- Ⓕ Breitbach's Country Dining
- Ⓖ Dubuque Family Restaurant
- Ⓗ The Moracco
- Ⓘ Tollbridge Inn

LODGING
- Ⓙ Gehlen House Bed & Breakfast
- Ⓚ Juniper Hill Farm
- Ⓛ Lighthouse Valleyview

DYERSVILLE

These tractors plow imaginary fields, but what they yield is as important as crops—fun and learning. Confused? We're talking about toy tractors. Known as the "Farm Toy Capital of the World," **Dyersville** is a small town with not only lots of toy tractors but more attractions than you'd expect given its size.

Toy-wise, the **National Farm Toy Museum**, 1110 16th Ave. SE, 319/875-2727, www.rcww.com/dyersville is ground zero. Its mission to display "The History of Agriculture Through Toys," the museum chronicles the life of Ertl Company founder Fred Ertl Sr., showcases an original assembly line once used to manufacture farm toys, and offers lots of "Li'l Farmer Play Areas" to occupy restless children. The world headquarters of the **Ertl Company**, Hwys. 136 and 20, 800/553-4886 or 319/875-5699, www.ertltoys.com, has a welcome center with exhibits. Call ahead to schedule a tour. Also visit the well-stocked **Ertl Toys Outlet Store**, located just half a mile north of the headquarters on Highway 136.

Dyersville's other major attraction, of course, is the **Field of Dreams Movie Site**, 28963 Lansing Rd., 888/875-8404, www.field-ofdreamsmoviesite.com. Thanks to Kevin Costner's 1989 baseball-worshipping film (based on the book Shoeless Joe by Iowa writer W. P. Kinsella), this rural Dyersville farm that provided the setting still inspires people to ask the question, "Is this heaven?" (Answer: "No, it's Iowa.")

There are still more attractions in this town. **Plaza Antique Mall**, Hwys. 20 and 136, 319/875-8945, features more than two hundred dealers hawking their wares in a 22,500-square-foot mall. **St. Francis Xavier Basilica**, 104 Third St. SW, 319/875-7325, is a Gothic church dating back more than a century. **Dyer/Botsford Doll Museum**, 331 First Ave., 319/875-2414, is the historic Victorian home of Dyersville's founder. It houses German Christmas decorations and more than nine hundred dolls.

For dining in Dyersville, try **Country Junction**, 913 15th Ave. SE, 319/875-7055, which offers down-home cooking, including a great breakfast. **Dyersville Family Restaurant**, 226 First Ave. E., 319/875-7110, is open from 5:30 a.m. for breakfast until 2 p.m.

Near Dyersville is **New Wine Township Park**, 16001 New Wine Park Ln., New Vienna, 319/921-3475 or 319/556-6745, with 167 acres' worth of primitive and modern campsites.

trails, modern campsites, and a trailer dump station. **Mud Lake Park**, 11000 Golf Lake Rd., 319/552-2746, has similar features but is larger, with 20 acres. **Swiss Valley Campground**, 13768 Swiss Valley Rd., 319/556-6745, is by far the largest Dubuque campground, with 60 acres; the campgrounds also have good cross-country skiing trails.

NIGHTLIFE

Dubuque Brewing Brew Pub, 500 E. Fourth St., 319/583-1218, serves up distinct flavors of locally produced beer. A charming corner bar is the **Grand Tap**, 802 Central Ave., 319/556-9537.

The **Spirit of Dubuque** riverboat offers sightseeing and dinner cruises in season, launching from the Ice Harbor. Call 800/747-8093 or 319/583-8093, or visit www.spiritofdubuque.com. Cruises run from May through October, with private charters available. For an evening's worth of entertainment on land, you might want to try a **Victorian House Tour & Progressive Dinner**. Call the Dubuque Guide Service at 800/226-3369 or 319/557-9545.

Taxi service is available by calling 319/582-1818 or 319/580-8005.

14
THE QUAD CITIES

If four cities wrapped into one is at times confusing for the tourist, the result-ing abundance of attractions more than makes up for it. The "Quad" refers to Davenport and Bettendorf in Iowa and Rock Island and Moline in Illinois. The Mississippi River splits the Quad Cities into Iowa and Illinois halves, and Interstates 80, 88, and 74 intersect here. The halfway point between Des Moines and Chicago, the Quad Cities are also within reasonable reach of other major Midwestern cities, such as St. Louis, Minneapolis, and Milwaukee.

This river area offers plenty to the traveler, as do the smaller suburban communities in the vicinity, like LeClaire in Iowa and Hampton, Silvis, East Moline, and Milan in Illinois. In the middle of the Mississippi is Arsenal Island, a U.S. Army factory since 1862, which now hosts tours and houses a museum.

The town of Bettendorf was named after the Bettendorf Axle & Wagon Company, which opened up shop in 1903. Davenport's Village of East Davenport, with 60 square blocks, is the state's largest historic district. Belgians founded Moline, which, as the home of the John Deere company (manufacturer of those green and yellow tractors), bills itself as the "Farm Implement Capital of America." Rock Island was once home to the Sauk and Fox Indian tribes.

The Quad Cities' riverfront area—all 65 miles of it—is the heart and soul of the area, and the rise of riverboat casinos in the '90s has led to a general eco-nomic resurgence along the waterfront. The shops and restaurants, riverside views, and other diversions on both sides of the Mississippi give the Quad Cities a distinct flavor that other communities in Iowa and Nebraska can't match.

A PERFECT DAY IN THE QUAD CITIES

Start your morning on the Illinois side of the Mississippi, at the John Deere Pavilion in Moline. The intriguing history of this company is representative of the region's rich agricultural past.

Back on the Iowa side, the Davenport Museum of Art is an essential stop, its exhibits worth at least an hour or two. Next head to downtown Davenport and the Village of East Davenport for lunch and an afternoon stroll. Front Street Brewery serves up fine fare.

At night, you'll find plenty of diversions at the downtown riverfront area in Davenport or in the District on Rock Island—the Rock Island Brewing Co. is highly recommended for its fresh-brewed beer and dynamite line-up of live bands.

SIGHTSEEING HIGHLIGHTS

★★★ DAVENPORT MUSEUM OF ART
1737 W. 12th St., Davenport, 319/326-7804
One of the oldest public art museums in the Iowa–Illinois region, the DMA opened in 1925 and holds more than 3,500 works within seven different collections: American art from the Colonial period to 1945; regional art by artists such as Grant Wood; European art from the fifteenth through nineteenth centuries; Mexican Colonial painting from the sixteenth through eighteenth centuries; Haitian art since 1940; Asian art from the eighteenth and nineteenth centuries; and art since 1945. There's also a Children's Center and Museum Shop.

> **Details:** *Open year-round Tue, Wed, Fri, and Sat 10–4:30, Thu 10–8, Sun 1–4:30. Donations encouraged. (1–2 hours)*

★★★ JOHN DEERE PAVILION
**1400 River Dr., The Commons, Moline, 309/765-1000
or 309/765-1005**
This modern, 14,000-square-foot exhibition hall focuses, of course, on the history of the green and yellow tractors and farm implements that have helped define agriculture throughout the nineteenth and

THE QUAD CITIES

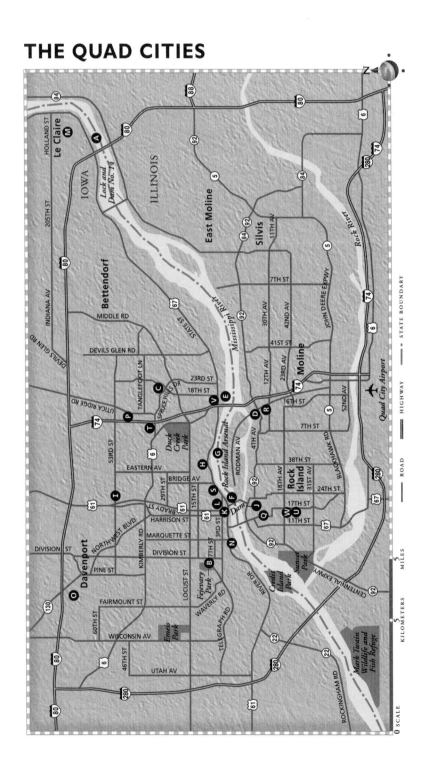

twentieth centuries. Vermont native and blacksmith John Deere launched the company in 1838, settling next to the Mississippi in order to use water power to help manufacture his first, primitive plows, which nonetheless possessed a unique, effective blade. Antique Deere tractors (nicknamed "poppers" for the distinct sound of their engines) and examples of the latest Deere farming technology are on display. The Pavilion also broadly traces the entire history of American agriculture. A John Deere Store is next door, peddling all kinds of green and yellow merchandise.

Details: *Open year-round Mon–Fri 9–6, Sat 9–5, Sun 12:30–5. Free. (1–2 hours)*

★★★ PUTNAM MUSEUM OF HISTORY & NATURAL SCIENCE
1717 W. 12th St., Davenport, 319/324-1933
Next door to the Davenport Museum of Art, Putnam features exhibits with themes ranging from the nearby Mississippi to the distant Nile. "River, Prairie and People" is an exploration of local history since the days when Native American settlements dominated the area. A mummy is on display in the Asian/Egyptian Gallery. With the Hall of Mammals, the Discovery Room, and

SIGHTS
- **Ⓐ** Buffalo Bill Cody Museum
- **Ⓑ** Davenport Museum of Art
- **Ⓒ** The Family Museum of Arts and Science
- **Ⓓ** John Deere Pavilion
- **Ⓔ** Lady Luck Casino
- **Ⓕ** President Riverboat Casino
- **Ⓑ** Putnam Museum of History & Natural Science
- **Ⓖ** Rock Island Arsenal Museum
- **Ⓗ** Village of East Davenport

FOOD
- **Ⓘ** Baba's
- **Ⓙ** Blue Cat Brew Pub
- **Ⓚ** Downstairs Family Dining
- **Ⓛ** Duck City Delicatessen & Bistro
- **Ⓜ** Francescon's
- **Ⓝ** Freight House Bistro
- **Ⓕ** Front Street Brewery
- **Ⓞ** Iowa Machine Shed
- **Ⓟ** Jumer's Restaurant
- **Ⓠ** Rexie's Gourmet House
- **Ⓡ** Sydney's Authentic Australian Pub Bar & Restaurant
- **Ⓝ** Upstairs Bistro

LODGING
- **Ⓢ** Fulton's Landing Guest House
- **Ⓣ** Hampton Inn– Davenport
- **Ⓟ** Jumer's Castle Lodge
- **Ⓔ** Lady Luck Casino Hotel
- **Ⓓ** Radisson on John Deere Commons
- **Ⓚ** Radisson Quad City Plaza
- **Ⓤ** Top O' the Morning Bed & Breakfast
- **Ⓥ** Twin Bridges Motor Inn
- **Ⓦ** Varner's Caboose Bed & Breakfast

Note: Items with the same letter are located in the same area.

Grandpa's Garage, Putnam holds a diverse range of permanent and temporary art exhibits.

Details: *Open year-round Tue–Fri 9–5, Sat 10–5, Sun noon–5. $4 adults, $3 seniors, $2 ages 5–17, free to under age 5. (1–2 hours)*

★★ BUFFALO BILL CODY MUSEUM
200 N. River Dr., LeClaire, 319/289-5580

The last-ever operating steam-powered tugboat on the Mississippi, the *Lone Star*, is docked next to this museum. You can enter and explore the vessel. In addition to steamboat history, the museum pays tribute to the life of William F. "Buffalo Bill" Cody.

Details: *Open May 15–Oct 15 daily 9–5; Oct 16–May 14 weekends 9–5. $2 adults, 50 cents children 6–15, free under 6. (1–2 hours)*

★★ THE FAMILY MUSEUM OF ARTS AND SCIENCE
2900 Learning Campus Dr. at 18th St., Bettendorf, 319/344-4106

Here's the one place on earth where you don't have to be afraid of a tornado—you can even touch one. Also learn about the human body (by walking in and around larger-than-life exhibits that represent the body), animal habitats, and weather. It's a museum for the whole family.

Details: *Open year-round Mon noon–8, Tue–Fri 9–8, Sat 9–5, Sun noon–5. $3 adults, $2 seniors, free under 3. (1–2 hours)*

★★ ROCK ISLAND ARSENAL MUSEUM
Bldg. 60, Rock Island Arsenal, 309/782-5021

This military museum traces the history of the munitions-manufacturing island. Built in 1816, Fort Armstrong was the first structure on Rock Island, and today the Fort Armstrong Blockhouse stands near the original site. The Col. Davenport House, the one-time home of Davenport's founder, is the oldest house in the Quad Cities. A national cemetery is also open to the public. The largest collection of military small firearms, including more than 1,300 pistols, is displayed in the museum itself. There's also a scale model of Fort Armstrong, plus military uniforms and equipment.

Details: *Open year-round daily 10–4. Free. (30 minutes–1 hour)*

★★ VILLAGE OF EAST DAVENPORT
River Dr. and Mound St., Davenport, 319/322-0546

For more than 150 years, this 120-acre historic district has encompassed six square blocks of establishments that today are restaurants and various specialty stores. Even if you don't want to shop, it's pleasant to stroll the charming, hilly neighborhood. Among the noteworthy shops is **Isabel Bloom Handcrafted Sculpture**, 1109 Mound St., 319/333-2040, which sells the work of the revered local artist who has earned a national reputation for her sculptures of people and animals.

Details: Open year-round. Individual business hours vary. Free. (1–3 hours)

★ LADY LUCK CASINO
1821 State St. Landing, Bettendorf, 800/724-5825 or 319/359-7280
More than eight hundred slot machines and nearly fifty table gambling options draw a steady crowd of luck-seekers to this casino. Buffet meals (plus the 70-item Curtain Call Cafe) and live entertainment in a 250-seat theater are also available.

Details: Open year-round daily 24 hours. Free. (15 minutes–1 hour)

★ PRESIDENT RIVERBOAT CASINO
212 Brady St., Davenport, 800/262-8711 or 319/328-6000
Open around the clock, the President is an authentic, historic riverboat that occasionally cruises the Mississippi while its customers wager. It's a historic landmark whose opening in 1991 helped spur the economic resurgence of the downtown Davenport area. Nearly eight hundred slot machines and fifty table games are on board.

Details: Open year-round daily 24 hours. Free. (15 minitues–1 hour)

FITNESS AND RECREATION
The Quad Cities boast nearly fifty miles of biking and hiking trails. The **Great River Trail** in Iowa begins at Credit Island in west Davenport and runs 6.5 miles with the Mississippi in sight. On the Illinois side of the Quad Cities, the Great River Trail stretches for 10 miles along the river, starting in Rock Island. This segment will eventually join a 60-mile trail that will lead all the way north to Palisades State Park near Savanna, Illinois.

EMPIRE in Mississippi Park, on the river shoreline on the East Moline/Hampton border, 309/752-1573, stands for East Moline Playground

Innovation Recreation Efforts. The 14,000-square-foot area features wooden structures, picnic shelters, a boat launch, and a bike path. **Hampton Park and Puttin' A Round**, 309/755-1212, next door, offers mini-golf, water games, and more.

With a name like "**Queen of Hearts**," you might think that this 400-passenger steamboat docked in Moline, Illinois, is a floating poker palace. In reality, the boat offers "non-gaming" cruises, including daily lunch and dinner cruises spring through fall. Some trips travel north to Galena, Illinois. Tuesday Family Fun Night features the live entertainment of comedians and magicians. The steamboat, located at 2501 River Dr., 800/297-0034 or 309/764-1951, is operated by Celebration River Cruises.

Connecting Moline, Bettendorf, and Davenport via the river, the **Channel Cat Water Taxi**, Moline, 309/788-3360 or 319/322-2969, is a 49-passenger water bus that takes regular hour-long loops on the Mississippi. An adult all-day pass costs just $3.50, and bicyclers are welcome. It runs from Memorial Day through Labor Day, Tuesday through Sunday, and on weekends in May and September.

Take to the air with **Scenic Seaplane Tours**, 3205 S. Shore Dr., Moline, 800/678-9747 or 309/799-3251. View the Quad Cities from above for around $15 per person.

FOOD

Riverside dining is naturally a recurring theme among the Quad Cities' restaurants, as is down-home, Midwestern food. There are plenty of worthy brew pubs and bistros, too.

The **Iowa Machine Shed**, I-80 and Northwest Blvd., Davenport, 319/391-2427, was the very first in the state's mini-chain of hearty family-style restaurants. For a change of pace, try **Baba's**, 2303 E. 53rd St., Davenport, 319/355-5929, offering a great range of Mediterranean food for lunch and dinner.

Front Street Brewery, 208 E. River Dr., Davenport, 319/322-1569, serves both fine English pub food and its own selection of homemade brews. Not far down the street, **Duck City Delicatessen & Bistro**, 115 E. Third St., Davenport, 319/322-3825, is open for lunch and dinner and offers slightly more exotic dishes like duck (of course), lamb, Thai chicken, and sushi.

Even closer to the river and steeped in river history, **Freight House Bistro**, 421 W. River Dr., Davenport, 319/324-4425, has it all: a view of the mighty Mississippi, a relaxed atmosphere, and great steak, seafood, and pasta.

A pair of restaurants gives you twice the choice. **Downstairs Family Dining**, 421 W. River Dr., Davenport, 319/324-4425, specializes in pizza, pasta, and outdoor seating on a wooden deck in warm weather. Next door, **Upstairs Bistro**, 421 W. River Dr., Davenport, 319/324-4425, features an Italian-themed menu, casual atmosphere, and a river view.

Jumer's Restaurant, Spruce Hill Dr. and Utica Ridge Rd., Bettendorf, 319/359-1607, bakes its bread daily, specializes in a Sunday brunch, and features the Library and Schwarzer Bar lounges that present live entertainment every night except Sunday.

Fine dining on the river is available at **Francescon's**, 627 N. Cody Rd., LeClaire, Iowa, 319/289-4721, which serves international cuisine and even has a 160-foot dock for those who wish to arrive by boat.

Didn't think you'd find the taste of the outback in the Quad Cities? Think again. The menu at **Sydney's Authentic Australian Pub Bar & Restaurant**, 425 15th St., Moline, 309/736-2252, features emu, kangaroo, and alligator, plus Aussie beers (such as Foster's) and wines.

Blue Cat Brew Pub, 113 18th St., Rock Island, 309/788-8247, has a selection of six hand-crafted beers, full lunch and dinner menus, and a second-floor pool hall. Blues bands play here on weekends, too.

Offering not only fine dining but also live entertainment on weekends, **Rexie's Gourmet House**, 623 17th St., Rock Island, 309/794-0244, is open for dinner Tuesday through Sunday.

LODGING

Hampton Inn–Davenport, 5202 Brady St., Davenport, 800/426-7866 or 319/359-3921, has reliable, clean accommodations and is conveniently located along I-74. Hampton Inns, as a rule, are among the more reliable mid-priced hotel chains.

Radisson Quad City Plaza, 111 E. Second St., Davenport, 319/322-2200, is a slightly upscale choice for businesspeople, budget-free travelers, and large groups. There's also a **Radisson on John Deere Commons**, 1415 River Dr., Moline, 800/333-3333 or 309/764-1000, which is newer, has a view of the Mississippi, and operates a T.G.I. Friday's restaurant and lounge on its ground floor.

Located next door to Lady Luck Casino, **Twin Bridges Motor Inn**, 221 15th St., Bettendorf, 319/355-6451, is an economical choice, with its own restaurant and lounge. **Lady Luck Casino Hotel**, 1777 Lady Luck Pkwy., Bettendorf, 800/724-5825 or 319/359-7280, was opened in late 1998 and boasts 259 rooms and an impressive laundry list of amenities.

For a truly distinctive night or two spent in the Quad Cities, it's tough to beat **Jumer's Castle Lodge**, 900 Spruce Hills Dr., Bettendorf, 800/285-6637 or 319/359-7141, where lodgers can seriously feel as if they're staying in an English castle. The dark woodwork and fireplace of the lobby exude coziness.

There are also delightful bed-and-breakfast lodgings in the Quad Cities area. **Fulton's Landing Guest House**, 1206 E. River Dr., Davenport, 319/322-4069, has five rooms for rent plus available space for meetings. **Varner's Caboose Bed & Breakfast**, 702 20th St., Rock Island, 309/788-7068, rents only one suite, but it's notable for allowing pets.

A larger bed-and-breakfast, with six rooms (not to mention a cheerful name), is **Top O' the Morning Bed & Breakfast**, 1505 19th Ave., Rock Island, 309/786-3513. It also has meeting rooms.

CAMPING

Interstate RV Park, 8448 Fairmount St., Davenport, 319/386-7292, has 28 electric campsites and 136 non-electric kinds—82 with water and 54 with sewer hookups. Volleyball and horseshoe courts and a recreation room are also on hand.

Buffalo Shores Recreation Area, Route 22 near Buffalo, Iowa, 319/381-2900, offers camping along the Mississippi River.

On the other side of the river, **Camelot Campground**, near Milan, Illinois, on Hwy. 92, 309/787-0665, has 123 campsites plus fishing, boating, baseball cages, basketball courts, and a video arcade.

NIGHTLIFE

The cities come alive for events like the Bix Run or the Mississippi Valley Blues Fest, but you'll find plenty of nightlife year-round. Casinos, cozy corner pubs, and other establishments ensure you'll enjoy your evenings as well as your days in the Quad Cities.

If live music or other entertainment is featured at **Col Ballroom**, 1012 W. Fourth St., Davenport, 319/322-4431, you'll most likely enjoy a well-spent evening in this charming, airy and historic venue.

Fox & Hound English Pub & Grille, 2144 W. Kimberly Rd., Davenport, 319/391-8722, serves up more than one hundred different beers from around the globe, is proud of its music selection, has 14 pool tables, offers both cork and electronic dartboards, features 33 TVs, and serves appetizers plus meat and pasta entrées. Do you need anything else?

America's Pub, 421 W. River Dr., Davenport, 319/322-0070, is a nightclub featuring dance music; a grill; and, often, live music.

Broadcasting live thoroughbred and harness racing daily, **Quad Cities Betting Parlor Sports Bar**, Rts. 5 and 92, East Moline, 309/792-0202, features races from 30 states and Canada.

Serving dinner and staging live entertainment, **Circa '21**, 1828 Third Ave., Rock Island, 309/786-7733, bills itself as a 1920s vaudeville house. **Rock Island Brewing Co.**, 1815 Second Ave., Rock Island, 309/793-1999, www.ribco.com, otherwise known as RIBCO, is reliable for both its drink specials and calendar of live bands.

15
BURLINGTON

Burlington was the first-ever capital of the Iowa Territory, in 1838, and so for a time this southeast region was the center of the Iowa universe. Before that, in 1837 and part of 1838, it was the capital of the Wisconsin Territory. Prior to that, in 1805, a man with the unique name of Zebulon Pike chose the area for a government fort. In 1833, the first settled community was established, named Flint Hills after the rich flint deposits found there.

When Flint Hills was renamed Burlington in 1834, it was to honor another, earlier city, Burlington, Vermont. The Mississippi and rail lines connected the town with surrounding communities, and Burlington today still touts its proximity to regional cities like Chicago and St. Louis.

Burlington still takes pride in its historic German and Irish neighborhoods and homes, unique curiosities like Snake Alley—the "Crookedest Street in the World"—and the scenic beauty of the rolling hills along the Mississippi River.

Southeastern Iowa in general is steeped in agricultural heritage, and its past is preserved in the region's architecture and transportation arteries that form so much of its character.

A PERFECT DAY IN BURLINGTON

Eat breakfast in downtown Burlington, then stroll the morning away in the Heritage Hill Historic District. Traverse the winding path of Snake Alley, and stop in at the Phelps Museum at the top of the hill. Smith's Cave Park & Preserve makes for a relaxing afternoon amid nature. Or stop by Crapo and Dankwardt Parks, just two miles south of Main Street; despite their odd names, both feature pleasing settings near the Mississippi River. Finish your perfect day with an evening of live music at the Blue Shop.

BURLINGTON SIGHTSEEING HIGHLIGHTS

★★★ HERITAGE HILL NATIONAL HISTORIC DISTRICT
Downtown Burlington, 319/752-0015
At downtown's north end, 29 square blocks encompass beautiful, majestic nineteenth- and twentieth-century homes of several styles—Victorian, Queen Anne, and Italian Villa. The Welcome Center, 400 Front St., dispenses brochures that detail a walking tour and an audiotape that guides you through Heritage Hill, among its homes.
Details: Open year-round daily. Free. (1–3 hours)

★★★ PHELPS HOUSE MUSEUM
512 Columbia St., 319/753-2449
Perched at the top of Snake Alley, Phelps House Museum is a Victorian home with eighteenth-century furnishings and a special "Medical Memories" exhibit that recalls the period when, from 1894 to 1899, the site contained the town's first Protestant hospital. William Garrett built the original part of the house in 1851 and in 1870 expanded it, doubling the size with a mansard roof and Italianate tower. (Incidentally, Garrett's father, David Rorer, coined the "Hawkeye" nickname to describe Iowans, now also the name of the University of Iowa mascot.) In 1974 Charles Phelps donated the house to the Des Moines County Historical Society.
Details: Open May–Oct Sat–Sun 1:30–4:30. $2 general admission. (1 hour)

★★ THE APPLE TREES MUSEUM
1616 Dill St., 319/753-2449
So named in recognition of the orchard that grew in nearby Perkins Park, this 1867 mansion has 39 rooms, including an ornate parlor. The Des Moines County Historical Society's collection is here, with Burlington-themed exhibits like Victorian furnishings, art glass, tools,

BURLINGTON

N

Gulfport ■

Mississippi River

ILLINOIS
IOWA

Mosquito Park ★

BLUFF RD

9TH ST
NORTH ST
CENTRAL AV
ARCH ST
COURT ST
8TH ST
7TH ST
6TH ST
4TH ST
SPRING ST
COLUMBIA ST
FRONT ST

T
F
C H
I
K
L
D
N O
M

MAIN ST
LOCUST ST
SOUTH ST
6TH ST
ANGULAR ST
MADISON RD
CENTRAL AV
MAPLE ST
9TH ST
13TH ST

To R

OSBORN ST
CORSE ST

JEFFERSON ST
MARKET ST
DIVISION ST
SUMMER ST
WEST AV
DILL ST
Perkins Park
B

GARFIELD AV
GARFIELD AV

STARR AV

PLANE ST
SPRAY ST
WEST AV
HAGEMANN AV

S

CURRAN ST
VALLEY ST
SHIELDS ST
FLINT HILLS DR

KIRKWOOD ST

P

COTTONWOOD
WINEGARD DR
Q

AGENCY ST

DIVISION ST

U

61

ROOSEVELT AV

W BURLINGTON AV

MT PLEASANT ST
GLASCOW ST
West Burlington ■

BROADWAY

34

Inset map (Burlington Region)

BURLINGTON REGION

Sperry
99
Gulfport G
15
Gladstone
96
Burlington
Danville T
61
16
Mt. Pleasant
34
W. Burlington
79
Geode State Park
Mississippi River
218
Donnellson
61
Fort Madison E
ILLINOIS

Fairfield
1
IOWA
16
Ottumwa A
34
Eldon
16
Bloomfield
2
Milton
15
MISSOURI
2
1
63

Legend

— STATE BOUNDARY
--- HIGHWAY
— ROAD
★ POINT OF INTEREST

0 SCALE
MILE
KILOMETER
1

antique dolls, and Native American artifacts. Original resident Charles E. Perkins was the president of the C, B&Q Railroad.

Details: Open May–Oct Wed and Sun 1:30–4:30. Free. (1 hour)

★★ LOCK AND DAM #18
Lock and Dam Rd., 309/873-2246

Built for a $9 million price tag in the 1930s, this is one of 29 such structures on the upper Mississippi River. Watch as barges move up and down the river, passing through the 600 feet of this lock and dam. In the winter this is also an ideal location from which to spot bald eagles migrating south, catching fish in the water around the dam.

Details: Four miles east of the Great River Bridge on Hwy. 34, then 4.5 miles north on Lock and Dam Rd. Open year-round daily. Free. (30 minutes–2 hours)

★★ SNAKE ALLEY
Between Washington and Columbia Sts., 800/82-RIVER

Ripley's Believe It or Not! labeled this famous stretch of Burlington street the "Crookedest Street in the World," and it's easy to see why. Snake Alley snakes 275 feet up—or down, depending on your

---

SIGHTS

- ⓐ American Gothic House
- ⓑ The Apple Trees Museum
- ⓒ Arts for Living Center
- ⓓ Catfish Bend River Casino II
- ⓔ Fort Madison Farmington & Western Railroad Rides & Museum
- ⓕ Heritage Hill National Historic District
- ⓖ Lock and Dam #18
- ⓗ Phelps House Museum
- ⓓ Port of Burlington Welcome Center

SIGHTS (continued)

- ⓘ The Secret Garden
- ⓙ Snake Alley
- ⓚ West Jefferson Street National Historic District

FOOD

- ⓛ Bakery Haus
- ⓜ Big Muddy's
- ⓝ Diggers Rest Coffeehouse
- ⓝ Jefferson Street Cafe
- ⓞ Salvador's

LODGING

- ⓟ Arrowhead Motel
- ⓠ Best Western PZAZZ!

LODGING (continued)

- ⓡ Lakeview Bed & Breakfast
- ⓢ Lincolnville Motel
- ⓣ Mississippi Manor Guest Inn
- ⓤ Ramada Inn
- ⓥ The Schramm House Bed & Breakfast

Note: Items with the same letter are located in the same area.

---

perspective—the side of a hill, turning five half-curves and two quarter-curves as it connects Columbia Street with Washington Street. The elevation from the top to the bottom of the hill is a 58-foot difference; the steepness inspired an architect, city engineer, and paving contractor to devise and construct the winding path in 1894.

Details: *Open year-round daily. Free. (15 minutes)*

★★ WEST JEFFERSON STREET NATIONAL HISTORIC DISTRICT
400–800 W. Jefferson St., 319/752-6365

Not as extensive as Heritage Hill, West Jefferson is a collection of 49 main buildings, mostly two- and three-story brick, which represent the look of the town's Main Street in Civil War days.

Details: *Open year-round daily. Free. (1 hour)*

★ ARTS FOR LIVING CENTER
Seventh and Washington Sts., 319/754-8069

Housed in a one-time German Methodist Episcopal Church, the center's gallery features a rotating schedule of exhibits of everything from student art to wood-fired pottery to prints and drawings. Group tours can be arranged, and there's a gift shop.

Details: *Open year-round Tue–Fri noon–5, Sat–Sun 1–4. Free. (1 hour)*

★ PORT OF BURLINGTON WELCOME CENTER
400 N. Front St., 319/752-8731

This 1928 building, once the Burlington Municipal Docks, now offers all kinds of information on the region and provides self-guided audiotape tours ($2 each) of the North and South Hill neighborhoods.

Details: *Open year-round daily 9–6. Free. (15 minutes)*

★ CATFISH BEND RIVER CASINO II
Port of Burlington, 800/372-2WIN

A 1,300-passenger steamboat with gaming, entertainment, and dining for as many as 400, Catfish Bend has slots, video poker, blackjack, Caribbean stud poker, craps, and roulette.

Details: *Open Nov–Apr in Burlington; May–Oct in Fort Madison (20 minutes south of Burlington). Free. (15 minutes–2 hours)*

OTHER SIGHTSEEING HIGHLIGHTS

★★★ FORT MADISON FARMINGTON & WESTERN RAILROAD RIDES & MUSEUM
Off Hwy. 2 between Fort Madison and Donnellson at 2208 220th St., 319/837-6689

Why simply learn about the old railroad days when you can relive them? This is an early 1900s railroad village, where you can even take a two-mile train ride in antique cars pulled by an authentic locomotive. A general store, print shop, and other historical buildings are on-site. Wilson Lake Park is next door. Horse-drawn wagon rides also available.

Details: Open Memorial Day weekend–Oct Sat–Sun noon–5; First three weekends in December include special "Santa Train" rides Sat–Sun noon–5; $6 adults; $5 ages 5–18; $1 under 5. (Ride and museum included in same price.) Train rides last 40 minutes and depart on the hour. (1–2 hours)

★ THE SECRET GARDEN
10182 Danville Rd., Danville, 319/392-8288

This is a large 1846 Sesquicentennial Farm (celebrating 150 years of Iowa's statehood) that features theme gardens, flowers in fields, barns, and a gift shop. Acres and acres of flowers are on display.

Details: Open Apr–Oct Tue–Sat noon–4; Nov–Dec Thu–Sat 9–5. Free. (1–2 hours)

★ AMERICAN GOTHIC HOUSE
American Gothic St., Eldon, 515/281-7650

One of the world's most recognized paintings is Grant Wood's *American Gothic*, the portrait of a serious-looking man and woman, the former grasping a pitchfork. The house in the background of the painting still stands today in the small town of Eldon, and the State Historical Society of Iowa has restored the exterior to its 1930s appearance. (The interior is closed to the public.)

Details: May only be viewed from the street. (15 minutes)

FITNESS AND RECREATION

Near rolling hills and the Mississippi River, the Burlington area offers a wide range of great outdoor options.

Despite their names, **Crapo** and **Dankwardt Parks**, two miles south of downtown on Main Street, Burlington, 319/753-8117, together form a century-old nature area of 100 acres along the west bank of the Mississippi that features beaches, many varieties of trees, and camping facilities.

For more structured outdoor activity, **Little Putt Miniature Golf**, 1228 N. Roosevelt Ave., Burlington, 319/754-7858, is a fine place to tee off on the green without having to drive the range.

More adventurous types should head to **Starr's Cave Park & Preserve**, just north of Burlington on Irish Ridge Rd., 319/753-5808. It's a 142-acre preserve with beautiful woodlands, cross-country skiing trails, a nature center with hands-on exhibits, Flint Creek, and, of course, Starr's Cave. The entire park is open daily from 6 a.m. to 10:30 p.m., while the nature center is open Sundays 2 to 5 or by appointment.

Burlington Free Public Library, 501 N. Fourth St., 319/753-1647, opened in 1898 and is Iowa's oldest public library. It also houses an art collection. The library is open daily from 9 to 5.

Down-home family fun is the specialty at **Grandpa Bill's Farm & 7 Ponds Park**, 13 miles north of Burlington off Hwy. 61, Sperry, 319/985-2262 or 319/985-2106, a century-old farmstead that now offers hayrack rides, mazes, a petting zoo, and Grandma Hazel's restaurant; admission costs $2. Next door, 7 Ponds Park has waterslides, a lake, fishing, and more; admission is $2.25.

FOOD

For those with light appetites and a need for a caffeine fix, **Diggers Rest Coffeehouse**, 314 Jefferson St., Burlington, 319/758-6067, serves not only java drinks but soups, sandwiches, and pastries. Internet access is available here, too.

For early risers who love all good things made with grains that rise, stop at **Bakery Haus**, 611 Jefferson St., Burlington, 319/752-2136, which opens at 7 a.m. Tuesday through Saturday.

Jefferson Street Cafe, 300 Jefferson St., Burlington, 319/754-1036, is open Monday through Saturday for lunch and dinner and features both casual and fine dining. Steaks, seafood, and pasta round out the menu.

Billed as "Burlington's only riverfront restaurant," **Big Muddy's**, 710 N. Front St., Burlington, 319/753-1699, is open for lunch and dinner six days a week, plus Sunday brunch. It's housed in a remodeled 1898 railroad freight house, which makes for a great rustic dining atmosphere.

For Mexican food try **Salvador's**, 210 N. Main St., Burlington, 319/754-5600, which also serves steaks, American cuisine, and, of course, margaritas—happy hour is daily from 4 p.m. to 7 p.m. There's also a supper buffet.

LODGING

Featuring an attention-grabbing if slightly goofy name, **Best Western PZAZZ!**, 3001 Winegard Dr., Burlington, 800/373-1223 or 319/753-2223, has 151 rooms, an indoor pool, and a sauna. Children under 19 stay free with their family.

Burlington's other large hotel is the **Ramada Inn**, 2759 Mt. Pleasant St., Burlington, 800/2-RAMADA or 319/754-5781, which has 169 rooms, a lounge, an indoor pool, and even its own mini-golf course.

There are also less expensive lodgings that offer a fine night's stay. **Lincolnville Motel**, 1701 Mt. Pleasant St., Burlington, 319/752-2748, has 33 rooms. **Arrowhead Motel**, 2520 Mt. Pleasant St., Burlington, 800/341-8000 or 319/752-6353, has 30 rooms. If you don't require myriad amenities, stay at one of these places.

The Schramm House Bed & Breakfast, 616 Columbus St., Burlington, 319/752-6353 or 319/754-0373, visit.schramm.com, run by Sandy and Bruce Morrison, occupies a large 1860 home at the top of Heritage Hill. The famous Snake Alley is just one block east, while the Mississippi is barely six blocks away. There are four fireplaces, two outdoor porches, and a study all available to guests. Each of the four guest rooms sports a different theme—the Brick and Tin Room, for instance, features a distinctive ceiling and walls. For memorable lodging to accompany your sightseeing, stay here.

Mississippi Manor Guest Inn, 809 N. Fourth St., Burlington, 319/753-2218, offers banquet facilities as well as five rooms. **Lakeview Bed & Breakfast**, 11351 60th St., Burlington, 800/753-8735 or 319/752-8735, is the third of the city's three main bed-and-breakfasts. Lakeview has four ready rooms.

CAMPING

Named after the beautifully sparkling rocks, **Geode State Park**, 12 miles west of Burlington on Hwy. 34, 319/392-4601, is a 1,640-acre park with 96 electric and 90 primitive campsites. Other features include a trailer dump station, rest rooms, and hiking trails.

A smaller park, the 47-acre **Lower Augusta Skunk River Access**, 6.5 miles south of Burlington and three miles west off Hwy. 61, 319/753-8260, has 20 electric and 27 primitive campsites, plus a trailer dump station, horse-shoe courts, and picnic areas.

Big Hollow Creek Recreation Area, eight miles north of Burlington and three miles west off Hwy. 61, 319/753-8260, has just eight primitive campsites but features handicapped access and an observatory.

NIGHTLIFE

34 Raceways, W. Hwy. 34, West Burlington, 319/753-5858, hosts races of IMCA late models, 360 Limited Sprint Cars, Modifieds, Hobby Stocks, and Thundercars every Saturday night from March through September. The track seats more than three thousand fans.

A great venue to blues bands and artists in other styles, the **Blue Shop**, 320 N. Fourth St., Burlington, 319/758-9553, provides an intimate setting for live music.

16
IOWA CITY
AND CEDAR RAPIDS

Iowa City and Cedar Rapids, linked by I-380, are steadily becoming a pair of cities that, together, deserve the title of Iowa's cultural capital. Just as Ames enhances Des Moines and the Quad Cities form a formidable Mississippi River center, the Iowa City and Cedar Rapids area is both unified and diverse.

Iowa City carries much of the cultural weight. It's hip, cool, and infused with 27,500 University of Iowa students, the state's largest university population, drawn from around the country and the world. But if you think that spells nothing but a rowdy bar crowd and heavy traffic on home game days, think again. The U of I's strong graduate school, particularly the renowned Writer's Workshop, has not only fostered an older student population but also helped nurture a community of writers, musicians, and other artists who make Iowa City their lifelong home.

Iowa City is the kind of town where you could potentially run into an internationally renowned folk musician (Greg Brown) or a famous poet (Jorie Graham). Good museums and night spots are in walking distance of each other. You can find a cup of coffee not brewed by Starbucks and plenty of record stores that cater to non-mainstream tastes.

The Iowa City suburb of Coralville, a mini-sprawl whose major feature is the immense Coral Ridge Mall (note its indoor ice rink), represents more recent commercial development that in some ways has competed with Iowa City's downtown shops.

IOWA CITY

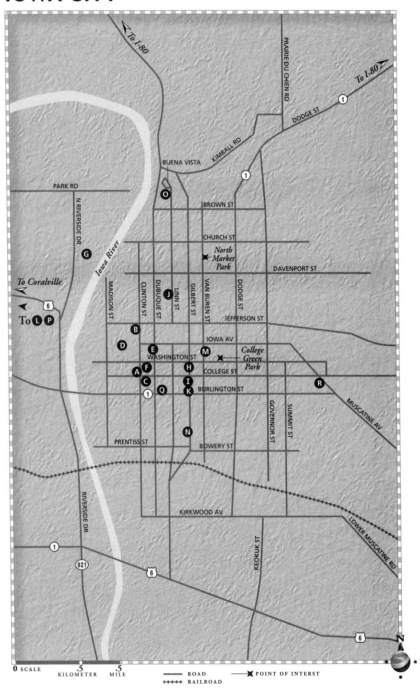

Cedar Rapids, located a half hour north of Iowa City, has a smaller student population but a long history as a river community and center for the milling industry. Your nose will definitely detect the distinct scent of cereal near the large Quaker Oats Company facilities, a longtime staple of the city's employment force.

Cedar Rapids' downtown, like Iowa City's, is also very much alive, as is the city's Czech and Slovak heritage. The popular Czech Village is one example of how this heritage has become an established, popular tourist attraction. With historic neighborhoods and clusters of live music and fine dining and lodging, Cedar Rapids is a good dual destination with Iowa City.

A PERFECT DAY IN IOWA CITY AND CEDAR RAPIDS

Start your day in Cedar Rapids, visiting the National Czech & Slovak Museum & Library. Steep yourself in more ethnic heritage at the Czech Village.

Spend the remainder of your day in Iowa City. Here, focus more on the present than the past. (Still, a quick visit to the Old Capitol Museum or another of the museums in the Pentacrest area at the center of the University of Iowa campus is worth your time.) The Ped Mall alone could occupy you for an entire afternoon and evening. Take time to look in on a few of the retail shops, especially Prairie Lights Books, the Record Collector, and the Iowa Artisans Gallery. If the weather's warm, grab an ice cream cone at the Great Midwestern Ice Cream Co.

For dinner, stop at either Masala for Indian cuisine or Sanctuary Restaurant & Pub for pizza and other enticing entrées. Enjoy an evening stroll in downtown Iowa City; meander into The Deadwood bar, the kind of place you find yourself falling into interesting conversations with complete

---

SIGHTS
- Ⓐ Iowa Artisans Gallery
- Ⓑ Iowa Hall—Museum of Natural History
- Ⓒ Lorenz Boot Shop
- Ⓓ Old Capitol Museum
- Ⓔ Prairie Lights Books
- Ⓕ Record Collector
- Ⓖ The University of Iowa Museum of Art

FOOD
- Ⓗ Brown Bottle
- Ⓘ Givanni's Cafe
- Ⓙ Hamburg Inn
- Ⓚ The Mill
- Ⓛ Mondo's Tomato Pie
- Ⓜ New Pioneer Co-op
- Ⓝ Sanctuary Restaurant & Pub

LODGING
- Ⓞ 2 Bella Vista Place
- Ⓟ Best Western Canterbury Inn & Suites
- Ⓠ Holiday Inn
- Ⓡ Morning Glory Bed & Breakfast

strangers. Most of the live music hosted by Gabe's, an upstairs club, is worth the inexpensive cover charge, and they serve Grain Belt beer, a lowbrow but tasty brew.

IOWA CITY SIGHTSEEING HIGHLIGHTS

★★★★ DOWNTOWN IOWA CITY PEDESTRIAN MALL
Clinton St. and Iowa Ave., 319/354-0863

The Ped Mall, as it's referred to, is a veritable garden of unique consumer and nightlife delights you won't find elsewhere in Iowa. **Prairie Lights Books**, 15 S. Dubuque St., 319/337-2681, is an independent, three-floor bookstore with a voluminous stock. The **Record Collector**, 125 E. Washington St., 319/337-5029, specializes in electronic music and collectible vinyl. **Lorenz Boot Shop**, 132 S. Clinton St., 319/339-1053, sells far more than just the standard footwear. The **Iowa Artisans Gallery**, 117 E. College St., 319/351-8686, features contemporary works by more than 150 Midwestern artists. Uniqueness is the general flavor of the Ped Mall. Street musicians gather, full-blown concerts are held outdoors in the summer, and locals sit and chat among the trees and benches. There's always a palpable buzz in the Ped Mall.

Iowa City was the first state capital, before Des Moines, and today it is Iowa's cultural capital, ahead of Des Moines. It has a certain bohemian flair that's distinct among Iowa communities.

> **Details:** *Roughly defined as the area bounded by Clinton St. (on the north), Iowa Ave. (east), Linn St. (south), and Burlington St. (west). Individual business hours vary. Free. (1–6 hours)*

★★★ OLD CAPITOL MUSEUM
24 Old Capitol St., 319/335-0548

The Old Capitol Museum has been restored to its mid-1800s glory, when it was the political center of Iowa, first of the territory and then the state. In the middle of the University of Iowa campus (in an area known as the Pentacrest), the Old Capitol features the House Chamber, Supreme Court Chamber, and the Territorial Library as well as offices for the governor and other officials. The building's main hall has a reverse spiral staircase that reaches to the top floor of the building. A gift shop with history-themed books is located on the lower level.

Details: Open year-round Mon–Sat 10–3, Sun noon–4, Saturdays with home football games 9–noon. Free. (1 hour)

★★ **IOWA HALL—MUSEUM OF NATURAL HISTORY**
Clinton and Jefferson Sts., 319/335-0480
Inside McBride Hall, the Museum of Natural History narrows in on "a billion years of Iowa's natural history." The Iowa Gallery Hall includes dioramas, while Bird Hall explores the lives of more than one thousand varieties of birds. Mammal Hall is also included.

Details: Next door to the Old Capitol Museum. Open year-round Mon–Sat 9:30–4:30, Sun 12:30–4:30. Free. (1–2 hours)

★★ **THE UNIVERSITY OF IOWA MUSEUM OF ART**
150 N. Riverside Dr., 319/335-1727,
www.uiowa.edu/~artmus
In this case, Cedar Rapids contributed to Iowa City's culture: Owen and Leone Elliott of Cedar Rapids were responsible for this museum's founding when they donated their art collection to the university in the 1960s with the stipulation that a new facility would be built. It opened in 1969. Noted for

The Museum of Natural History at the University of Iowa is the oldest university museum west of the Mississippi River.

its collections of twentieth-century European and American painting and sculpture as well as African sculpture, the University of Iowa Museum of Art also hosts rotating exhibits in the Carver Wing, added in 1976.

Details: Open year-round Tue–Sat 10–5, Sun noon–5. Free. (1 hour)

CEDAR RAPIDS SIGHTSEEING HIGHLIGHTS

★★★ **NATIONAL CZECH & SLOVAK MUSEUM & LIBRARY**
30 16th Ave. SW, 319/362-8500, www.ncsml.org.

KALONA

The largest Amish–Mennonite settlement west of the Mississippi River, Kalona is an easy 17-mile drive south of Iowa City and makes for a pleasant day's worth of rustic sightseeing.

The **Kalona Historical Village**, Hwy. 22 and Ninth St., Kalona, 319/656-2519, preserves the 1800s style of the old railroad town that was settled by its religious founders and is the centerpiece of any tour. The Kalona Depot, Iowa Mennonite Museum and Archives, Wahl Museum, and Grout Church, plus other buildings that reflect the community's past life, are all part of the Village experience. It's open Monday through Saturday and costs only $4 for adults, $2 for children.

A man named John Meyers determined the town's name by naming a railroad station on his land after one of his bulls. Today you'll find horse-drawn buggies clomping along the streets. Also, in the fields in the surrounding countryside, you'll see farmers hard at work. There are actually four main groups of Amish and Mennonite settlers today that make up Kalona's traditional population, and each group's relationship with technology differs slightly.

An annual Fall Festival is held in Kalona the last Friday and Saturday of September, featuring homemade food and crafts, as well as demonstrations of historical working methods from the community's past.

The **Kalona Historical Society**, 319/656-2519, is the center for all things relating to the town's historical tourist spots.

Appropriately, this attraction is located in the Czech Village (see below). Dedicated in 1995 by Presidents Clinton, Havel (Czech), and Kovac (Slovak), this is the largest such collection in the country of folk costumes and other artwork. Bohemian textiles, glassware, and a restored nineteenth-century immigrant home are also on display. Its research library has a collection of related books and periodicals in Czech, Slovak, and English.

Details: Open May–Dec Tue–Sat 9:30–4, Sun noon–4. $5 ages 19–64, $4 age 65 and older, $3 ages 5–16, free under 5. (1–3 hours)

★★ CZECH VILLAGE
16th Ave. SW, 319/362-2846

This retail district of small businesses along the Cedar River has a long history as a center for the area's large Czech population. Sykora Bakery, Polehna's Meat Market, and the Saddle & Leather Shop are just a few of the oldest businesses in the village, while Al's Red Frog Bar is a popular restaurant and watering hole. The Czech Village Association has helped guide and unify the village over the last couple of decades. It's a fine example of Old World style serving the modern world's everyday needs.

Details: Exit I-380 at Wilson Ave. SW and follow signs. Individual business hours vary. Free. (1–2 hours)

FITNESS AND RECREATION

Plenty of trails, both urban and rural, snake through the Iowa City–Cedar Rapids area.

The **Cedar Greenbelt National Recreation Trail**, 6665 Otis Rd. SE, Cedar Rapids, 319/362-0664, has trails that stretch through a 210-acre natural preserve. **Bever Park & Children's Zoo**, 2701 Bever Ave. SE, Cedar Rapids, 319/398-0247, is 90 acres packed with friendly barnyard animals, a primate house, swimming and wading pools, tennis courts, trails, gardens, and concession stands.

Coralville Lake & Devonian Fossil Gorge, 3.4 miles north of I-80 Exit 244 on Dubuque St., Iowa City, 319/338-3543, has a wide range of facilities, including hiking and biking trails, an outdoor swimming pool, and a Frisbee golf course on its 8,400 acres. Within Iowa City, **City Park**, along the Iowa River on Park Rd., 319/356-5110, also offers a large variety of outdoor possibilities. This park offers easy access if you'd like to stay close to the Iowa City attractions and not invest much travel time toward outdoor fun.

FOOD

Iowa City boasts some of the most charming and diverse restaurants in the state. Cedar Rapids, more dominated by national chains, features less variety, but there are still fine eateries to be found there.

One of Roseanne Barr's favorite restaurants when she briefly called Iowa home in the early '90s, the **Hamburg Inn**, 214 N. Linn St., Iowa City, 319/337-5512, serves hearty, old-fashioned breakfasts, hamburgers, and thick shakes. It's inexpensive and well worth a stop.

CEDAR RAPIDS

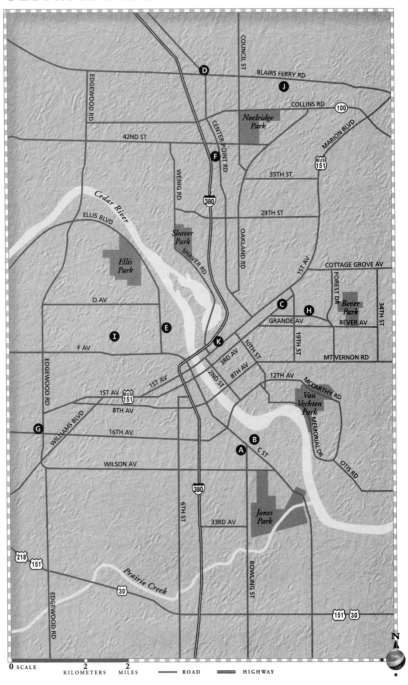

COUNCIL ST

BLAIRS FERRY RD

D

J

COLLINS RD

100

EDGEWOOD RD

CENTER POINT RD

42ND ST

Noelridge Park

MARION BLVD

BUS 151

35TH ST

F

WENIG RD

380

29TH ST

Cedar River

ELLIS BLVD

Shaver Park

SHAVER RD

OAKLAND RD

1ST AV

COTTAGE GROVE AV

Ellis Park

FOREST DR

Bever Park

34TH ST

O AV

C

H

BEVER AV

GRANDE AV

I

E

F AV

K

3RD AV

10TH ST

19TH ST

MT VERNON RD

EDGEWOOD RD

1ST AV

2ND ST

8TH AV

12TH AV

McCARTHY RD

1ST AV BUS 151

Van Vechten Park

8TH AV

WILLIAMS BLVD

MEMORIAL DR

G

16TH AV

A

B

C ST

WILSON AV

OTIS RD

380

6TH ST

Jones Park

218 151

33RD AV

BOWLING ST

30

Prairie Creek

30

EDGEWOOD RD

151 30

N

0 SCALE   2   2
KILOMETERS   MILES   ━━ ROAD   ══ HIGHWAY

Even though it's a grocery store, **New Pioneer Co-op**, 22 S. Van Buren St., Iowa City, 319/338-9441, www.newpi.com, has a great selection of natural foods you should check out, perhaps in preparation for a picnic. Not only is **Sanctuary Restaurant & Pub**, 405 S. Gilbert St., Iowa City, 319/351-5692, a great place for gourmet pizza, it also features live music in an intimate setting as well as an extensive wine and beer selection. **The Mill**, 120 E. Burlington St., Iowa City, 319/351-9529, also hosts great live music on the weekends and serves food and fine coffees—as it has for the last 36 years.

Brown Bottle, 115 E. Washington St., 319/351-6704, is a family-owned and -operated Italian-themed restaurant. Although a bit more upscale and costly than your average family restaurant, it's not extremely fancy. Both **Givanni's Cafe**, 109 E. College St., Iowa City, 319/338-5967, and **Mondo's Tomato Pie**, 516 E. Second St., Iowa City, 319/337-3000, are operated by the same local ownership, and both restaurants serve good, flavorful food.

Homemade brew and national trivia games are the norm at **Cedar Brewing Company**, 500 Blairs Ferry Rd. NE, 319/378-9090, Cedar Rapids, www.beerstuff.com/cbc. The American menu is full of tasty and zesty appetizers and entrées. **Spring House Family Restaurant**, 3980 Center Point Rd. NE, Cedar Rapids, 319/393-4995, has been owned and operated by the same family for almost 30 years, and its hearty, down-home food will stick to your ribs.

European cuisine is the fare at **Cafe De Klos**, 821 Third Ave. SE, Cedar Rapids, 319/362-9340, housed in a delightful Victorian home. At **Zindricks Czech Restaurant**, 86 16th Ave. SW, Cedar Rapids, 319/365-5257, the cooking is authentic to the old Czech and Slovak ways. It's open for lunch and dinner Monday through Saturday and for Sunday brunch.

A solid pizzeria/steakhouse with a 40-year history, **Flamingo Pizza Palace**, 1211 Ellis Blvd. NW, Cedar Rapids, 319/365-6333, also features seafood and BBQ, plus a full bar. It's a mid-priced eating stop.

SIGHTS
Ⓐ Czech Village
Ⓑ National Czech & Slovak Museum & Library

FOOD
Ⓒ Cafe De Klos
Ⓓ Cedar Brewing Company
Ⓔ Flamingo Pizza Palace
Ⓕ Spring House Family Restaurant
Ⓖ Zindricks Czech Restaurant

LODGING
Ⓗ 2325 Grande Ave. Homestay
Ⓘ Belmont Hill Bed & Breakfast
Ⓙ Collins Plaza Hotel & Convention Center
Ⓚ Crown Plaza Five Seasons Hotel

THE AMANA COLONIES

Settled more than 150 years ago by German immigrants seeking religious freedom in the middle of America (after initially settling near Buffalo, New York, but needing more land), the Amana Colonies are easily accessible from either town. To reach the seven colonies—South Amana, West Amana, High Amana, Middle Amana, East Amana, Amana, and Homestead—from Cedar Rapids, take Highway 151 south; from Iowa City, take Highway 6 northwest.

All the colonies are rich in history and still steeped in tradition—preserving both has made tourism a key component in the Amanas' economic lifeblood. The **Museum of Amana History**, Amana, 319/622-3567, occupies three nineteenth-century buildings. The **Communal Agriculture Museum**, South Amana, 319/622-3567, exhibits farm implements, photos, maps, and other examples of how the community, before 1932, lived off the land as an equal-share commune. After that, your next logical stop is the **Communal Kitchen and Coopershop Museum**, Middle Amana, 319/622-3567, with the only existing kitchen in the colonies preserved from the days of communal living.

The Amana Colonies specialize in hearty German family-style dining, and visiting here without sampling the cuisine is like going to Egypt and skipping the pyramids. Best of all the Amanas' restaurants is the **Ox Yoke Inn Restaurant**, 4420 220th Trail, Amana, 800/233-3441, which has also been a historic landmark since 1940. The hearty fare should leave you full for a couple days. **Brick Haus Restaurant**, 728 47th Ave., Amana,

LODGING

In Iowa City, you might want to consider staying near the downtown area, simply for the convenience of being within walking distance of some of the city's best attractions. (Coralville, however, has most of the hotels in the area, especially along and near I-80.)

Because it's right next to the downtown Ped Mall area in Iowa City, **Holiday Inn**, 210 S. Dubuque St., Iowa City, 800/848-1335 or 319/337-4058, is a popular choice. You can just glance out your window to see if it's a hopping night on the town.

Also near downtown is the logically named **2 Bella Vista Place**, 2 Bella Vista Pl., Iowa City, 319/338-4129, a four-room bed-and-breakfast inn

---

800/622-3471 or 319/622-3278, is another fine family-style brunch and dinner choice, as is **Amana Barn Restaurant**, 4709 220th Trail, Amana, 319/622-3214. At Iowa's oldest brewery, the **Millstream Brewing Co.**, Amana, 319/622-3672, tours and samples are available.

The Amana Colonies feature more than 70 specialty stores, including the recommended **Amana Furniture Shop**, Amana, 319/622-3291, which gives free tours and has a large clock-making shop. The **Amana Woolen Mill**, Amana, 800/222-6430 or 319/622-3432, is Iowa's only woolen mill and a great place to pick up quality bedcovers for the cold winter months—especially if you contend with such weather as Midwesterners do.

Celebrations and festivals are scattered throughout Amana's warm months, including, of course, the annual German-themed **Oktoberfest**.

If you're planning an overnight stop in the Amanas, the **Amana Holiday Inn**, I-80 Exit 225, 800/633-9244 or 319/668-1175, is part of "Little Amana," next to a cluster of shops with Amana merchandise near the interstate. In the Amanas themselves, **Baeckerel Bed & Breakfast**, 507 Q St., South Amana, 800/391-8650 or 319/622-3597, is an 1860 home that rents out three rooms. **Rose's Place Bed & Breakfast**, Middle Amana, 319/622-6097, has its own three rooms in a renovated 1870s Sunday school building.

with a view of the Iowa River. Another fine in-town bed-and-breakfast is **Morning Glory Bed & Breakfast**, 1113 E. College St., Iowa City, 319/354-1296.

In the Iowa City suburb of Coralville, **Best Western Canterbury Inn & Suites**, 704 First Ave., Coralville, 800/798-0400 or 319/351-0400, favors an Old English theme throughout its 100-plus rooms.

Collins Plaza Hotel & Convention Center, 1200 Collins Rd. NE, Cedar Rapids, 800/541-1067 or 319/393-6600, is the upscale, plush choice. It has a seven-story atrium and offers a pricey yet restful stay. Another hotel long on amenities is **Crowne Plaza Five Seasons Hotel**, 3501 First Ave. NE, Cedar Rapids, 800/2CROWNE or 319/363-8161, which offers coffee makers, complimentary newspapers, and rooms that cater to the needs of business travelers.

Cedar Rapids has bed-and-breakfast options as well. **Belmont Hill Bed & Breakfast**, 1525 Cherokee Dr. NW, Cedar Rapids, 319/366-1343, is an 1882 Victorian home with gardens on its grounds. Another lodging named in honor of its address, **2325 Grande Ave. Homestay**, 2325 Grande Ave. SE, Cedar Rapids, 319/363-5389, is closed during the summer months (June 15 through September 15).

CAMPING

The location of **Colony Country Campground**, 1275 Forevergreen Rd., Iowa City, 319/626-2221, is convenient to many of the region's attractions. It has 4.5 acres with 34 electric and 11 primitive campsites.

If you're willing to venture away from the cities, **Lake McBride State Park**, 3525 Hwy. 382 NE, Solon, 319/644-2200, hosts not just camping but other outdoor activities like swimming, fishing, and sailing. It has plenty of room, with 40 electric and 82 primitive campsites on more than two thousand acres.

Two and a half miles west of Cedar Rapids, **Morgan Creek Park**, 7515 Worchester Rd., Palo, 319/398-3505, features a sports field, an arboretum, and campsites spread throughout its 230 acres. South of Iowa City, **Wildwood Campground**, Hwy. 1 S., 1 mile west of Kalona, 319/656-2001, offers scenic views and 78 campsites with electric facilities.

NIGHTLIFE

The Iowa City Ped Mall district fuels a thriving nightlife scene, and it's not just one big collegiate party. With character that can be soaked in as easily as the brews on tap, **The Deadwood**, 6 S. Dubuque St., 319/351-9417, Iowa City, is a dark and voluminous bar with a well-stocked jukebox and deep booths you can sink into to escape the outside world. Across the street, **Dublin Underground Public House**, 5 S. Dubuque St., 319/337-7660, Iowa City, is a cool basement bar. The **Q Bar**, 211 Iowa Ave., Iowa City, 319/337-9107, hosts live bands, but the wide array of bar games (video, darts, pool, and so on) ensures no boredom during the day, too.

Away from the Ped Mall, **Fitzpatrick's Brewing Co.**, 525 S. Gilbert St., Iowa City, 319/356-6900, was Iowa's first brew pub, and it still churns out great-tasting stouts, lagers, and wheat ales. Plus, it has a great outdoor courtyard.

For live music, it's tough to beat the low-fi charm and band line-up at **Gabe's**, 330 E. Washington Ave., Iowa City, 319/354-4788. There's one bar downstairs, and another bar and the music venue upstairs. Plenty of roots rock, punk, and other styles of national artists stop by. Although technically a music store, **Sal's Music Emporium**, 624 Dubuque St., Iowa City, 319/338-7462, hosts lots of free in-store concerts. Many of the bands that play at Gabe's on a given night stop here first earlier in the evening. It's just south of the downtown area.

In Cedar Rapids, check the schedule of **CSPS**, 1103 Third St. SE, Cedar Rapids, 319/364-1580, www.legionarts.org, a live music venue that consistently imports world-class talent, at least every couple of weeks.

Cedar Rapids' only brew pub is the **Cedar Brewing Company**, 500 Blairs Ferry Rd. NE, Cedar Rapids, 319/378-9090, which also serves lunch and dinner. Jazz bars can be hard to find in Iowa, but **Eddie Piccard's**, Mt. Vernon Rd. and Memorial Dr. SE, Cedar Rapids, 319/369-4932, swings nightly and isn't cheap. It also serves dinner.

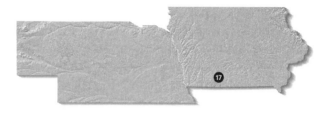

17
MADISON COUNTY

This is the land of John Wayne and Clint Eastwood—a place of famous, rickety yet romantic bridges.

The Bridges of Madison County—both the book by Iowa native Robert Waller and Clint Eastwood's subsequent movie—unveiled rural Winterset's covered bridges to the rest of the country and inspired an annual influx of thousands of tourists. Just as *Field of Dreams* transformed a simple baseball field in Dyersville into a golden tourist goose, Hollywood has made Madison County one of the most popular tourist destinations in the state.

Winterset itself has long been known as the birthplace of "the Duke," Western movie icon John Wayne. In his recommended book *John Wayne's America*, author Gary Wills deconstructs the larger-than-life movie star's ongoing impact on our country's culture. In the first chapter he writes: "(Wayne) was at least a man from nowhere. The nowhere was Winterset, Iowa."

Calling Winterset "nowhere" is undoubtedly an exaggeration. The town's rural charm is catching; its town square, quaint shops, down-home eateries, and friendly citizens are things to celebrate and enjoy. Outside of town, Madison County offers a mixture of woods and prairie grasslands. In addition, there are creeks and rivers that interrupt much of the county's gentle terrain. And the six nearby covered bridges contribute to the scenery's romantic feel. It's a perfect place to go for a relaxing afternoon drive.

A PERFECT DAY IN MADISON COUNTY

After breakfast, tour the covered bridges. Their popularity is not due only to Hollywood; they really do make for interesting sightseeing in the middle of the peaceful countryside. Driving between the bridges is quick and easy, and you get to see plenty of picturesque farm scenery. Photo opportunities abound. Back in Winterset, stop for lunch at the Northside Cafe, stroll the great town square, and then drop by the John Wayne Birthplace. Howell Dried Florals & Green House might not sound appealing unless you're in the market for plants, but its vast collection of dried flowers is delightful. The colorful bunches hang in the loft of a barn and stretch high up into the rafters.

SIGHTSEEING HIGHLIGHTS

★★★★ MADISON COUNTY COVERED BRIDGES
Rural Winterset, 800/298-6119 or 515/462-1185

Six bridges, each more than a century old, dot the backroads of rural Winterset, all within 15 minutes of town. Nineteen bridges were built during a 30-year span, between 1855 and 1885, and were covered to help protect the flooring lumber from the elements and

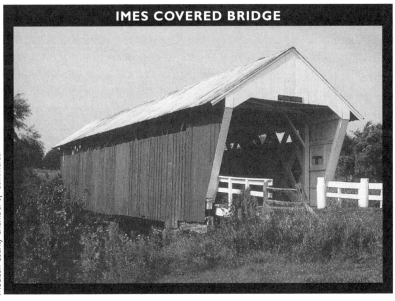

IMES COVERED BRIDGE

Madison County Chamber of Commerce

MADISON COUNTY/WINTERSET

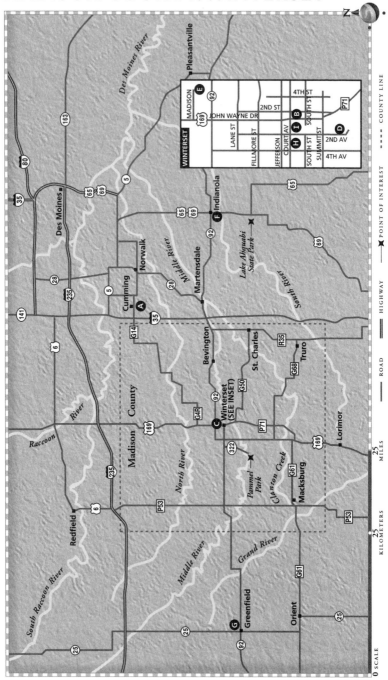

N

Pleasantville

WINTERSET
MADISON
E 92
JOHN WAYNE DR
169
4TH ST
2ND ST
SOUTH ST
P71
B
LANE ST
FILLMORE ST
COURT AV
JEFFERSON
H I
D
SUMMIT ST
SOUTH ST
2ND AV
4TH AV

Des Moines River

80
163
35
69
65
69
5
Des Moines

Indianola F
92
65 69
65
69
Lake Ahquabi State Park
Norwalk
28
Middle River
Martensdale
69
28
235
5
Cumming
A
35
141
6
G14
Bevington
St. Charles
R35
Truro
G68
South River
Madison County
92
Winterset (SEE INSET)
G50
G4R
C
P71
169
Lorimor
169
North River
Raccoon River
322
Pammel Park
Clanton Creek
G61
Macksburg
235
6
P53
P53
Redfield
Middle River
Grand River
G61
South Raccoon River
Greenfield
Orient
25
G
25
25
92

COUNTY LINE
POINT OF INTEREST
HIGHWAY
ROAD
MILES 25
KILOMETERS 25
0 SCALE

therefore extend the life of the bridge. (The bridges' roofing and wall materials were cheap compared to the cost of constructing a new floor.)

Cedar Covered Bridge, built in 1883, is the only one of the six bridges still open to vehicular traffic. **Roseman Covered Bridge** is the famous bridge featured most prominently in the well-known movie, and was renovated in 1992 for that purpose to the tune of more than $150,000. **Imes Covered Bridge**, built in 1870, is the oldest remaining bridge and it was moved to its present locale just east of St. Charles in 1977. Also featured in the film, **Holliwell Covered Bridge** is the longest bridge, spanning 122 feet. **Cutler-Donahoe Covered Bridge** sits at the entrance to Winterset City Park. **Hogback Covered Bridge**, just northwest of Winterset, was also renovated in 1992.

Bring a camera to snap photos like Robert Kincaid did in the book and movie. Unless you visit during the annual Covered Bridge Festival during the second full weekend in October, you'll likely be able to tour the bridges in peace, with only a couple other groups of tourists at most—except at the more heavily-traveled Roseman Covered Bridge. Next door is the small Roseman Covered Bridge Shop, accessed via a narrow trail.

Details: Open year-round daily, on public roads. Phone the above numbers for a map, or stop by the Madison County Chamber of Commerce, 73 Jefferson St., Winterset. From I-80, take Exit 100 (Hwy. P53) west six miles past Winterset, then turn south at the Roseman sign, following additional signs to the bridge. Free. (1–2 hours)

SIGHTS

- Ⓐ Francesca's House
- Ⓐ Groth's Gardens
- Ⓐ Howell Dried Florals & Green House
- Ⓑ John Wayne Birthplace
- Ⓒ Madison County Covered Bridges
- Ⓓ Madison County Museum and Historical Complex

FOOD

- Ⓒ Northside Cafe
- Ⓑ Rookies' Pub & Grille

LODGING

- Ⓕ Apple Tree Inn Motel
- Ⓖ Brass Lantern
- Ⓗ Eagle's Nest Luxury Suite on the Square
- Ⓘ A Step Away
- Ⓒ Village View Motel

Note: Items with the same letter are located in the same area.

★★★ FRANCESCA'S HOUSE
3271 130th St., Cumming, 515/981-5268

This is the actual farmhouse in which Clint Eastwood wooed Meryl Streep in *The Bridges of Madison County*—where much of the filming for the movie took place. The "set," down to the same props, remains. Remember the yellow Formica kitchen table? It's still here. Remember the bathtub where Francesca soaked and dreamt of Kincaid as the water dripped? It's here, too. The house was built in 1870 by Nicholas Johnson and was in turn purchased, along with 1,000 acres, by Joseph Meade in 1910. His family still owns the property. Warner Bros. movie scouts reportedly viewed 150 other potential sites before settling on this one.

> **Details:** *Take Hwy. 169 north of Winterset 2.5 miles to G4R and turn right. Follow for 13.6 miles and turn right at gravel road with "Francesca's House" sign. Go a half mile east to the first house on the left. Open May–Oct daily 10–6. $5 ages 13–54, $3 age 55 and older, $3 ages 2–12, free under 2. Grounds tour $4 per car. (30 minutes–1 hour)*

★★★ HOWELL DRIED FLORALS & GREEN HOUSE
3146 Cumming Rd., Cumming, 515/981-0863, www.howellfloral.com

On these 15 acres, three generations of the Howell family have grown Christmas trees and a stunning variety of flowers. Browse the massive attic of a 1910 barn where the flowers are hung to dry; the rainbow of floral shapes and vivid colors rises high above your head, reaching to the peak. Erin's Roses Gift Shop is located on the barn's first floor. Just outside is a petting zoo with amiable goats.

*Howell's hosts a **Spring Open House** the second weekend in May, a **Full Open House** the second weekend in September, and a **Christmas Open House** the first weekend in November.*

> **Details:** *Near Francesca's House (see above). Open year-round Mon–Sat 10–5, Sun 1–5. Free. (1 hour)*

★★ MADISON COUNTY MUSEUM AND HISTORICAL COMPLEX
815 S. Second Ave., Winterset, 515/462-2134

Built in 1904, this museum today includes 14 buildings situated on 18 acres on the south edge of Winterset. The Bevington-Kaser House, finished in 1856, is a beautiful mansion that serves as one of the main attractions. A barn, post office, log cabin school, gas station, blacksmith shop, and other buildings are also part of the complex. A train depot recalls nineteenth-century transportation. The museum also displays fossils, minerals, Native American artifacts, and pioneer antiques on its grounds. Standing and walking among the buildings—gazing across the rooftops, hearing the cluck of chickens from the barn area—gives you a sense, more than any indoor museum experience, of the look and feel of pioneer life in Madison County.

Details: Open May–Oct Mon–Sat 11–4, Sun 1–5. Year-round office hours weekdays 9–4. $3 mansion or museum or $5 for both, free under 13 with adult. (1–3 hours)

★★ **JOHN WAYNE BIRTHPLACE**
216 Second St., Winterset, 515/462-1044
www.johnwaynebirthplace.org
This four-room house where the Duke was born displays photos and other memorabilia from his life and movies—including the eye patch he wore in *True Grit*. Letters from fellow movie stars—Jimmy Stewart, Maureen O'Hara, Ronald Reagan—can also be seen. Wayne was born here in 1907, as Marion Robert Morrison. Don't worry, pilgrim—there's a gift shop next door.

Details: Open year-round daily 10–4:30. Guided tour $2.50 adults, $2.25 seniors 55 and over, and $1 children 12 and under. (15–30 minutes)

★ **GROTH'S GARDENS**
2451 Cummings Rd., Cumming, 515/462-4445
The gardens on this century-old farm contain more than three hundred varieties of wildflowers, perennials, herbs, and other flora. The mums reportedly grow as big as basketballs.

Details: Open Apr 15–Labor Day Mon–Fri 10–6, Sat 9–6, Sun 1–5. Free. (30 minutes–1 hour)

FITNESS AND RECREATION

In town, the 75-acre wooded **Winterset City Park**, East Ct. and 10th Street, Winterset, 515/462-3258, includes the Cutler-Donahoe Covered Bridge and Clark Tower, a three-story limestone tower that stands on a bluff.

ANTIQUING AND SIGHTSEEING WEST OF WINTERSET

If you're willing to stray west of Winterset in the name of a little antiques shopping and sightseeing, plenty of distractions are waiting for you.

__Walnut's Antique Drive__, downtown Walnut, one mile south of I-80 Exit 46, 712/784-2100, is probably the most impressive destination. This charming small Iowa town is chock full of locally owned shops brimming with an assortment of antiques—furniture, Christmas decorations, linens, toy railroad setups, and more. Antiques are Walnut's business, and business is good. Literally dozens of shops are open year-round, most from 10 a.m. to 5 p.m. on Monday through Saturday and from noon to 5 p.m. on Sunday.

Some of the shops include __Antique Furniture Emporium__, 712/784-3839, __Country Classics Christmas Store__, 800/937-9318, __Farm Fresh Antiques__, 712/784-2275, __The Granary Antique Mall__, 712/784-3331, __Isabel's Doll Works__, 712/784-3005, __Victorian Rose Antiques__, 712/784-3900, and __The Collectible Closet__ 712/784-2221.

If you fancy a meal during your antiquing trip, stop by __The Villager Restaurant__, 712/784-2200. If you stay long enough to end up needing accommodations, __Walnut Creek Inn Motel & 30 Space RV Park__, 712/784-2233, offers a wide range of affordable accommodations, even if you're driving a giant home on wheels. For more upscale accommodations, try __Antique City Inn Bed & Breakfast__, 400 Antique City Dr., Walnut, 712/784-3722, which is located in a beautiful Victorian home and run by Sylvia Reddie. Lunch and dinner can be arranged, too. Rooms cost around $50; the special carriage house costs more.

Everything in Walnut is fairly close together and easy to find. The name "Antique City Drive" is appropriate; most of the shops are located on that main street or just off it, in one central and easy-to-find location. Just exit off the interstate.

If you decide to go to Walnut, you might also want to stop next door in Elk Horn. This charming small town proudly proclaims its Danish heritage with a few fine attractions. There are fewer antiques shops here.

The Danish Windmill Museum and Welcome Center, 4038 Main St., Elk Horn, 800/451-7960 or 712/764-7472, www.netins.net/showcase/danishmill, was originally built in Denmark in 1848 and transported here in 1975. The history of this structure is compelling, but its inner workings are fascinating as well. It's open from 9 to 5 Monday through Saturday and from noon to 5 on Sunday. Spring and summer hours expand to 8 to 7 Monday through Saturday and 10 to 7 on Sunday.

The Danish Immigrant Museum, 2212 Washington St., west edge of Elk Horn, 800/759-9192 or 712/764-7001, dkmuseum.org, is a beautiful modern structure filled with artifacts and information relating to the Danish heritage of the local populace. The 20-acre site includes one of the world's tiniest churches, with only about a half-dozen pews.

If you're more adventurous still, stray even farther, south of I-80, to the tiny town of Lewis, where you'll find the **Hitchcock House**, 712/769-2323. No, it's not the boyhood home of the famous director of suspenseful, psychological thrillers like Psycho and North by Northwest. The Hitchcock House was built in 1856 by Reverend George B. Hitchcock and became an important stop on the "Underground Railroad," the secret network of homes and buildings that during the Civil War helped harbor runaway slaves as they escaped from the South. This brown sandstone structure overlooks the East Nishnabotna River, and the Mormon Trail is just one mile south. There's also a full basement and large fireplace. Although Hitchcock House was left vacant in the 1960s, state grants helped restore it in the 1980s. It's open from 1 p.m. to 5 p.m. daily (except Mondays) from mid-April through mid-October. It sits on a 65-acre grounds that also contain a two-mile nature trail leading down to the East Nishnabotna.

If instead you'd like to roam the rest of Madison County with a little assistance, **Madison County Farm & Country Tours**, 1510 270th St., Winterset, 515/462-3515, can help. Movie locales, the covered bridges, and local farm history are all part of the itinerary. Minivan tours leave from 821 N. John Wayne Drive.

FOOD
Northside Cafe, 61 Jefferson St., Winterset, 515/462-1523, is the infamous café where Clint Eastwood, as Robert Kincaid, endured the scrutiny of curious townsfolk. It's open Monday through Saturday from 5:30 a.m. (seriously) to 8 p.m. and Sunday from 6 a.m. to 2 p.m.

    Rookies' Pub & Grille, 105 E. Madison St., Winterset, 515/462-2226, serves lunch and dinner, a mixture of appetizers, sandwiches, and salads. Takeout is also available.

LODGING
Village View Motel, Hwy. 92 E., Winterset, 515/462-1218, offers 16 affordable rooms in the heart of the county. Right on the town square, **Eagle's Nest Luxury Suite on the Square**, 322 W. Court Ave., Winterset, 888/462-5900, lives up to its name, with a whirlpool and king-size bed.

    A Step Away, 104 W. Court Ave., Winterset, 515/462-5956, is a charming bed-and-breakfast inn, also within city limits.

    A little to the west, the **Brass Lantern**, 2446 State Hwy. 92, Greenfield, 515/743-2031, is a charming bed-and-breakfast guest house with two rooms, a large indoor pool, and 20 acres of homestead. Queen beds, air conditioning, a VCR, and phone are standard. Terry and Margie Moore are the friendly proprietors.

    Some 25 miles east of Winterset, **Apple Tree Inn Motel**, Hwys. 65 and 69, Indianola, 800/961-0551, offers 60 rooms.

CAMPING
Criss Cove County Park, eight miles south of Winterset at Hwy. 169 and Rd. G61, 515/462-3563, open from April 15 to November 1, features 16 electric campsites and a playground. **Pammel State Park**, four miles southwest of Winterset on Hwy. 322, 515/462-3536, has hiking trails, picnic shelters, and a lodge as well as 20 electric and 2 primitive campsites.

NIGHTLIFE

Situated on Cumming's Main Street, the **Cumming Tap**, is also just a few steps off the Great Western Bike Trial that stretches into the Des Moines metro. **Rookies' Pub & Grille** (see Food, above) is a relaxed, friendly night spot to stop by during your Madison County touring. The Des Moines metro area, nearby, offers a full menu of urban nightlife diversions; see Chapter 18 for details.

18
DES MOINES

Situated at the confluence of the Des Moines and Raccoon rivers, the city of Des Moines and its suburbs make up Iowa's largest metro area. The capital city, Des Moines is home to a variety of cultural attractions you won't find anywhere else in the state, but its people exude the rural friendliness for which Iowa is famous.

Des Moines is largely known for the landmarks within the city limits. From various points around the metro area, you'll see the golden dome of the majestic Iowa State Capitol. Less than a block from the seat of today's state government stands the most important reminder of yesterday's Iowa, the Iowa State Historical Building. On Des Moines' western side you'll find, all in a cluster, the renowned Des Moines Art Center, the Science Center of Iowa, and tranquil Greenwood Park. Des Moines' various distinct neighborhoods reflect different eras in the city's history, even as they buzz with modern activity. From the upscale flair of the specialty retail shops and restaurants in Valley Junction (an old railroad neighborhood) in West Des Moines to the restored Victorian homes of Sherman Hill (where many live and work in the same building), Iowa's central city will reward those who take time to venture beyond its major thoroughfares and new developments.

Downtown Des Moines can sometimes appear deserted in the early evenings, but in the summer it's a center for outdoor gatherings. Seniom Sed (Des Moines spelled backwards) is an example. Each Friday around 5 p.m.

people gather in Nollen Plaza to listen to live music, drink beer, and chat. The nightlife on Court Avenue revolves around live music, dancing, and dining; on the best nights, it truly beats like the heart of a thriving city. Even in bad weather, downtown Des Moines is easily navigated on foot, thanks to the year-round shelter provided by the above-street-level Skywalk.

Since World War II, the Des Moines area has sprawled; many Iowans have abandoned agriculture for office jobs in the city, trading in their John Deere tractors for Ford Explorer SUVs. Just 20 years ago, most of the land west of Valley West Mall in West Des Moines was farmland. Now West Des Moines (Iowa's fastest-growing city) stretches west well beyond I-35, and the expanding Waukee suburb is creeping west toward the not-so-distant town of Adel. The popular Living History Farms open-air museum in Urbandale, once surrounded by modern farms, is now an agricultural oasis within a booming suburb of strip malls.

A PERFECT DAY IN DES MOINES

Start your day with breakfast at one of two places with great character—Waveland Cafe if you're looking for lots of tasty calories to fuel a full day of sightseeing, or Zanzibar's Coffee Adventure if you prefer a light breakfast and a wide range of gourmet coffee options. You can grab a newspaper at either spot.

If it's a summer Saturday, definitely head to the farmer's market on Court Avenue, if only to soak in the pervasive vibe of community among the strolling throng and to sample much of what Iowa is known for—the greens, tomatoes, and flowers grown in the rich soil.

Start your sightseeing at the Iowa State Capitol, afterward popping next door to the Iowa State Historical Building; both attractions open fairly early. Even those who aren't history buffs will appreciate the Historical Building's attractive and logically arranged displays that bring alive the state's past.

Closing in on lunchtime, head to the Sherman Hill neighborhood just northwest of downtown Des Moines. You can stroll around and view the beautiful Victorian homes in various stages of restoration, maybe tour the Hoyt Sherman Place mansion, and order a light (or heavy, if you want) lunch at Chat Noir, a great European-style eatery. If weather allows, dine outside at a table on the porch.

After lunch, head to the Des Moines Art Center and take your time viewing the paintings, sculptures, and beauty of the gallery itself. You can also stroll outside the museum and into nearby Greenwood Park, following the terrain (and a paved road) down to a pond.

Dining out is popular in Des Moines, which supports more than its share

DES MOINES

Des Moines River

Des Moines River

Raccoon River

Water Works Park

Drake University

To Greenwood Park

WASHINGTON ST
CLEVELAND AV
HUTTON ST
E 15TH ST
E 14TH ST
E 12TH ST
E 9TH ST
PENNSYLVANIA AV
E 6TH ST
E 4TH ST
2ND AV
6TH AV
9TH ST
10TH ST
CROCKER ST
CROCKER ST
CENTER ST
17TH ST
19TH ST
24TH ST
25TH ST
28TH ST
31ST ST
31ST ST
42ND ST
KEOSAUQUA WY
FOREST AV
UNIVERSITY AV
BEAVER AV
COTTAGE GROVE BLVD
CENTER ST
WOODLAND AV
INGERSOLL AV
GRAND AV
TONAWANDA DR
HIGH ST
SE 15TH ST
GRAND AV
LOCUST ST
WALNUT ST
MULBERRY ST
15TH ST
COURT AV
SCOTT AV
E ELM AV
ELM ST
SW 9TH ST
SE 9TH ST
SE 6TH ST
SE 1ST ST
FLEUR
TERRACE RD
W RIVER DR
E RIVER DR

A B C D E F G H I J K L M N O P Q R S T

SCALE
0
1 MILE
1 KILOMETER

RAILROAD
POINT OF INTEREST
HIGHWAY
ROAD

of restaurants. Visit one of two Italian spots—Chuck's Italian-American Restaurant on the north side or Baratta's Restaurant & Pizzarea, tucked within a residential neighborhood on the south side. You'll leave either place, which both feature great service and food, with a pasta-induced smile on your face.

In the summer, if you're lucky enough to be in Des Moines when the Iowa Cubs (yeah, the Chicago Cubs' farm team) are playing a home game at Sec Taylor Stadium, don't miss it. The ballpark is in great shape, and you don't have to battle Major League–sized crowds or prices.

ORIENTATION

You should have little problem navigating around Des Moines. Interstate 235, before it curves to the north on the east side of the city to intersect with I-80 and I-35, cuts the city into north and south halves. Except during Des Moines' 15-minute "rush hour," there's no better way to get across town quickly than on the freeway.

Ingersoll Avenue and Grand Avenue are major east–west arteries just south of I-235; Army Post Road is another east–west road at the very southern edge of the city. North of I-235, University Avenue, Hickman Road, and Euclid Avenue (which turns into Douglas Avenue farther west) are all major east–west streets.

Major north–south streets include 22nd Street (which turns into 86th Street as it goes north) in West Des Moines, Clive and Urbandale to Merle Hay Road, Fleur Drive, and NE/SE 14th Street in Des Moines proper.

SIGHTS

- **A** Botanical Center
- **B** Hoyt Sherman Place
- **C** Iowa State Capitol
- **D** Salisbury House
- **E** State of Iowa Historical Building
- **F** Terrace Hill

FOOD

- **G** 801 Steak & Chop House
- **H** A Dong Restaurant
- **G** Basil's Cafe
- **I** Big Tomato Pizza Co.
- **J** Chat Noir Cafe

FOOD (continued)

- **K** Court Ave. Brewing Co.
- **L** Drake Diner
- **M** Noah's Ark Restaurant & Lounge
- **N** Raccoon River Brewing Co.
- **O** SomeWhere Else
- **P** A Taste of Thailand

LODGING

- **Q** Best Western Starlite Village
- **R** Carter House Inn
- **S** Holiday Inn Downtown
- **N** Hotel Fort Des Moines
- **T** Savery Hotel and Spa

Note: Items with the same letter are located in the same area.

Just remember that when crossing from West Des Moines into Des Moines on the freeway, or vice versa, the street numbers can be a little confusing. Otherwise, the Des Moines street grid is fairly logical.

DES MOINES SIGHTSEEING HIGHLIGHTS

★★★ HOYT SHERMAN PLACE, IN THE SHERMAN HILL NATIONAL HISTORIC DISTRICT
1501 Woodland Ave., 515/243-0913 or 515/244-0507

The anchor of the beautiful tree-lined and home-filled Sherman Hill neighborhood is this sprawling 1870s mansion, art gallery (added in 1907), and theater (added in 1923). Original owner Hoyt Sherman, brother of Civil War General William Tecumseh Sherman, was a wealthy businessman who helped build much of Des Moines' early infrastructure. You can tour the mansion's one-time living quarters or, if your timing is right, take in a music or theater performance in the charming 1,360-seat auditorium. You can't miss it—the mansion has a huge front yard and parking lot and is across the street from Methodist Medical Center. You should also stroll around Sherman Hill, which is full of lovely Victorian homes as well as residents who are usually friendly and eager to talk. A neighborhood renaissance of sorts began in the late 1970s, and people of all ages and walks of life now live in Sherman Hill. Succinctly put, it's a funky 'hood.

Twenty-nine different kinds of marble were used in the original construction of the Iowa State Capitol.

Details: *Exit I-235 at Martin Luther King Pkwy., go south to Woodland Ave., then east five blocks. Open year-round weekdays 8–4. Free. (1 hour)*

★★★ IOWA STATE CAPITOL
E. Ninth St. and Grand Ave., 515/281-5591

Proudly perched at the top of Des Moines, elevation-wise, the Iowa State Capitol features a 275-foot-tall gold-leafed dome—the largest of all the country's state capitols—that is surrounded by four smaller domes. You'll catch glimpses of the big dome from various points throughout the city. You can tour the Supreme Court chambers, the two-story law library, and monuments on the capitol

---

grounds. The rooms are decorated with native Iowa woods and have recently undergone extensive restoration. A scale model of the USS *Iowa* battleship is on display inside, as are dolls of past Iowa First Ladies (seriously!).

Details: *Open year-round Mon–Fri 8–4:30, Sat–Sun 8–4. Free. (1 hour)*

★★★ SALISBURY HOUSE
4025 Tonawanda Dr., 515/279-9711 or 515/274-1777

Once featured on A&E Network's *America's Castles* series, this 42-room English Tudor–style castle brings a rare taste of the British Isles to Des Moines. Built in the 1920s by Carl and Edith Weeks, its exterior stonework spans two continents, with flint from the Cliffs of Dover in England and blackstone from nearby Indiana. The whole castle was modeled after the King's House in Salisbury, England. Its airy Great Hall, with wooden beams high above your head that were transported from the White Heart Inn (ask about this English inn's literary connections), is the architectural centerpiece of the interior. The library contains an impressive collection of 700 first-edition books and 3,000 rare books in all.

Details: *Tours Jun–Aug Mon–Thu 2, Fri 10, Sun 1 and 2:30. $5 age 13 and older, $2 ages 6–12, free under 6. (1–2 hours)*

★★ BOTANICAL CENTER
909 E. River Dr., 515/242-2394

The geodesic dome you can see just north of I-235 near downtown Des Moines is the Botanical Center, perpetually on the grow with more than 15 thousand plants, plus fine feathered friends.

Details: *Open year-round Mon–Fri 10–6, Sat–Sun 10–9. $1.50 adults, 50 cents children 6 and over including students with ID, 75 cents 65 and over, and free under 5. (30 minutes–1 hour)*

★★ STATE OF IOWA HISTORICAL BUILDING
600 E. Locust St., 515/281-5111 or 515/281-6412

The open, airy State of Iowa Historical Building makes a strong case for paying attention to what has already happened in our Land Between Two Rivers. Multiple floors introduce you to Iowa's farm and city life, peace and war time, and political and social history. The gift shop is well stocked, and the Terrace Cafe offers inexpensive lunches on weekdays (and a great view of downtown).

Details: *Open year-round Tue–Sat 9–4:30, Sun noon–4:30. Free.*
(1–2 hours)

★★ TERRACE HILL
2300 Grand Ave., 515/281-3604

A Victorian mansion built in 1869 by the state's first millionaire, Benjamin F. Allen, Terrace Hill has been Iowa's gubernatorial palace since 1972. A grand staircase is the mansion's centerpiece. Historic furnishings and artwork are spread around 21 rooms and two floors that are open to the public. The third floor is typically off-limits, housing the living quarters of the governor and his family. A visitors center and gift shop are located next door in a carriage house, and gardens dot the surrounding grounds.

Details: *Open Mar–Dec Tue–Sat 10–1:30. $3 age 13 and older, $1 ages 6–12, free under 6. (30 minutes–1 hour)*

GREATER DES MOINES SIGHTSEEING HIGHLIGHTS

★★★ DES MOINES ART CENTER
4700 Grand Ave., 515/277-4405

The Art Center building itself is, appropriately enough, an exhibit in its own right. Commonly regarded as the city's most architecturally distinctive building, it was built in stages and designed by three different architects. Eliel Saarinen pioneered the initial structure in the 1940s. I. M. Pei added to that in the 1960s. And Richard Meier departed drastically (and less successfully, by many accounts) with the museum's most recent addition in the 1980s. While Saarinen's and Pei's structures hug the landscape and meld well with each other, Meier's addition is a taller, more brash structure full of attitude and busy staircases and railings.

The Art Center is located on a hilltop, next to the entrance to Greenwood Park. Inside, permanent collections of nineteenth- and twentieth-century paintings and sculptures are on display, including works by Francis Bacon, Henri Matisse, Claude Monet, Auguste Rodin, and Frank Stella. Local artists are also featured in exhibits. The center hosts film series and other events in Levitt Auditorium. The Art Center Restaurant (overlooking a reflecting pool and courtyard) is open for lunch Tuesday through Saturday and for dinner on the first Friday night of each month, when the museum throws a party with live music called Arts After Hours.

Details: Open year-round Tue, Wed, Fri, and Sat 11–4; Thu and the first Friday of each month 11–9; Sun noon–4. Free. (1–2 hours)

★★★ LIVING HISTORY FARMS
2600 NW 111th St., Urbandale, 515/278-5286 or 515/278-2400, www.lhf.org

Its name tells the story: This 600-acre open-air museum is a living re-creation of 300 years of Iowa's agricultural past, including the maize-planting Native Americans and early twentieth–century farmers. Follow a path that leads you through a 1700 Iowa Indian village, an 1850 pioneer farm, a 1900 farm, and the modern Henry A. Wallace Crop Center. (If you're not up for a lot of walking, there is also motorized transportation—that is, wagons pulled by tractors.) Museum workers, in costume and in character, will make you feel welcome at each stop, as though you're a guest who just happened to travel back in time. Also on site are the 1875 frontier town named Walnut Hill (featuring a general store, church, barn, and other buildings along its Main Street) and the Martin Flynn 1867 Italian Villa–style mansion. A newly built State of Iowa Welcome Center is situated at the entrance.

Details: Exit I-35/80 at Hickman Rd. Open May–Oct daily 9–5. $8 ages 13–59, $7 age 60 and older, $5 ages 4–12, free under 4. (1–3 hours)

★★ HISTORIC VALLEY JUNCTION
Fifth St., 515/222-3642

This one-time railroad neighborhood has plenty to offer all kinds of people: charming, upscale retail shops, good restaurants, and a pedestrian-friendly atmosphere. You could spend all afternoon here just browsing antiques. An exhaustive costume shop, The Theatrical Shop, is ground zero for Halloween in Des Moines. On Thursday nights in the summer, Valley Junction comes alive with its own farmer's market featuring live music and extremely popular kettle popcorn. A wee bit weary? Stop for a pint at A. K. O'Connors, an Irish bar.

Details: Exit I-235 at 63rd St. (Des Moines), drive south and look for the Valley Junction signs. Open year-round daily. Free. (1–2 hours)

★★ SCIENCE CENTER OF IOWA
4500 Grand Ave., 515/274-4138

This museum welcomes curious kids of all ages, or simply the young at heart, with more than 33 thousand square feet of hands-on exhibits that explore and explain the mysteries of science. There are 11 images from the Hubble Space Telescope, a working Foucault pendulum, and a small stable of native Iowa animals, especially turtles. The Sargent Space Theater is a planetarium and, on weekends, hosts laser shows to the tunes of Pink Floyd, Metallica, the Beastie Boys, and their ilk.
Details: Just south of Des Moines Art Center. Open year-round Mon–Sat 10–5, Sun noon–5. $5.50 adults, $3.50 children 3–12 and seniors 60 and over, and free under 3. (1 hour)

★ ADVENTURELAND PARK
I-80 and Hwy. 65, Altoona, 800/532-1286 or 515/266-2121

OK, so it's no mega-huge Worlds of Fun, but Adventureland is home to such heart-pounding rides as the Tornado roller coaster, the Raging River, and the newer Space Shot. It's a great kids' destination and offers plenty of thrills for adults, too. With more than a hundred rides, shows, and attractions, it's Iowa's biggest amusement park.
Details: Open Memorial Day–Labor Day daily 10–10; Apr–Memorial Day and Labor Day–Sep weekends 10–8. $19.50 age 10 and older, $18 ages 4–9, free under 4. (2–5 hours)

★ BLANK PARK ZOO
7401 SW Ninth St., 515/285-4722

If you can stop at the more impressive Henry Doorly Zoo in Omaha, skip this, but Blank Park Zoo is one of Iowa's major zoos, with more than eight hundred animals—giraffes, wallabies, monkeys, and otters among them. An African Boardwalk, Big Cats Exhibit, and Australian Walkabout are among the theme attractions on its 22-acre grounds. Nearby is the green, rolling landscape of Blank Park.
Details: Open May–Oct 15 daily 10–5. $4.25 ages 12–64, $3.50 age 65 and older, $2.75 ages 2–11, free under 2. (1–2 hours)

★ PRAIRIE MEADOWS RACETRACK & CASINO
1 Prairie Meadows Dr., Altoona, 800/325-9015 or 515/967-1000, www.prairiemeadows.com

You have to play to pay, right? Er, maybe that's not exactly how casinos describe the attraction of their floors full of slot machines, cheap food, and simulcast racing. If gambling's your thing, Prairie Meadows is central Iowa's center for said activity, whether you prefer living, breathing horses or the bells and whistles of the slot machines.

Details: *I-80 Exit 142. Open year-round 24 hours. Free. (15 minutes–1 hour)*

FITNESS AND RECREATION

Indoor or outdoor, wet or dry, the Des Moines area has a recreation location fit for you.

The **Great Western Trail**, 515/999-2557 or 515/961-6169, is 17 miles of crushed limestone that stretches south from Des Moines (with a trailhead at Park Avenue on the city's south side) to the town of Martensdale. Bicyclers can stop at the Cumming Tap in the town of Cumming for a pit stop and refreshments. Another fine trail is the **Raccoon River Valley Trail**, 515/755-3061 or 515/465-3577, 35 miles of asphalt from Waukee to Yale. You'll pass through both Adel and Redfield.

Saylorville Lake, 5600 NW 78th Ave., 515/964-0672, is full of trails, picnic shelters, campgrounds, and water-sport opportunities. Does Iowa have sandy beaches? Yes, and there's one at Saylorville. Don't expect the Gulf Coast, though—you're in a landlocked state, remember?

Need an indoor sports haven to escape the extremes of Iowa's weather while you work out? **Grand Slam U.S.A.**, 3025 Justin Dr., Urbandale, 515/278-1070, is hidden in a suburban strip mall, but it's packed with batting cages and two basketball courts—the latter with adjustable-height rims, so anybody can slam dunk like Shaq, or whoever their favorite NBA star is.

Sleepy Hollow Sports Park, 4051 Dean Ave., 515/262-4100, is Des Moines' year-round outdoor recreation complex. Summer brings sand volleyball, winter brings snowboarding. Meanwhile, **White Water University**, 5401 E. University Ave., 515/265-4904, focuses solely on summer (from Memorial Day to Labor Day), with water slides, go-carts, mini-golf, and more.

FOOD

Just north of Sherman Hill, **A Dong Restaurant**, 1905 Cottage Grove Ave., 515/284-5632, serves tasty, affordable Vietnamese food in a casual, friendly atmosphere. Its small parking lot is located in back. On the south edge of Sherman Hill, **Chat Noir Cafe**, 644 18th St., 515/255-5900, serves bruschetta and other light, refreshing fare on the first floor and porch of a historic, renovated Victorian home.

GREATER DES MOINES

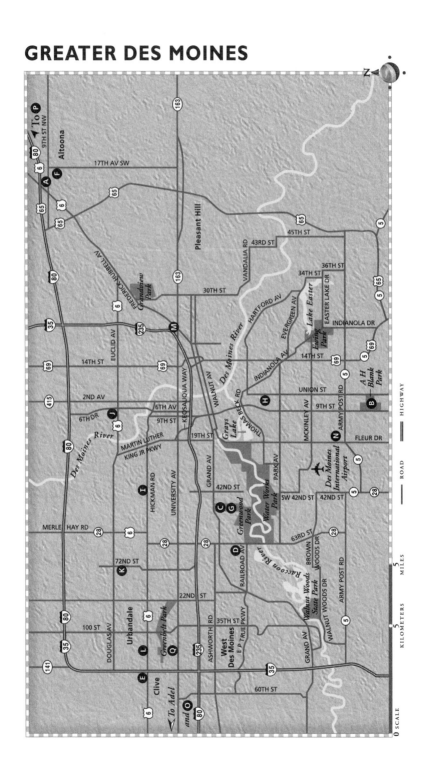

To P
9TH ST NW
Altoona
80
6
65
A
F
17TH AV SW
65
65
65
6
80
Pleasant Hill
163
163
45TH ST
65
43RD ST
VANDALIA RD
30TH ST
36TH ST
34TH ST
FREDRICK HUBBELL AV
Grandview Park
6
235
35
M
EUCLID AV
14TH ST
2ND AV
6TH AV
6TH DR
J
6
9TH ST
MARTIN LUTHER
KING JR PKWY
19TH ST
HICKMAN RD
I
UNIVERSITY AV
MERLE HAY RD
28
6
28
28
72ND ST
K
22ND ST
100 ST
DOUGLAS AV
Urbandale
L
6
Greenbelt Park
Q
235
ASHWORTH RD
35TH ST
West
Des Moines
E P TRUE PKWY
E
Clive
To Adel
and O
O
60TH ST
141
35
80

Des Moines River
69
KEOSAUQUA WAY
WALNUT AV
Des Moines River
Grays Lake
Water Works Park
42ND ST
C
G
Greenwood Park
D
RAILROAD AV
GRAND AV
Raccoon River
Walnut Woods State Park
WALNUT WOODS DR
GRAND AV

163
HARTFORD AV
Lake Easter
EASTER LAKE DR
INDIANOLA DR
Ewing Park
14TH ST
EVERGREEN AV
INDIANOLA AV
UNION ST
H
9TH ST
MCKINLEY AV
N
ARMY POST RD
FLEUR DR
Des Moines International Airport
SW 42ND ST
42ND ST
63RD ST
BROWN
WOODS DR
ARMY POST RD
5
5
5
5
5
5
5
69
69
69
A H Blank Park
B
55
28
28
28
THOMAS BECK RD
PARK AV

SCALE
0
KILOMETERS
5
MILES
5

ROAD
HIGHWAY

Close to Drake University, **Drake Diner**, 1111 25th St., 515/277-1111, has a solid menu of hamburgers, sandwiches, and other fare with a decidedly 1950s flair. It's housed in an authentic-looking diner with a screened-in porch.

A Taste of Thailand, 215 E. Walnut St., 515/243-9521, has become a staple on the Des Moines restaurant scene thanks to its flavorful dishes and selection of more than a hundred bottled beers. Also in the downtown area, **Court Ave. Brewing Co.**, 309 Court Ave., 515/282-BREW, and **Raccoon River Brewing Co.**, 200 10th St., 515/283-1941, are Des Moines' best brew pubs, serving good food and locally produced libations.

For lunch downtown, nothing beats **Basil's Cafe**, 801 Grand Ave., 515/244-2070. Located on the Skywalk level of the Principal Financial building, Basil's Italian pasta concoctions and homemade breads consistently impress. If you show up around noon on a weekday, be prepared to find a ravenous mob of employees on their lunch break. For fine dining in the same building, **801 Steak & Chop House**, 801 Grand Ave., 515/288-6000, specializes in fine meats sautéed in delicious juices.

Part of the popular Ingersoll Avenue strip, **Noah's Ark Restaurant & Lounge**, 2400 Ingersoll Ave., 515/288-2246, serves top-of-the-line steaks, seafood, and pasta. And you can't beat the calzone appetizer. Some of the best pizza in town is sold by the slice after midnight at **Big Tomato Pizza Co.**, 2613 Ingersoll Ave., 515/288-7227, in a locally owned carry-out/delivery business that feeds the hungry masses on the nightlife scene. Just across the street, **SomeWhere Else**, 2716 Ingersoll Ave., 515/282-9399, is another late-night eatery with soups, sandwiches, and fried snacks.

Along with Noah's Ark, there are a few Italian restaurants in Des Moines that form the cornerstone of the city's eating scene. Nestled into a

SIGHTS

- Ⓐ Adventureland Park
- Ⓑ Blank Park Zoo
- Ⓒ Des Moines Art Center
- Ⓓ Historic Valley Junction
- Ⓔ Living History Farms
- Ⓕ Prairie Meadows Racetrack & Casino
- Ⓖ Science Center of Iowa

FOOD

- Ⓗ Baratta's Restaurant & Pizzarea
- Ⓘ Bistro 43
- Ⓙ Chuck's Italian-American Restaurant
- Ⓚ El Rodeo
- Ⓛ Iowa Machine Shed Restaurant
- Ⓜ Latin King Restaurant

LODGING

- Ⓝ Airport Holiday Inn & Conference Center
- Ⓞ Comfort Suites at Living History Farms
- Ⓞ Grey Goose Bed & Breakfast
- Ⓟ Lacorsette Maison Inn Bed & Breakfast
- Ⓠ Wildwood Lodge

Note: Items with the same letter are located in the same area.

quiet residential area on the south side, **Baratta's Restaurant & Pizzarea**, 2320 S. Union St., 515/243-4516, will probably make you feel right at home with its friendly service and cozy tables. Try their ribs, even if that's not your normal dish.

Farther east, **Latin King Restaurant**, 2200 Hubbell Ave., 515/266-4466, offers a similar food selection with a little more pomp and circumstance. On the north side, **Chuck's Italian-American Restaurant**, 3610 Sixth Ave., 515/244-4104, is a wonderfully low-key establishment that pours Old Style beer from the tap and cooks its pizzas in full view of a street-side window. If you're with a group of friends, definitely stop to eat here and order at least one of the specialty pizzas.

Myth: *Iowa food, even in Des Moines, is all meat and potatoes.*
Fact: *The city features everything from Vietnamese and Thai to cutting-edge gourmet styles.*

If you're planning to dine at only one fine restaurant in Des Moines, you'd better make reservations at **Bistro 43**, 4345 Hickman Rd., 515/255-5942. This popular place is big in gourmet delights, but small in size. Cooks and diners share the same room and wonderful aromas.

Don't neglect that Iowa meat-and-potatoes chow during your visit. The home of hearty family-style dining that fully reflects the state's farm heritage is the **Iowa Machine Shed Restaurant**, 11151 Hickman Rd., Urbandale, 515/270-6818. Lots of knick-knacks are for sale in the lobby gift shop, too. Not quite as far west, authentic Mexican dining in an airy, lively atmosphere is the specialty of **El Rodeo**, 7420 Douglas Ave., 515/251-7647.

LODGING

The Des Moines area has a large contingent of fine hotels, most reasonably priced, even on weekends. There are also nearby bed-and-breakfast inn options in this urban pocket of Iowa.

Hotel Fort Des Moines, 10th St. and Walnut St., 800/532-1466 or 515/243-1161, www.hotelfortdm.com, is on the National Register of Historic Places and a revered 240-room mainstay on the city's lodging scene. Raccoon River Brewing Company is just next door. Another pricey but luxurious option for downtown lodging is **Savery Hotel and Spa**, 401 Locust St., 800/798-2151 or 515/244-2151.

If you want to drive into town and roll right off of I-235 and into your hotel room, check out **Best Western Starlite Village**, 929 Third St., 800/528-1234 or 515/282-5251, or the **Holiday Inn Downtown**, 1050 Sixth Ave., 800/HOLIDAY or 515/283-0151, both located near downtown and just off the freeway. (In fact, they face each other across the freeway.) Neither is especially notable, but their location is handy.

Across Fleur Drive from Des Moines International Airport, **Airport Holiday Inn & Conference Center**, 6111 Fleur Dr., 515/287-2400, is notable not only for its handy locale but for its Crystal Tree Restaurant & Lounge, which serves a fine Sunday champagne brunch. Location is part of the charm of the **Carter House Inn**, 640 20th St., 515/288-7850, a bed-and-breakfast housed in the 1878 Italianate Victorian home of Rick and Cindy Nelson. Ask to view the videotape of the inn being moved—in a single piece—to its present site in the Sherman Hill neighborhood.

If you're out in the 'burbs, **Comfort Suites at Living History Farms**, 11167 Hickman Rd., Urbandale, 800/395-7675 or 515/276-1126, is an attractive hotel that remembered to include charm along with all of its modern amenities. This mid- to high-priced option has a great indoor pool, too. In the same area, **Wildwood Lodge**, 11431 Forest Ave., Clive, 800/728-1223 or 515/222-9876, is a new hotel that's meant to make you feel like you're staying in the remote northern wilderness. It's charming in a kitschy sort of way.

West of Des Moines is the **Grey Goose Bed & Breakfast**, 1740 290th St., Adel, 515/833-2338, a renovated 1920s farmhouse on a scenic 40-acre farm. East of Des Moines, **Lacorsette Maison Inn Bed & Breakfast**, 629 First Ave. E., Hwy. 6, Newton, 515/792-6833, is a Mission-style mansion known for its antiques, whirlpools, and fine dining.

CAMPING

With horseback riding, electricity, showers, and RV hookups, the camping at **Jester Park**, along the southwest shore of Saylorville Lake and three miles east of Granger, 515/999-2557, is easy and scenic. There's also a renovated barn designed for picnics. Open April through October.

Ledges State Park, six miles south of Boone on Hwy. 164, 515/432-1852, has more than 90 campsites (half are electric, half are primitive) on its picturesque grounds. The hilly terrain offers better-than-normal views for Iowa. And like all state parks, it's open year-round.

Privately owned, **Timberline Best Holiday Trav-L Park**, 3165 Ashworth Rd., Waukee, 515/987-1714, has 10 acres of wooded trails and offers everything from electricity to showers to groceries.

NIGHTLIFE

Downtown nightlife revolves around Court Avenue, which features a tight cluster of bars and dance clubs. **Court Ave. Brewing Co.**, 309 Court Ave., 515/282-2739, features live acoustic music a few nights per week in its bar. Sunday nights are usually acoustic; on weekends the musicians plug it in and turn it up a notch. **Papa's Planet**, 208 Third St., 515/284-0901, is a Top 40 dance club where singles eyeball each other over cheap draught beer and well drinks. **Java Joes Coffeehouse**, 214 Fourth St., 515/288-5282, serves not only coffee but beer and, on many afternoons and evenings, free live music. It serves a good, healthy lunch menu, too. Also downtown, **The Garden**, 112 SE Fourth St., 515/243-3965, southeast of Court Avenue, is not just a popular gay dance club, it's the best dance club in the city, period. Its multiple rooms host everything from throbbing DJ music to live stage shows by drag queens.

It's a goofy name, but **Super Toad Entertainment Center**, 1424 E. Euclid Ave., 515/264-8623, is a voluminous bar and music venue that country fans should check out. On weeknights you can line dance to live music. The venue also hosts national acts of all styles, from country legend Merle Haggard to metal veterans Megadeth.

Blues fans gravitate towards **The Grand**, 1501 Grand Ave., 515/280-1024. Its cozy stage hosts some of the best blues talent you'll find anywhere in the country, week after week. Meanwhile, **Hairy Marys**, 2307 University Ave., 515/279-5507, is the hip live music hangout for the rock and punk crowd. Incidentally, its owners also run Big Tomato Pizza Co. and GT Lounge, both on Ingersoll Avenue.

If you're in the mood for dancing that requires actual steps, you can't go wrong at the historic **Val Air Ballroom**, 301 Ashworth Rd., West Des Moines, 515/223-6152, where big band, swing, and exotic music flavors rule. The dance floor and disco ball are both large and impressive, the retro decor stylish, and the overall experience highly memorable.

Also in West Des Moines, **Billy Joe's Pitcher Show**, 1701 25th St., West Des Moines, 515/224-1709, is more than a movie theater that shows second-run films in a lounge-style room. Jaegermeister is on tap, and *Rocky Horror Picture Show* is screened exclusively at midnight on weekends.

If you're looking for laughs, **Funny Bone Comedy Club**, 8529 Hickman Rd., Urbandale, 515/270-2100, hosts local and national comedians, like local radio and TV personality the Round Guy and 1970s sitcom icon Jimmy "Dyn-o-mite!" Walker.

APPENDIX

Consider this appendix your travel tool box. Use it along with the material in the Planning Your Trip chapter to craft the trip you want. Here are the tools you'll find inside:

Planning Map. Make copies of this map and plot out various trip possibilities. Once you've decided on your route, you can write it on the original map and refer to it as you're traveling.

Mileage Chart. This chart shows the driving distances (in miles) between various destinations throughout the region. Use it in conjunction with the Planning Map.

Special Interest Tours. If you'd like to plan a trip around a certain theme—such as nature, sports, or art—one of these tours may work for you.

Calendar of Events. Here you'll find a month-by-month listing of major area events.

Resources. This guide lists various regional chambers of commerce and visitors bureaus, state offices, bed-and-breakfast registries, and other useful sources of information.

PLANNING MAP: Iowa/Nebraska

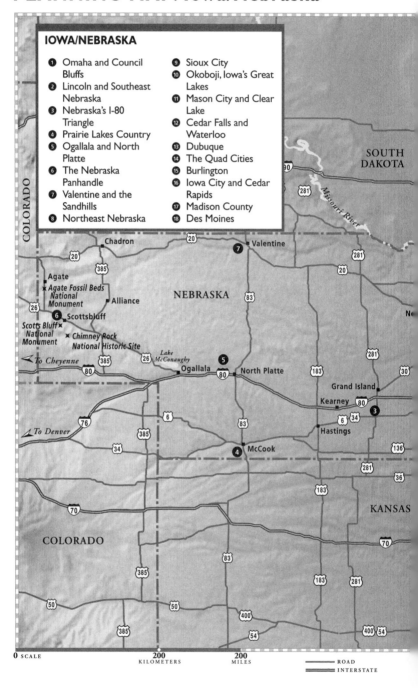

IOWA/NEBRASKA

- ❶ Omaha and Council Bluffs
- ❷ Lincoln and Southeast Nebraska
- ❸ Nebraska's I-80 Triangle
- ❹ Prairie Lakes Country
- ❺ Ogallala and North Platte
- ❻ The Nebraska Panhandle
- ❼ Valentine and the Sandhills
- ❽ Northeast Nebraska
- ❾ Sioux City
- ❿ Okoboji, Iowa's Great Lakes
- ⓫ Mason City and Clear Lake
- ⓬ Cedar Falls and Waterloo
- ⓭ Dubuque
- ⓮ The Quad Cities
- ⓯ Burlington
- ⓰ Iowa City and Cedar Rapids
- ⓱ Madison County
- ⓲ Des Moines

SOUTH DAKOTA

COLORADO

Chadron

Valentine

NEBRASKA

Agate
Agate Fossil Beds
National
Monument

Alliance

Scottsbluff

Scotts Bluff
National
Monument

Chimney Rock
National Historic Site

To Cheyenne

Lake McConaughy

Ogallala

North Platte

Grand Island

Kearney

To Denver

Hastings

McCook

COLORADO

KANSAS

Missouri River

0 SCALE

200
KILOMETERS

200
MILES

ROAD

INTERSTATE

WISCONSIN

MINNESOTA

Minneapolis
St. Paul

Mississippi River

La Crosse

Effigy Mounds National Monument

Sioux Falls

Spirit Lake

Okoboji

Clear Lake
Mason City

To Madison

Missouri River

Sioux City

IOWA

Ft. Dodge

Ames

Waterloo

Cedar Falls

Dubuque

To Chicago

Cedar Rapids

Des Moines

Winterset

Indianola

Iowa City

Davenport

Rock Island
Moline

Omaha

Council Bluffs

Galesburg

Lincoln

Nebraska City

Burlington

Beatrice

Homestead National Monument

St. Joseph

MISSOURI

Topeka

Kansas City

Mississippi River

Missouri River

St. Louis

N

STATE BOUNDARY
POINT OF INTEREST

IOWA/NEBRASKA MILEAGE CHART

	Burlington, IA	Cedar Falls, IA	Cedar Rapids, IA	Clear Lake, IA	Des Moines, IA	Dubuque, IA	Hastings, NE	Iowa City, IA	Lincoln, NE	Mason City, IA	Ogallala, NE	Okoboji, IA	Omaha, NE	Sioux City, IA	Valentine, NE
Cedar Falls, IA	162														
Cedar Rapids, IA	104	59													
Clear Lake, IA	255	91	152												
Des Moines, IA	185	107	130	113											
Dubuque, IA	151	98	69	191	194										
Hastings, NE	477	399	421	404	291	486									
Iowa City, IA	76	89	30	182	112	85	403								
Lincoln, NE	376	298	320	303	190	385	107	302							
Mason City, IA	237	72	133	8	121	173	412	163	311						
Ogallala, NE	644	566	588	572	459	653	203	570	274	579					
Okoboji, IA	402	238	299	147	260	338	358	329	257	155	525				
Omaha, NE	319	241	264	247	134	328	162	246	61	255	329	200			
Sioux City, IA	382	219	327	202	197	316	254	309	153	210	421	105	96		
Valentine, NE	595	453	540	484	410	550	234	522	306	492	183	366	298	238	
Waterloo, IA	339	261	283	266	153	347	155	265	54	274	322	198	20	94	277

SPECIAL INTEREST TOURS

With *Iowa/Nebraska Travel•Smart* you can plan a trip of any length—a one-day excursion, a getaway weekend, or a three-week vacation—around any special interest. To get you started, the following pages contain five special-interest itineraries geared toward a variety of interests. For more information, refer to the chapters listed—chapter names are in boldface, and chapter numbers appear inside black bullets. You can follow a suggested itinerary in its entirety, or shorten, length, or combine parts of each, depending on your starting and ending points.

Discuss alternative routes and schedules with your travel companions—it's a great way to have fun even before you leave home. And remember: Don't hesitate to change your itinerary once you're on the road. Careful study and planning ahead will help you make informed decision as you go, but spontaneity is the extra ingredient that will make your trip memorable.

MISSISSIPPI TOUR

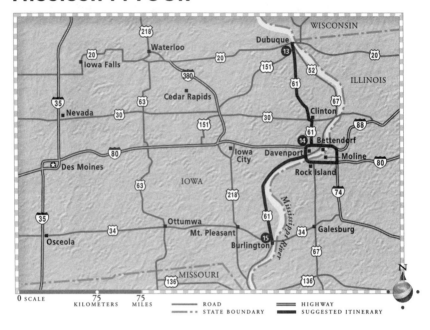

No American river quite enchants like the mighty Mississippi, and your eastern Iowa travels offer the perfect opportunity to explore the attractions that preserve and promote the river way of life.

⑬Dubuque (Mississippi River Museum, Diamond Jo Casino, the Tollbridge Inn)

⑭The Quad Cities (Rock Island Arsenal Museum, the Great River Trail, the Queen of Hearts steamboat, Freight House Bistro)

⑮Burlington (Lock and Dam #18, Port of Burlington Welcome Center, Catfish Bend River Casino II)

Time needed: 1 day

MUSIC CLUB TOUR

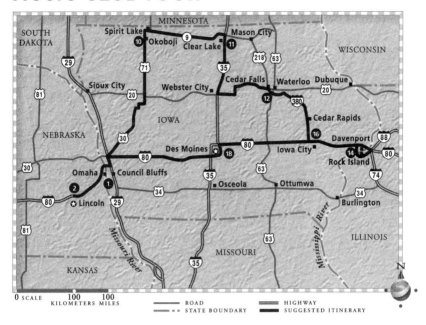

Iowa might be the state that hosted "The Day the Music Died," as Don McLean described the Buddy Holly–Ritchie Valens–Big Bopper plane crash in 1959 just north of Clear Lake, but Iowa and Nebraska today offer live music spots that still thrive. Stringing some of these destinations together will help you see a good sampling of the region's urban culture.

❶Omaha and Council Bluffs (The Ranch Bowl, the Dubliner Pub, the Stork Club, the 18th Amendment Saloon)
❷Lincoln and Southeast Nebraska (The Zoo Bar, Knickerbockers)
❿Okoboji, Iowa's Great Lakes (The Roof Garden)
⓫Mason City and Clear Lake (Surf Ballroom)
⓬Cedar Falls and Waterloo (Steb's)
⓮The Quad Cities (The Col Ballroom, Rock Island Brewing Co.)
⓰Iowa City and Cedar Rapids (Gabe's, Sal's Music Emporium, CSPS)
⓲Des Moines (The Grand, Hairy Marys, Val Air Ballroom, Java Joes Coffeehouse)

Time needed: 6–8 days

ART TOUR

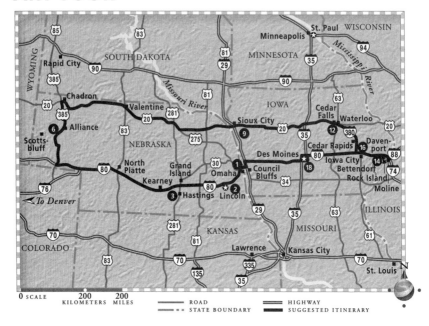

O SCALE 200   200
       KILOMETERS MILES

▬▬▬ ROAD   ▤▤▤ HIGHWAY
▬ ▪ ▪ STATE BOUNDARY ▬ SUGGESTED ITINERARY

"Art" doesn't just mean a painting on a wall in a fine art museum. The wrecked but carefully arranged autos that make up Carhenge near Alliance, Nebraska, are a good example of unconventional, art that you shouldn't pass up.

❶Omaha and Council Bluffs (Joslyn Art Museum, the Antiquarium)
❷Lincoln and Southeast Nebraska (Sheldon Memorial Art Gallery & Sculpture Garden)
❸Nebraska's I-80 Triangle (The Museum of Nebraska Art)
❻The Nebraska Panhandle (Carhenge & Car Art Reserve)
❾Sioux City (Sioux City Art Center)
⓬Cedar Falls and Waterloo (University of Northern Iowa Gallery of Art, Hearst Center for the Arts, Waterloo Museum of Art)
⓮The Quad Cities (Davenport Museum of Art)
⓰Iowa City and Cedar Rapids (University of Iowa Museum of Art, National Czech & Slovak Museum & Library)
⓲Des Moines (Des Moines Art Center, Hoyt Sherman Place)

Time needed: 5–8 days

PIONEER HERITAGE TOUR

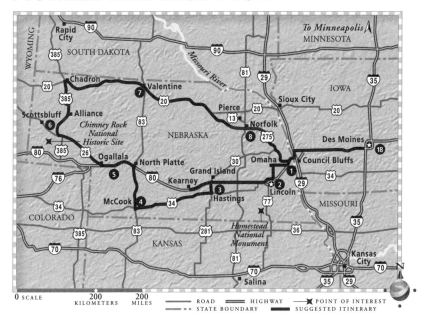

Trace the path of early settlers across Nebraska and Iowa.

❶**Omaha and Council Bluffs** (Western Historic Trails Center, Lewis & Clark Monument and Scenic Overlook)

❷**Lincoln and Southeast Nebraska** (The Museum of Nebraska History, Thomas P. Kennard House, Rock Creek Station State Historical Park)

❸**Nebraska's I-80 Triangle** (Harold Warp Pioneer Village, Stuhr Museum of the Prairie Pioneer, Plainsman Museum)

❹**Prairie Lakes Country** (Museum of the High Plains)

❺**Ogallala and North Platte** (Buffalo Bill Ranch State Historical Park, Boot Hill)

❻**The Nebraska Panhandle** (Chimney Rock Historical Site, Museum of the Fur Trade, North Platte Valley Museum)

❼**Valentine and the Sandhills** (Cherry County Historical Society Museum)

❽**Northeast Nebraska** (Pierce Historical Museum Complex)

❿**Des Moines** (State of Iowa Historical Building)

Time needed: 4–6 days

AGRICULTURAL TOUR

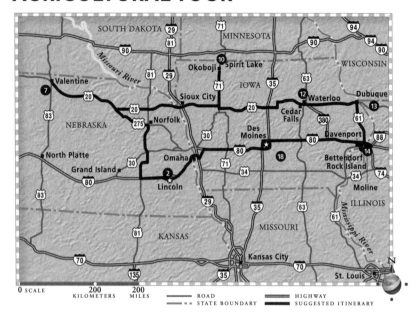

No industry has been as important to Nebraska and Iowa as agriculture. Without a doubt, Iowa's fertile soil and Nebraska's vast grazing lands have provided both economic and social anchors. Only in the last few decades have independent agricultural operators largely given way to big business interests. Around the region, a wide variety of attractions preserve the history and spirit of these independent operators.

❷Lincoln and Southeast Nebraska (Homestead National Monument)
❼Valentine and the Sandhills (Sandhills Guest Ranch Bed & Breakfast)
❿Okoboji, Iowa's Great Lakes (Clark Museum of Area History/Clark's Antique Acres)
⓬Cedar Falls and Waterloo (Antique Acres, John Deere Waterloo Works)
⓭Dubuque (National Farm Toy Museum, Ertl Company)
⓮The Quad Cities (John Deere Pavilion)
⓲Des Moines (Living History Farms, Iowa Machine Shed)

Time needed: 3 days

CALENDAR OF EVENTS

January
Iowa
Bald Eagle Appreciation Days
  Third weekend in January
  Keokuk
  800/383-1219
Snowfest
  Fourth weekend in January
  Cresco
  800/373-6293

Nebraska
Quack-Off (Duck Race on Ice)
  Last Saturday in January
  Avoca
  402/275-3221

February
Iowa
Buddy Holly Tribute
  First weekend in February
  Clear Lake
  515/357-6151

Nebraska
Freeze-Out Picnic
  First Sunday in February
  Capitol Hill Park, Brownville
  402/825-4131 or 402/825-6001
Valentine's Day Celebration
  February 14
  Valentine
  402/376-2969

March
Iowa
St. Patrick's Day Celebration

St. Patrick's Day weekend
  Emmetsburg
  712/852-4326
Waverly Midwest Horse Sale
  Last full week in March
  Waverly
  319/352-2804

Nebraska
High School State Basketball
Tournament
  First and second weekend in March
  Pershing Auditorium, Lincoln
  402/489-0386

April
Iowa
Kalona Quilt Show and Sale
  Last weekend in April
  Kalona
  319/656-2240
Battle of Pea Ridge: Civil War
Reenactment
  Last weekend in April
  Keokuk
  319/524-5599

Nebraska
Crane Watch
  First half of April
  Rowe Sanctuary and Fort Kearny,
  Kearney
  800/652-9435

May
Iowa
Tulip Time Festival

First weekend in May
Pella
515/628-2409
Tulip Festival
  Second weekend in May
  Orange City
  712/737-4510
North Iowa Band Festival
  Third weekend in May
  Mason City
  515/423-5724

Nebraska
81 Cruisers Annual Rod Run
  First Saturday in May
  Downtown Geneva
  402/362-6194
Lincoln Czech Festival
  First Saturday in May
  East Park Plaza Mall, Lincoln
  402/488-6309
Willa Cather Spring Conference
  First Saturday in May
  Willa Cather Pioneer Memorial,
  Red Cloud
  402/746-2653
Arbor Day Celebration
  First weekend in May
  Nebraska City
  402/873-3000
Heartland Storytelling Festival
  Second weekend in May
  Homestead National Monument of
  America, Beatrice
  402/223-3514

June
Iowa
Jesse James Days
  First weekend in June

Corydon
515/872-1338
Frontier Days
  First weekend in June
  Fort Dodge
  515/573-4231
My Waterloo Days Festival
  First two weekends in June
  Waterloo
  319/233-8431
Le Festival de l'Heritage Français
  First Saturday in June
  Corning
  515/322-5229
Glenn Miller Festival
  Second weekend in June
  Clarinda
  712/542-2461
Grant Wood Art Festival
  Second Sunday in June
  Stone City, Anamosa
  319/462-4267
Donna Reed Festival for the
Performing Arts
  Second full week in June
  Denison
  712/263-3334

Nebraska
Loup City Polish Days
  Second weekend in June
  Loup City
  308/745-1050
Nebraska State Country Music
Championship
  Second weekend in June
  Otoe County Fairgrounds,
  Syracuse
  402/234-5277
Nebraska High School Rodeo Finals

Last full week and weekend in June
Custer County Fairgrounds,
Broken Bow
308/872-5287

July
Iowa
Riverboat Days
First weekend in July
Clinton
319/242-7052
Saturday in the Park
First Saturday in July
Sioux City
800/593-2228
Iowa Games
Third weekend in July
Ames
800/964-0332
RAGBRAI (Register's Annual Great
Bike Ride Across Iowa)
Last week in July
Across Iowa
800/474-3342
Bix Beiderbecke Memorial Jazz
Festival
Last weekend in July
Davenport
888/BIX-LIVS
National Balloon Classic
Last weekend in July and first
weekend in August
Indianola
800/FLY-IOWA

Nebraska
Celebrate America's Birthday
July 4
Stuhr Museum, Grand Island
308/385-5316

Cornhusker State Games
Second full week in July
Lincoln
402/471-2544
Art in the Park
Second Sunday in July
Harmon Park, Kearney
308/234-2662

August
Iowa
Knoxville Nationals (Sprint Car)
Second week in August
Knoxville
515/842-5431
Iowa State Fair
Second and third week in August
Des Moines
800/545-FAIR
Old-Time Country Music Contest,
Festival and Pioneer Exposition
Last week in August
Avoca
712/762-4363

Nebraska
Nifty '50s Celebration
First weekend in August
Main Street, Ponca
402/755-2224
Carhenge Classic Car Show
First Saturday in August
Alliance
308/762-1520
National Country Music Festival
Second weekend in August
East City Park, Ainsworth
402/387-2844
Wine & Wings Festival
Last weekend in August

Cuthills Vineyards, Pierce
402/329-6774

September
Iowa
Midwest Old Thresher Reunion
First weekend in September
Mount Pleasant
319/385-8937
Dragon Boat Festival
Second weekend in September
Dubuque
319/583-6345
Clay County Fair
Third weekend in September
Spencer
712/262-4740

Nebraska
Kass Kounty King Korn Karnival
Second weekend in September
Main Street, Plattsmouth
402/296-4155
Chimney Rock Pioneer Days
Second weekend in September
Library Park, Bayard
308/586-2830
Applejack Festival
Third weekend in September
Nebraska City
402/873-3000

October
Iowa
Oktoberfest
First weekend in October
Amana Colonies
800/245-5464
Madison County Covered Bridge
Festival

Second weekend in October
Winterset
515/462-1185

Nebraska
Blue Grass and Country Music
Festival
First weekend in October
Christensen Field, Fremont
402/727-7626
Pumpkin Festival
First Sunday in October
Town Hall, Elyria
308/728-5438

November
Iowa
National Farm Toy Show
First weekend in November
Dyersville
800/533-8293
Julefest
Last weekend in November
Elk Horn and Kimballton
800/451-7960

Nebraska
Celebration of Lights
Third Thursday in November
Downtown Hastings
402/463-1692

December
Iowa
Sinterklass Day and Christmas Tour
of Homes
First Saturday in December
Orange City
712/737-4510

Nebraska

Christmas on the Prairie
First weekend in December
Saunders County Museum, Wahoo
402/443-3090

Sights and Sounds of Christmas
First Sunday in December
Dana College, Blair
402/426-7216

Star City Holiday Parade
First Sunday in December
Downtown Lincoln
402/434-6900

RESOURCES

Iowa

Association of County Conservation Boards, 405 S.W. 3rd St., Suite 1, Ankeny, IA 50021; 515/963-9582.

Central Iowa Tourism Region, P.O. Box 454, Webster City, IA 50595; 800/285-4808, www.iowatourism.org.

Eastern Iowa Tourism Association, P.O. Box 485, Vinton, IA 52349; 800/891-EITA, www.easterniowatourism.org.

Iowa Association of Campground Owners, Oakwood RV Park, 5419 240th St., Clear Lake, IA 50428; 515/357-4019; www.gocampingamerica.com.

Iowa Bed & Breakfast Innkeepers Association, 250 W. Maple Dr., Hartley, IA 51346-1359; 800/888-INNS.

Iowa Department of Natural Resources, Wallace State Office Building, Des Moines, IA 50319-0034; 515/281-5145, www.state.ia.us/dnr.

Iowa Department of Transportation Customer Service Center; 800 Lincoln Way, Ames, IA 50010; 800/532-1121 or 515/244-9124.

Iowa Lodging Association/Iowa Bed & Breakfast Guild, 9001 Hickman Rd. #2B, Des Moines, IA 50322; 800/743-IOWA.

Iowa State Patrol, Des Moines, IA; 515/281-5824; emergency phone 800/525-5555; cellular emergency number *55.

Western Iowa Tourism Region, 502 E. Coolbaugh St., Red Oak, IA 51566; 888/623-4232.

Winter Road Conditions; 515/288-1047 outside of Iowa or 800/288-1047 toll-free in Iowa.

Nebraska

Nebraska Association of Bed & Breakfasts, RR 2 Box 17, Elgin, NE 68636-9301; 402/843-2287; www.bbonline.com/ne/nabb.

Nebraska Department of Economic Development Division of Travel & Tourism, P.O. Box 94666, Lincoln, NE 68509; 402/471-3796 or 800/228-4307.

Nebraska Department of Roads, 1500 Hwy 2, P.O. Box 94759, Lincoln, NE 68509-4759; 402/471-4567.

Nebraska Game/Parks Commission Omaha Metro Office, 1212 Deer Park Blvd., Omaha, NE 68108-2020; 402/595-2144; www.ngpc.state.ne.us/.

Nebraska Restaurant Association, www.nebraska-dining.org.

Nebraska Travel and Tourism Division, Department of Economic Development, P.O. Box 94666, Lincoln, NE 68509; 800/228-4307.

INDEX

Adventureland Park, 206

Agate Fossil Beds National Monument, 76

Amana Colonies, 184–185

American Gothic House, 171

Antiquarium, 15–17

Antique Acres, 129

Apple Trees Museum, 167–169

Arbor Day Farm, 39

Arbor Lodge State Historical Park and
    Arboretum, 39

Arts for Living Center, 170

Ashfall Fossil Bed State Historical Park, 97–98

Belle of Sioux City, 107–108

Blank Park Zoo, 206

Bluedorn Science Imaginarium, 133

Boot Hill, 69–70

Botanical Center, 203

Bowring Ranch, 88–89

Boys Town (Father Flanagan's Boys Home),
    20–21

Buffalo Bill Cody Museum, 160

Buffalo Bill Ranch State Historical Park, 65–67

Burlington, Iowa, 166–174

Cabela's, 78–79

Carhenge & Car Art Reserve, 76

Catfish Bend River Casino II, 170

Cedar Falls, Iowa, 128–141

Cedar Rapids, Iowa, 175–187

Centennial Hall, 88

Central Iowa College Towns, Scenic Route,
    213–214

Champion Mill Historical Park, 57

Charles H. MacNider Museum, 121–122

Cherry County Historical Society Museum, 88

Chimney Rock National Historic Site, 77

Clark Museum of Area History/Clark's
    Antique Acres, 114–115

Clear Lake, Iowa, 119–127

Cody Trading Post, 67

Council Bluffs, Iowa, 14–31

Crystal Lake Cave, 149

Cuthills Vineyards, 98

Czech Village, 181

Davenport Museum of Art, 157

Des Moines Art Center, 204–205

Des Moines, Iowa, 198–214

Diamond Jo Casino, 146–147

Dickinson County Museum, 115

Downtown Iowa City Pedestrian Mall, 178

Dubuque Arboretum and Botanical
    Gardens, 149

Dubuque Greyhound Park & Casino, 149

Dubuque Museum of Art, 145

Dubuque, Iowa, 142–155

Dyersville, Iowa, 154

Eagle Point Park, 147–148

East Davenport, Village of, 160–161

Edgerton Explorit Center, 50

Elkhorn Valley Museum & Research Center, 98

Fairview, The Bryan Museum, 36

Family Museum of Arts and Science, 160

Fenelon Place Elevator (Fourth Street Elevator), 145–146

Folsom Children's Zoo & Botanical Gardens, 36–37

Fort Kearny State Historical Park, 50

Fort Madison Farmington & Western Railroad Rides & Museum, 171

Fort Niobrara National Wildlife Refuge, 87

Francescas's House, 192

Frank Lloyd Wright Stockman House, 122

Galena, Illinois, 146–147

Gardner State Historic Site, 114

Genoa Museum, 98–99

Gerald R. Ford Birthsite & Gardens, 21

Great River Road, Scenic Route, 140–141

Groth's Gardens, 193

Grout Museum of History and Science, 132–133

Harold Warp Pioneer Village, 47–49

Hastings Museum, 50–51

Hearst Center for the Arts, 129–131

Henry Doorly Zoo, 17–18

Heritage Hill National Historic District, 167

Higgins Museum, 115–116

Historic Fourth Street, 105

Historic General Dodge House, 21

Historic Haymarket, 33–35

Historic Old Market, 18–19

Historic Pottawattamie County "Squirrel Cage" Jail and Museum, 23

Historic Valley Junction, 205

Homestead National Monument of America, 39–41

Howell Dried Florals & Green House, 192

Hoyt Sherman Place (Sherman Hill National Historic District), 202

Hyde Memorial Observatory, 37

Ice House Museum, 131–132

Iowa City, Iowa, 175–187

Iowa Great Lakes Maritime Museum, 115

Iowa Great Lakes, 113–114

Iowa Hall—Museum of Natural History, 179

Iowa State Capitol, 202–203

Iowa Trolley Park, 124

Iowa's Great Lakes, 111–118

James Arthur Vineyards, 41

John Deere Pavilion, 157–159

John Deere Waterloo Works, 133

John G. Neihardt Center, 99

John Wayne Birthplace, 193

Johnny Carson Home, 99

Joselyn Art Museum, 19

Kalona, Iowa, 180

Kenfield Petrified Wood Gallery, 70

Kinney Pioneer Museum, 122–123

Lady Luck Casino, 161

Lake McConaughy State Recreation Area, 65

Lakes Art Center, 115

Lee G. Simmons Conservation Park & Wildlife Safari, 20

Lewis & Clark Monument and Scenic Overlook, 24

Lincoln County Historical Museum and Western Heritage Village, 67

Lincoln's Children's Museum, 37

Lincoln, Nebraska, 32–45

Little Red Schoolhouse, 132

Living History Farms, 205
Living Memorial Gardens, 79
Lock and Dam #18, 169
Loess Hills, Scenic Route, 30–31

Madison County Covered Bridges, 189–191
Madison County Museum and Historical
   Complex, 192–193
Madison County, Iowa, 188–197
Mason City, Iowa, 119–127
Massacre Canyon Historical Marker, 60
Mathias Ham House, 149
Meredith Wilson Boyhood Home, 123
Mississippi River Museum, 143–145
Museum of Nebraska Art, 47
Museum of Nebraska History, 33
Museum of the Fur Trade, 77
Museum of the High Plains, 57–59

National Czech & Slovak Museum & Library,
   179–180
National Museum of Rollerskating, 38
Nebraska Panhandle, 73–84
Nebraska State Capitol, 35
Nebraska's I-80 Triangle, 46–55
Norfolk Arts Center, 100
North Platte Valley Museum, 77–78
North Platte, Nebraska, 64–72
Northeast Iowa, 136–137
Northeast Nebraska Zoo, 100
Northeast Nebraska, 95–103

Ogallala, Nebraska, 64–72
Okoboji, Iowa, 111–118
Old Capitol Museum, 178–179
Ole's Big Game Steakhouse & Lounge, 67–69
Omaha, Nebraska, 14–31
Our Lady of Fatima Shrine, 60

Panorama Point, 79
Parks of Pride Arboretum, 99
Phelps House Museum, 167
Pierce Historical Museum Complex, 99–100
Plainsman Museum, 51–52
Port of Burlington Welcome Center, 170
Prairie Lakes Country, Nebraska, 56–63
Prairie Meadows Racetrack & Casino, 206–207
President Riverboat Casino, 161
Putnam Museum of History & Natural Science,
   159–160

Quad Cities, Iowa, 156–165

Riverside Zoo, 78
Rock Creek Station State Historical Park, 41
Rock Island Arsenal Museum, 160
Rosebud Casino, 88

Salisbury House, 203
Sandhills Spirit of the West, 89
Sandhills, Nebraska, 85–94
Science Center of Iowa, 205–206
Scotts Bluff National Monument, 75–76
Secret Garden, 171
Senator George Norris Historical Site, 59
Sergeant Floyd Monument, 108
Sergeant Floyd Welcome Center and Museum,
   105–107
Sheldon Memorial Art Gallery & Sculpture
   Garden, 37–38
Sidney Historic Downtown District, 78
Sioux City Art Center, 105
Sioux City Public Museum, 107
Sioux City, Iowa, 104–110
Snake Alley, 169–170
Southeast Nebraska, 32–45
Spirit of Brownville Missouri Riverboat
   Cruises, 38–39
State of Iowa Historical Building, 203–204

Strategic Air Command Museum, 19–20
Stuhr Museum of the Prairie Pioneer, 49–50
Surf Ballroom, 123–124

Terrace Hill, 204
Thomas P. Kennard House, 38
Tri-state Marker & Nebraska's Highest Point
   (Panorama Point), 79

Union Pacific Bailey Yard, 69
University of Iowa Museum of Art, 179
University of Nebraska State Museum
   (Morrill Hall), 36
University of Northern Iowa Gallery of Art,
   132
University of Northern Iowa Museum, 129

Valentine, Nebraska, 85–94
Van Horn's Antique Truck Museum, 123
Victorian Home & Carriage House Museum,
   132

War Eagle Monument, 108
Waterloo Museum of Art, 133–134
Waterloo, Iowa, 128–141
West Jefferson Street National Historic
   District, 170
West of Winterset, Antiquing and Sightseeing,
   194–195
Western Historic Trails Center, 21–23

Map Index

Agricultural Tour, 222
Art Tour, 220

Burlington: sights, food, lodging, 168
Cedar Falls/Waterloo: sights, food, lodging,
   130

Cedar Rapids: sights, food, lodging, 182
Clear Lake: sights, food, lodging, 126
Council Bluffs: sights, food, lodging, 22

Des Moines, greater: sights, food, lodging, 208
Des Moines: sights, food, lodging, 200
Dubuque, downtown: sights, food, lodging,
   144
Dubuque: sights, food, lodging, 152

Grand Island: food, lodging, 53
Great River Road, scenic route, 140

Highway 20, scenic route, 84

I-80 Triangle/Kearney: sights, food, lodging, 48
Iowa City: sights, food, lodging, 176

Lincoln: sights, food, lodging, 34
Loess Hills, scenic route, 30

Madison County/Winterset: sights, food,
   lodging, 190
Mason City: sights, food, lodging, 120
Mississippi Tour, 218
Music Club Tour, 219

Nebraska Panhandle: sights, food, lodging, 74
North Platte: sights, lodging, 68
Northeast Nebraska: sights, food, lodging, 96

Ogallala Region: sights, food, lodging, 66
Okoboji Region: sights, food, lodging, 112
Omaha, greater: sights, food, lodging, 16

Pioneer Heritage Tour, 221
Planning Map, 214–215
Prairie Lakes Country: sights, food, lodging, 58

Quad Cities: sights, food, lodging, 158

Scottsbluff/Gering/Terrytown: sights, food,
    lodging, 80
Sioux City: sights, food, lodging, 106
Southeast Nebraska: sights, lodging, 40

Valentine Region: sights, food, lodging, 86

KYLE MUNSON

ABOUT THE AUTHOR

Kyle Munson was born in eastern Iowa, spent his childhood in southwest Iowa (near Omaha/Council Bluffs), and now lives smack in the middle of the state, in Des Moines. Ever since his parents were wheeling him around the Iowa State Fair in a stroller, he has traveled all over Iowa and Nebraska, exploring sites from Omaha's Henry Doorly Zoo to the distinct clubs and shops of downtown Iowa City.

From an early age, Kyle fell in love with both music and writing, which he now combines in his job as music critic for *The Des Moines Register* and as a freelance writer. Neither a devout Nebraska Cornhusker nor Iowa Hawkeyes fan, Kyle was the perfectly neutral choice to write a book that digs into the best sites of both states. He has canoed the scenic Upper Iowa River. He has stood atop the majestic Scotts Bluff National Monument. He loves to spend hours at a time amid the bursting shelves of the Antiquarium bookshop, record store, and art gallery in downtown Omaha. This guidebook is the sum of those and many more moments.